CHARLEMAGNE
First of the Moderns

CHARLEMAGNE
From an engraving after Meissonier

CHARLEMAGNE
FIRST OF THE MODERNS

BY

CHARLES EDWARD RUSSELL

WITH ILLUSTRATIONS

BOSTON AND NEW YORK
HOUGHTON MIFFLIN COMPANY
The Riverside Press Cambridge
1930

The Riverside Press
CAMBRIDGE · MASSACHUSETTS
PRINTED IN THE U.S.A.

PREFATORY NOTE

No other figure of antiquity means so much in so many ways to the modern world as Charlemagne. No other had such a profound effect upon all times succeeding his own down to these of ours. For centuries the world was content to accept about this curious and compelling person the mass of romance and fiction begun by his contemporaries and augmented by each generation thereafter. In the end he ceased to be real and became mythical and fantastic.

Scholarship has always known better and often it has protested. In modern times it has become more and more dissatisfied with sources of information once accepted as unquestionable. More recently the devastating inquiries of Professor Halphen of the University of Bordeaux have all but eliminated one of these ancient repositories of fable, the Monk of Saint Gall, and cast much doubt upon even Einhard, the Emperor's secretary, once deemed oracular. The undermining of so much accepted testimony may seem to have left us with rather a maimed and certainly a most unstable basis for the estimating of Charlemagne's character. Yet from the man's indubitable deeds and still more from his remarkable letters or Capitularies, it should be possible to discern his psychology, purposes, methods, and view of life and this is the attempt here.

He found Europe a kind of seething mad-house of conflicting races; he left it unified and organized. He found it in an almost incomparable ignorance; he started it upon the road to education and light. He found it a political chaos and left it the ordered state. What instigated him to these achievements, how he effected them, and his peculiar attitude toward them are to be found best in these letters hereinafter described.

PREFATORY NOTE

The footnotes are added to assist those that may wish to do comparative or extended reading. The term 'Einhard's *Annals*' used in these notes is employed because there is no other accepted name for the records with which it is now fairly certain Einhard had nothing to do. For convenience, the paging followed in all these references to Einhard's *Life*, *Annals*, Paulus Diaconus, the Monk of Saint Gall, and the other annalists is that of the Leipsic edition of Dr. Abel. The paging in the references to Vétault is that of the fourth edition of his work; to Gibbon, that of the variorum edition of 1867; to Hallam, that of the standard edition of 1880.

I should be remiss if I did not here acknowledge the generous and sympathetic help received in the preparation of this work from Dr. Walter Kaemmerer, director of the Stadt-Archiv of Aachen, and from members of his staff. Nor should I omit a note of grateful remembrance of the good old city of Aachen, where still dwells the ancient spirit of hospitality to the stranger and of good comradeship toward him that comes to search the records of Charlemagne's capital.

CONTENTS

ILLUSTRATIONS

ILLUSTRATIONS

CHARLEMAGNE
First of the Moderns

CHARLEMAGNE'S SIGNATURE

The A of Karl is to be found at the center of the cross. The clerk's part of
the signature reads, 'Signum Caroli gloriosissimi regis' (The mark of
the most glorious King Charles).

CHARLEMAGNE

.·.

CHAPTER I

ROYALTY IN THE MAKING AND THE UNMAKING

A FOUR-WHEELED cart was jolting down a country road to
Soissons, in northern France; a crude, primitive, ponderous
cart that bumped and creaked; a wretched and dirty cart,
drawn by dull oxen, guided by an ox-faced peasant, dull as
his beasts and not less dirty. The ill-made road wound
through a region fertile of soil, potential of happiness, and
sad as death, because it was blighted by a dull, ill-made
government and a crushing burden of taxation. A man sat
in the cart; a man with wonderful long reddish hair and a
wonderful reddish beard, long and thick. Otherwise, little
distinguished him from the ox-faced peasant that drove him
on. And yet he was a king, the last of a long line of famous
kings, and the cart that, bumping and joggling, carried him
over the ill-made road, was bearing him to the assembly of
his nobles, there to be deposed.[1]

Childeric III was his name, King of the Franks, defender
of the faith, titular lord over some millions of people that
were wretched, ill-housed, ill-fed, and strangers to joy, and
over some hundreds that were not wretched at all but comfortable, well-housed, well-fed, and, by the millions, well-
served. It was the well-fed that were about to do the depos-

[1] Einhard (Eginhard), *De Vita et Gestis Caroli Magni*, pp. 89, 90; Dieffenbach and
Vogt, *Geschichte des Mittelalters*, pp. 299, 302–03; Dr. Thomas Hodgkin, *Charles the
Great*, p. 55; Alphonse Vétault, *Charlemagne*, pp. 72, 103–04; Gibbon, chap. XLIX,
p. 387.
    As to the taxation, J. I. Mombert, *A History of Charles the Great*, pp. 395–96.

ing of King Childeric III. The rest had nothing to say about it, being but pawns in the pleasant but somewhat sanguinary scheme of life then enforced by the comfortable. Why the well-fed should be well-fed and why the pawns should be pawns, none of the pawns ever inquired. In later years, certain descendants of theirs compassed that question, with others; notably in the Place de la Concorde. But here in northern Europe, year of grace 751, all they knew was that they were pawns and born to toil, sweat, fight, serve, shed blood, and say nothing.

Childeric III, King of the Franks, thus summarily disposed of, ended the dynasty of the Merovingians that for two hundred years had ruled in fact or in name over a vast territory comprising central and northern France, southwestern Germany, and much other fair domain. In that region some years afterward was to arise the greatest figure and greatest intellect of the Middle Ages. His wonderful and romantic story is here to be recounted, and we shall not see it in its real perspective nor him in his direct relationship to the life of our own day unless we remind ourselves first of the nature of the world he came to dominate and next of the strange, fateful ways by which it seemed to have been made ready for his reshaping hand.

Go we then back to familiar, outjutting points of history, needful to these ends and affording first the suggestion that men must on the whole learn less readily than monkeys. There was never an ape that would burn his paws more than once in the same fire; but in every age of which we have record has been some nation perfectly willing to invite the destructions that wait upon imperialism. Either so, or the yearning to dominate subject races is ineradicable in the human breast, for dead in the face of invariable experience is all such ambition.

The most memorable of these tragic futilities, the ancient Roman Empire, having reached in the year 395 A.D. a state of gangrenous expansion where it could no longer hold to-

2

gether, broke in the middle. Theodosius, its dying Imperator,[1] divided it as Eastern and Western Empires between his sons Arcadius and Honorius, the Eastern capital being Constantinople and the Western, Rome. Down went the two halves to disaster almost side by side, but fringed about with a difference. The Eastern perished at heart and slowly, corrupted and corrupting under the blight of the worst traditions of Asia, and ruled by a succession of Oriental despots in a sickly atmosphere of intrigue, plots, lies, assassinations, abominable cruelties, and bestial vices. The Western crumpled before the wild men of the Northern woods.

For generations these had been beating in successive waves upon the Roman periphery, driving it farther inward. On the populations that should have opposed them the debasing poisons of the imperial state had worked perfectly. There was no longer left a manhood that could withstand the sheer physique of the barbarian. When Alaric in 410 climaxed the long struggle with the capture of Rome, other wild men had already overrun the Gaul that Cæsar conquered. France, southern Germany, Burgundy, Switzerland, northern Italy, swarmed with the newcomers that had begun to assimilate themselves with the resident populations.

At Rome the fierce-eyed conquerors took into their own hands the ancient imperial machinery. For a time they retained the hollow forms under which it had revolved. There was still a nominal emperor, but the real government was a military dictatorship. In 476 the faded and flaccid emblem of vanished power was in the hands of a boy fifteen years old, probably half-witted, but bearing the imposing name of Romulus Augustulus. The head of the army and therefore real ruler of the state was Odoacer the Hun. Upon him the extreme absurdity of the existing situation seems at last to have wrought to action. After enduring for a year the spectacle of a boy emperor playing about in the ancient purple, Odoacer abolished the inane and profitless show, retired lit-

[1] Gibbon, chap. xxix, p. 306; Bryce, *The Holy Roman Empire*, pp. 7–8.

3

tle Romulus Augustulus to his native obscurity, and ended the Western Empire.[1]

From that time on, there was but one emperor known to man, the particular assassin, conspirator, degenerate, or mountebank that happened to occupy the throne at Constantinople. To him the old Western organization, or what was left of it, was supposed, by a shadowy fiction, to be subject; but in the main all persons outside of his own territories speedily forgot his existence. Rome itself was ruled by the successors of Odoacer with the title of Patrician. At Ravenna sat a functionary called the Exarch, who, by another fiction, was pretended to represent Constantinople in the affairs of that part of Italy. And for the rest, chaos reigned or rioted.

The old Roman system of provincial government in these outlying regions had fallen to pieces at the touch of the barbarian's club. The tribal chiefs he had brought with him supplied in most places the only semblance of authority and law. Here and there a Roman colony still groped along the old ways or compromised with the invaders, who continued to arrive spasmodically in skin-clad contingents.

One seeking for redeeming traits among this branch of our ancestry is likely to have small reward for his pains. The virtues that Tacitus reported among them, or their like,[2] were mostly primitive or illusory and at best contributed little to an ordered state. To be brave without judgment of reason, to be loyal without discernment to a petty and unenlightened tyrant, are no great stays to a struggling civilization.[3] It appears that the woodsmen were almost inconceivably ignorant, brutal, sensual, and greedy; and the moral stamina actually existing among them may be gauged

[1] Gibbon, chap. xxxvi, pp. 96–98; Bryce, pp. 22–25; Dieffenbach and Vogt, pp. 66–67.

[2] Michelet, *Histoire de France*, vol. i, p. 134. He points out a fact too generally overlooked that the people described by Tacitus were not in the main the people that descended upon the Empire. It is hardly likely, for instance, that Tacitus ever saw or heard of a Saxon.

[3] 'The Chief fought for victory, his followers for the Chief.' *Ibid.*, p. 133.

by the fact that if they destroyed with a blow the structure of the old Roman system, in their own turn they succumbed as quickly before its vices.[1]

Yet sometimes in the horde of petty chieftains that commanded the invaders, having in general little idea above plunder and roast pig, arose a man of ambition, of parts, and almost of vision, who busied himself to defeat the fellows of his order, not so much to get their meat supplies as to enlarge his own power and territories. Among them, and above all the rest, appears the redoubtable figure of Clovis or Chlodovech, chief at the beginning of his career of the people called Salians.[2]

These were Franks,[3] and the Franks were a great division of the Germanic tribes that had pushed out of the forests and moved to the west of south, settling chiefly along the Lower Rhine, but also in other places inviting for fertility or plunder. About the middle of the fifth century, the chieftain of a little group of Salian Franks was a wise and crafty old man named Merwig. He had one son, Childeric, who died in early manhood leaving a son named Chlodovech. This youth it was Merwig's task to train for the succession, with such effective results that the grandsire's name, transformed into Merovingian, became the family appellation of a long line of kings and left on history more than one indelible mark.[4]

Merwig died in 481 when his pupil was only fifteen years old. Assuming the active command at that age, he showed

---

[1] Conf. Hodgkin, p. 12; Dieffenbach and Vogt, p. 70.

[2] This branch came from the region on the river Saale; hence the name.

[3] According to the Frankish sagas, the race originally inhabited Sicambria on the Sea of Asov. They had for their first princes Marchomer, a son of Priam, and Sunno, a son of Antenor. This links them handily to the royal house of Troy to which every aspiring tribe in Europe traced its lineage. The everlasting Pharamond reappears later in the legend as Marchomer's heir, which is well, since without a reference to Pharamond no Middle Age throne seems to have been able to function. Conf. Dieffenbach and Vogt, pp. 69–70. It seems to have been the old dreamer, Fredegar, or the anonymous continuer of his *Annals*, that first gave to the public the secret of the Frankish birth. Conf. Abel's edition, p. 5.

[4] Guizot, *The History of France from the Earliest Times to the Year 1781*, American edition, p. 128.

at once that he was of the true order of genius. He began to train his little army to an efficient mobility before him all unknown among even the ablest practitioners of the bludgeon and the bow.

Four years later he left Flanders with his organized band and invaded France at the exact time when, dissensions having weakened the governing powers, an invasion was likeliest to succeed. What was left of authority, Roman and barbarian, gathered to oppose him under a Roman named Syagrius. A great battle was fought at Soissons, and the nineteen-year-old Salian so outmaneuvered and outfought the more experienced chieftains opposed to him that he won a memorable victory. From the lost battle-field Syagrius fled to Alaric, King of the Visigoths, whose protection he claimed. Clovis demanded that he should be surrendered. Alaric yielded him up. Clovis had him put to death.

He was now master of northern France as well as of Flanders, this extraordinary youth. He pushed southward, overwhelming every force that tried to check him and adding territory after territory to his dominions. To the record of his military exploits there are few fellows in history. Almost his entire life was spent in fighting and he was never defeated. Petty kings, princes, princelings, dukes, counts, wild tribes and those not so wild, he sent reeling right and left. With a restless and insatiable thirst for conquest he enlarged a kingdom that already seemed for those days abnormal. He conquered Champagne, Lorraine, Alsace, Baden, Württemberg, western Bavaria, northern Switzerland. He crossed the Rhine and at the battle of Tolbiac crushed the Alemannians. When his son Theodoric had broken the power of the Thuringians, he ruled from the Bay of Biscay to the river Inn, and from the Ems to the Upper Rhone.[1]

When he had been a boy undergoing tutelage from Merwig, the Franks, in many divisions and subdivisions, occupied most of the territory from what is now Brussels to

[1] Hodgkin, pp. 5–7; Dieffenbach and Vogt, p. 70.

6

what is now Metz, and from what is now Frankfort to the northern boundaries of Burgundy. Among them were scores of small chieftains like Merwig. Now the Frankish territory was more than doubled in area and over all was but the one head, one authority, one lord, Chlodovech or Clovis, its first king.

He had not proceeded far upon his career when the eternal feminine crossed it, and as the consequences were momentous in history we should have the full story.

Chilperic, King of the Burgundians, had two sons and a daughter, Clotilde the Fair. He had also a brother, one Gondebaud. Some one should descant philosophically upon Good Brother and Bad Brother. From Genesis IV onward they persistently recur in all human records. In this instance, the performance went beyond tradition. Gondebaud the Bad coveted the throne of Chilperic the Good. So Gondebaud slew his brother and took possession of what he had coveted. The wife of Chilperic he disposed of by tying rocks around her neck and throwing her into the Rhine. Her two sons he had assassinated.[1] This left only Clotilde.

For some reason unrevealed he did not murder her, but sent her to Geneva, then part of the Burgundian territory. There she lived in obscurity and virtual exile, wholly absorbed, we are told, in good works.

Clovis heard of this maiden, her surpassing beauty, her wisdom and modesty, and determined to make her his wife, if that might be. At Geneva she was so closely guarded that it was impossible for him to see her. So he sent to woo in his stead a wise and wily Roman, one Aurelian, whom he felt he could trust.

Aurelian clothed himself in rags, took the ring of Clovis, and, playing the rôle of a poor mendicant, besought the aid of the charitable Clotilde. She received him kindly and, believing him to be a holy man, washed his feet. Then Aurelian, bending over her, whispered in her ear:

[1] Guizot, p. 135.

7

'Lady, I have great matters to reveal to thee if thou wilt grant me secret audience.'

'Say on,' said Clotilde.

'Clovis, King of the Franks, hath sent me to thee. If it be the will of God, he would raise thee to his high rank by marriage, and that thou mayest be certified thereof, he sendeth thee this ring.'

The wise and perspicacious Clotilde must have seen, opening of a sudden before her, the chance of revenge for father, mother, and brothers slain. With great joy, we are told, she accepted the ring, gave her own in exchange and the lucky messenger three hundred sous in gold. Then her woman's wit went round to work, and she told Aurelian exactly what Clovis must do to win her. Let him demand her in marriage of her uncle Gondebaud, but do it quickly; let the messengers that should make the demand take her away at once, lest Aridius, Gondebaud's counselor, should return.

Aridius, a shrewd, schemeful old man, happened at the moment to be in Marseilles.

Clovis followed exactly the tactics outlined by his fiancée, made the demand, secured an unwilling consent, and by his messengers carried the lady away.

In a few days Aridius came back and, when he heard the news, cast ashes upon his head and betook himself to the King.

'Yes,' said Gondebaud, 'we have given our niece Clotilde in marriage to Clovis, King of the Franks, that we may have the support of this great power.'

'Support!' cried Aridius, 'thou hast taken steps to thy ruin. Dost thou not see that as the wife of Clovis she will move heaven and earth to be revenged for her father, mother, and brothers? Recall thy decision. Send a swift troop to overtake thy niece and bring her back before it is too late.'

The dull Gondebaud, terrified by the revelation of his own stupidity, sent forth his troop in haste with strictest orders to bring Clotilde back before she could pass the Burgundian frontier.

8

She was traveling in a lumbering and ponderous vehicle of the age, a kind of chariot. The troop was on horseback, traveling three times as fast. There was scarcely a chance that she could escape.

Yet she did — by native wit. She had conceived in her mind what Aridius would be likely to say and do, and she thought she could circumvent him. When she had been a few days in the lumbering chariot, she professed to be weary of it, insisted that she and her escort should be mounted upon horses, and thus with diligent speed made her way safely out of her uncle's clutches.

Before she crossed the border she did a thing so characteristic of her times and people that to omit it would be a pity. She induced her escort to lay waste with fire and sword a part of the Burgundian dominion and then tripped easily over the dividing line.

Once married to the impetuous and neurotic Frank, she lost no time in pursuing her object.

A feud had broken out between Gondebaud and his brother Godegisil. Clovis fomented it, probably under the tuition of his lady wife, supporting the revolting brother. Then of a sudden he entered with his army the Burgundian territory, defeated Gondebaud at the battle of Dijon, and pursued him to Avignon, where he had taken refuge. Clovis started a siege. The wily Aridius now took charge. He fled to Clovis, pretended to have abandoned the cause of his master, won the confidence of the Frank, and finally proposed an arrangement by which Gondebaud should become a vassal and Burgundy should be added to the Frankish territory. On these terms peace was made and Gondebaud was allowed to live — which seems to have been an error.[1]

Clotilde was a Christian, a fact that one might perhaps not suspect from this narrative. She now set herself diligently

[1] Guizot, p. 135. To the engagement of Clovis and Clotilde, he is following Gregory of Tours; but the story of Aurelian and the pursuit is from Fredegar, who continued the narrative of Gregory.

to convert her pagan husband. According to tradition, she wrought this miracle [1] — with incalculable results upon the Christian world. How she achieved it, which would be the most interesting part of the story, is not revealed, but the surmise is reasonable that in his case argument was hardly the means of grace, he being immune to any less ponderable than a pike or halberd. There is a story that at first the battle at Tolbiac went against him, and he vowed that if he won he would become a Christian. However this may be, it appears that once convinced, he had all the traditional fervor of the proselyte, and still more. He was not content to embrace the cross alone, but ordered three thousand of his nobles and retainers to come with him into the fold, and all were baptized together.

His access of faith cannot be said to have mollified his manners, sweetened his disposition, or changed his belief that the essential of life was to fight and by whatsoever means to win. A pretext to fight was to him as sweet as hidden well-water to the wayfarer. In embracing Christianity, he had taken what was called the Catholic side in a controversy then dividing the Church. The Visigoths had erected in southern France and northern Spain a kingdom and stronghold that they enlisted on the other or Arian side of this debate. Clovis said that he felt it his duty to combat these heretics and bring them to a knowledge of their errors. Their King was Alaric II. Clovis made war upon him. In a great battle fought near Poitiers in 507, he routed the Gothic forces, inflicted upon them a terrific slaughter, and with his own hands slew the unfortunate Alaric. [2] As the cruel murderer Gondebaud fought on the side of Clovis in this engagement, it is to be supposed that by the loss of his kingdom he had atoned for his crimes.

Arianism having been handsomely defeated (with the

[1] Hallam, chap. I, p. 17; Dieffenbach and Vogt, pp. 70–71; Gibbon, chap. XXXVIII, pp. 165–66.

[2] Dieffenbach and Vogt, p. 72.

10

sword) in the Visigothic Kingdom, Clovis annexed that also and returned content.

His slaying of Alaric was not much for the times, being no more than the death of one man; but some of his other exploits seem to have impressed an age not easily susceptible. Although marked with a touch of crudity, it is to be admitted that his methods had the essence of an almost flawless efficiency.

As we have noted, the region occupied by the Franks when he started upon his career was assorted into many small kingdoms. On his return from his first successful expedition to the south, he encountered the fact that these small royalties were absorbing an allegiance that he thought should be his. First, then, he set his hand to the task of ridding himself and his plans of these encumbrances.

One of them was the little Kingdom of Terouanne, of which Chararic was monarch. When Clovis had been organizing his expedition against Syagrius, Chararic declined to join it. Clovis now revenged this error by attacking Chararic, defeating him, and taking him and his son prisoners. Both he ordered to be shorn and thrust into a monastery, that being the customary fate of defeated rulers not slain with the axe, poisoned, or strangled.

Chararic was greatly cast down. He saw nothing about life in a monastery that ought to allure the soul of aspiring royalty. His son tried to cheer him by reminding him of the mutations of fortune and that Clovis would probably be overtaken by retribution, adding the wish that it might be soon and sure. When this remark was repeated to Clovis, he had father and son beheaded and annexed their kingdom.[1]

Sigebert, King of the Ripuarian Franks, had a son named Cloderic. Clovis sent a secret and trusted emissary to Cloderic to whisper in his ear:

'Thy father hath become old and his wound maketh him to limp in one foot. If he should die the kingdom would come to thee of right — with my friendship.'

[1] Guizot, p. 145.

As Sigebert slept in his tent, Cloderic had him murdered. He then sent word to Clovis:

'My father is dead and I have his kingdom and treasures. Send to me some of thy people and I will gladly give into their hands whatsoever among these treasures shall please thee best.'

Clovis sent some of his men, well instructed. Cloderic exhibited the treasures. One was a coffer wherein his father had been wont to pile up gold pieces.

'Plunge thy hand to the bottom,' said one of Clovis's men, 'that nothing escape thee.'

Cloderic bent forward and Clovis's man split his skull with a battle axe.

Clovis immediately called at Cologne a meeting of the leading Ripuarian Franks.

'Alas, what hath happened!' said he. 'As I was sailing on the river Scheldt, Cloderic, son of my relative Sigebert, the King, said to his father that I was minded to slay him and urged him to flee. As he fled across the forest, his son sent bandits that fell on him and slew him. Cloderic, also, is dead, smitten I know not by whom as he was opening his father's treasures. I am altogether innocent in it all. I could not shed the blood of my relatives, for it is a crime. But since it hath so happened, I give unto you counsel, which ye will follow if it seem to you good. Turn ye to me and live under my protection.'[1]

It is not astonishing that they perceived at once the great wisdom of this advice and Clovis annexed another kingdom.

Ragnacaire, King of Cambrai, came next. He had served Clovis against Syagrius, but that made no difference. Clovis made war on him as easily as upon the others. In the battle, Ragnacaire was defeated and fled, but was captured by his own soldiers, who dragged him and his brother Rignier, their hands tied behind their backs, before Clovis.

Clovis frowned heavily and said to Ragnacaire:

[1] Guizot, pp. 144–45.

12

'Wherefore hast thou dishonored our race by letting thy-self wear bonds?' and clove his skull with one blow of his axe. He then turned to Rignier the brother.

'If thou hadst succored thy brother, assuredly he need not have been bound,' and felled him also with the same axe.[1]

Next was Rignone, King of Le Mans. Clovis ordered him to be killed, but did not with his own hands do the slaying.[2]

'So Clovis,' remarks the chronicler, 'remained sole King of the Franks, for all the others had disappeared.'

Most of his victims had been near kinsmen. When he had killed the last he cried aloud:

'Woe is me! who am left as a traveler among strangers and who have no longer relatives to lend me support!'[3] There seems no doubt that he was truly of the stuff whereof conquerors are made.

Once while he was still a pagan, his soldiers looted the church at Reims, where the noble Saint Remi was archbishop. Among the treasures taken was a vase that, being a holy relic, was especially prized by the archbishop and his staff. Saint Remi boldly demanded of Clovis the return of this sacred article. Clovis consented — moved by superstition, probably. When it came to the distribution of the booty, Clovis claimed the vase. A wild man, also probably intoxicated, struck the vase with his axe and shouted:

'Thou shalt have thy due lot and share and no more.'

Clovis submitted with a sweet and gracious meekness to this insult, but he got the vase.

A year later he summoned to a review and inspection all his chiefs. The wild man that had opposed him came with the rest. When Clovis, going down the line, came to this man, he cried:

'None hath brought here arms so ill-kept as thine. Nor lance, nor sword, nor battle axe is in condition fit for service!' and he wrested the battle axe from the man's grasp, and flung

[1] Guizot, p. 145.   [2] *Ibid.*
[3] *Ibid.* These narratives follow Gregory of Tours.

it on the ground. As the man stooped to pick it up, Clovis with both hands raised his own axe and brought it down upon the unlucky man's skull, saying:

'Thus didst thou to the vase of Reims.' [1]

After this, we are told, the officers and soldiers were impressed with a new sense of loyalty, which, of course, was but natural in one that desired to keep one's skull in one piece.

Cynical writers and others [2] have asserted that the conversion of this red-handed murderer was never anything but cold policy, inasmuch as it greatly increased his prestige and power with those that could do most to further his ambition. A point about this that has escaped most of the commentators is emphasized by M. Vétault.[3] It is that whatever may have been the external appearance of the incessant battlings of clan against clan, nation against nation, the real and underlying struggle was always between the germ of Christian civilization and the remnants of paganism; between a conception of life that at least admitted conscience and responsibility, and a conception of life based on the alimentary canal. One or the other of these ideas was certain to conquer; the two could not coexist; and the labors of many missionaries had widely spread the beginnings of the outlines of the conscience conception before ever Clovis saw Clotilde.

But one thing protrudes through all speculations about the first King of the Franks: murderer, tyrant, bully, and bandit, he was a force, he embodied energy, he was no loller on day beds. At first some of his descendants seemed to reproduce his own qualities, a circumstance rare enough to be noted with awe. His sons reversed the common practice by adding to his dominions instead of losing them, until at the height of their glory the Kingdom of the Franks stretched from the Atlantic Ocean to the heart of Germany and was the dominant and virtually the only efficient power in Europe.[4]

---

[1] Guizot, p. 130.
[2] Hallam, chap. I, p. 17; Hodgkin, p. 6.
[3] *Charlemagne*, p. 27.   [4] Hodgkin, p. 7.

Almost as soon as this empire had been cemented, it began to drop to pieces. There being in it no authority but the autocratic will of the ruler, nothing but the strong hand of a Clovis could keep the elements of such a nation from disintegrating. Phenomena like Clovis are not for every generation.

His father, Childeric, had married a fair Thuringian, said to have been of prophetic powers. On their wedding night, she said to her lord and master:

'Rise now, quietly, and get thee into the court of the palace, observe what thou seest there and come back and tell thy servant.'

He did as he was bidden, returned and said that he had seen in the court a lion, a unicorn, and a leopard. She said:

'Return now quietly to the court and bring word again to thy servant what thou seest there.'

He obeyed a second time and reported that he had seen a bear and a wolf. His bride said:

'Go then once more, thy servant begs thee, and bring her word what thou seest.'

From his third visit he returned, saying he had seen first a dog and then many meaner animals that pursued and harassed the dog.

'What thou hast seen,' said his bride, 'is the foreshadowing of the future. There will be born to us a son that will resemble the lion; his sons will be like the unicorn and the leopard. After them will come the bear and the wolf, and then the dog, unable to check the attacks of the multitude of other animals, which signify the people released from all awe of their princes.'

This is the tradition,[1] which is manifestly *post facto* in origin, as is usual in such cases. Nevertheless it accurately pictures the sure decline in the royal stock. By the time the grandsons had been reached, feebleness was painfully apparent. After that came a line of chiefly imbeciles, gluttons,

[1] Vétault, pp. 25–26, following the ancient annalist, Fredegar.

15

and degenerates, their lives so vicious that all died in their youth [1] and of some constitutional exhaustion. *Fainéants* some of the historians call them; *insensati* or imbeciles the rest, being not so kind. It is a strange fact but unescapable that the Nordic morale, which had prosperously withstood privation, exposure, forced marches, and ferocious fighting, perished in the malaria of an assured sloth.[2] The once over-spiring Clovian ambition had come to mean no more than that these creatures should have their meats, their wine, their women, be drunken always, divert themselves as often as might be with beastly orgies, and so pass out and be forgotten.[3]

Four principal capitals of the kingdom had been established at the death of Clovis — Soissons, Orléans, Paris, and Metz. In or near one or another of these the King of the Franks was now pursuing his sodden pleasures and ignoring the affairs of state. But for the interposition of a wholly unauthorized power, the governing machinery would have gone to wreck, the restraint that the fear of a master had imposed upon the half-tamed hordes would have broken, the Kingdom of the Franks have ended, the chaos that Clovis found have come again.

The circumstance is strange and represents one of the narrow chances of history. Clovis the absolute, Clovis the capable, had employed about him as head servant, chief steward and overseer of butlers and cooks, an officer called the Mayor of the Palace; or in plainer terms to our ears, the major-domo.[4] Now the descendants of stout old Merwig, first of the Merovingians, declined into voluptuaries, idiots, or

[1] Dr. Hodgkin has compiled a list of some of them. Few lived to be more than twenty-five years old. Some were fathers at fifteen and died at twenty (page 13).

[2] Michelet, p. 221.

[3] Michelet, p. 220; Guizot, *History of France*, pp. 144–45. Guizot stresses the significant fact that from the death of Clovis to the accession of Charlemagne was a span of 241 years, in which time there were twenty-eight Merovingian kings, an average of eight years to a reign.

[4] Gustave Freytag, in his *Karl der Grosse* (page 4), has some brief but wise comments on this. Also *vide* Einhard, p. 9.

16

crapulent dolts, the head servant began to perform more and more of the duties the King should have performed,[1] and so kept the enginery in motion instead of allowing it to stop on a dead center.

As the line of Clovian wretches stretched out, it grew always worse. The major-domos had therefore a more ample opportunity to advance themselves and exalt their office. After a time they made their place hereditary. Then from head servants they became prime ministers. Next they absorbed all exercise of power. Then they shut up the kings in remote farmhouses, exhibiting them occasionally to the open-mouthed multitude and allowing them an empty name of authority. Finally, the kings became mere pieces of all but forgotten stage furniture and the mayors ruled alone.

Einhard (or Eginhard [2]), a chronicler with whom we shall have much to do hereafter, has left us a fair description of this royal state. 'In some public ceremony,' he says, 'seated on his throne, with his long hair floating about him and his long flowing beard, he nevertheless represented nothing but the effigy of a monarch. He gave audience to foreign ambassadors and made, when they departed, responses as if they were his own words; but he said only what he had been instructed, or rather commanded, to say. With the exception of the empty name of king and of an allowance for his daily board, which the mayor of the palace regulated to suit himself, he had of what he could call his own only a villa, supported by a moderate revenue. It was there that he held his court, composed of a very small number of domestics charged to perform the most indispensable services under his orders. He never went out except in a cart drawn by oxen and conducted by an ox-driver, exactly like the peasants.' [3]

To this depth, in the hands of his spineless progeny, had sunk all the absolutism of Clovis. The dog of the vision had

[1] The matter is fully discussed in Dieffenbach and Vogt, pp. 296–97.
[2] The French chroniclers use Eginhard; the German, Einhard.
[3] *Life*, pp. 8–9; Vétault, p. 72.

become more like a goat, a weasel, or a badger. We are accustomed to overlook the fact, but the divinity that doth hedge a king is historically as otherwise a myth. At recurrent intervals in the long and uninspiring story of monarchy appears a man that has a conscience hard enough and hands large enough to grasp and wield the scepter. The rest of the time it is moved, if at all, by schemers, parasites, prostitutes, and concubines. Caligula to Ivan and Charles the Second. Vices inseparable from the system were now at their worst in the realm that had once resounded with the triumphs of the hardy. Yet the odd fact is that at the time when government seemed at its dullest and weakest and civilization lost in a trackless morass, Europe, groping in this darkest midnight of the Dark Ages, was close upon the beginning of the road of democracy and light she has traveled ever since.

Not in one ordered straight line; it seems that advance is not made in that fashion. Inasmuch then as the human race progresses upon the plan of a spiral, around and around, continually treading near if somewhat above the ground it has trodden before, the first point reached in this story should have in these times a peculiar interest. For certain root tendrils of events as real and terrible to us as the World War reach back and touch the man with the red hair and beard sitting in the ox-cart on the Soissons road. And as we retrace the spirals to their beginnings, we may recognize in the environment more than one feature that will seem not only most familiar but having a significance of cheer. Because, when we have looked attentively upon the gloomy wreckage out of which mankind emerged triumphantly in those days, we are likely to conclude that after all civilization must be indestructible. And so with composure, if not with amusement, we can read the forecasters of evil that see it now about to be swallowed in whatsoever tempests, black, brown, or yellow. Since it survived from the fifth to the ninth century, nothing can kill it.

CHAPTER II

THE RIVAL QUEENS AND THE WILD HORSE

WHAT kind of kingdom it was that the mayors ruled from the Frankish palace, how they ruled it, what state of society surrounded them, what order of mind dominated the world of that day, what kind of men and women most flourished in it, whether the conclusions of the last chapter seem fair and just, with other enlightenment pertinent to the theme, may be gathered from a series of incidents that came next in the story of the mayoralty and the persons that held it.

Grim old Clovis had followed precedent and apportioned his empire among four of his sons, of whom, strange to say, only one was illegitimate. In the end, the four divisions were reunited under the youngest, who was also the most capable of the heirs, but not before there had been started in the Frankish world a momentous cleavage.[1]

One of the provinces of the kingdom had attained about this time to the name of Neustria. It lay in what is now western France, bordering along the English Channel and the Atlantic and stretching from the Loire back to the Seine and a little beyond, comprising Flanders, Normandy, Champagne, and adjacent regions. Another province was called Austrasia and lay next to the eastward of Neustria. It comprised what is now western Germany, from the valley of the Meuse to Czecho-Slovakia, and north of the Danube. As things were then, one might be called the heart of France and the other the heart of Germany.

The antithetical impulse between them was of race and language. Neustria, truly enough, had been conquered by

[1] Gibbon, chap. XXXVIII, pp. 180–83; Hallam, chap. I, p. 19 (footnote); Hodgkin, pp. 8–9; Dieffenbach and Vogt, pp. 291–92.

19

Franks, who were Teutons, but the conquerors had been absorbed into the conquered, who were Gauls with a background of four or five centuries of Romanic culture. Manners, language, and ideas that emerged were predominantly Latin. The Teutonic strain in the Neustrian Franks had largely disappeared. They had been essentially Romanized.[1]

The Teutons that dwelt in Austrasia had been subjected to no such transmutation; they clung to the speech and manners they had brought out of the forests.[2] The more highly cultured Neustrians regarded the Austrasians with contempt as uncouth barbarians.[3] The brawny Austrasians resented with interest the Neustrian assumption of superiority; if they had less music they had more muscle. Daily life, habits, psychology, government, organization (if any) in the two peoples were fundamentally different. Both were subject, and in equal degree, to the Clovian scepter, but each had a certain latitude of local autonomy common in the loose arrangements of that day. Before long each had a monarch, and these, representing peoples of different ideas and speech, began to come into conflict.

And thus was launched upon Europe the struggle between Latin and Teuton, France and Germany, that has endured to this day, that has figured in almost every European war in fourteen hundred years, that came to its tremendous crises from 1914 to 1918, and even in peace has absorbed more of the world's anxious attention than any other international strife that ever existed.

The association of these opposing forces under the youngest son of Clovis was brief. When again they came to be separated, each had erected within itself what may be called the mayoralty scheme of government. Each had its manikin monarch in a farmhouse or other safe retreat; each had a mayor, or something akin thereto, to engineer its real affairs.

[1] Léon Gautier, Intro. to Vétault, p. 10.
[2] Conf. Hodgkin, p. 9.
[3] H. Carless Davis, *Charlemagne, the Hero of Two Nations*, p. 22.

20

Ordinarily this arrangement proceeded with *éclat*, some smoothness, and not too much murder. Sometimes when the peep-show king tired of being peep-show or when a man came upon the scene, the conditions were far otherwise and might be riotous.

An eminent modern historian has compared France and Prussia in 1866–1870 to two express trains started at opposite ends of a single track. The beginning of that flight was thirteen hundred years earlier and signaled by women; for women repeatedly throughout this strange passage of history from Clotilde to Eugénie have exercised the deciding influence. The two women that now marshaled the initial conflict between France and Germany, Frank and Teuton, were Fredegonde, Queen of Neustria, and Brunhilda, Queen of Austrasia.[1]

These dominating figures, who might be taken as the grim, awesome, unforgettable symbols of a lost and terrific age, were able, ambitious, restless, reckless, scheming, unscrupulous, and sisters-in-law. Everything, therefore, was provided for a duel of hate between them, and as the opportunities fell in, they made up a long-stretched-out drama that for vicissitude and savage intensity is not to be matched among the sagas. Both were bad, which was no novelty in their station, but by common consent the palm for depravity between them has been awarded to Fredegonde, who in evil shines with an almost incomparable luster.[2]

Of each, the influence over her royal husband, a more or less degenerate Clovian, was virtually paramount, and the intrigues at home and abroad incessant.

An incident related in a matter-of-fact way by one of the

[1] They are also known as Fredegond and Brunhaut and Fredegondis and Brunechildis, which latter are the forms the learned Dr. Hodgkin prefers, doubtless on good grounds. But since it is as Fredegonde and Brunhilda that they figure in familiar stories and legends, I have followed that usage here. It is a poor name in the old chronicles that has not at least three spellings.

[2] Conf. Michelet. 'She appears to us like a Scandinavian Walkyrie, beautiful and murderous, surrounded by the superstitions of the heathen' (page 173). And again, 'la Walkyrie, charmante et terrible' (at page 139).

old chroniclers of the time sheds light not only on the queenly character but upon the general state of society. Theodoric, languid King of Burgundy, was a grandson of Brunhilda. Another grandson, not much better, was Theudebert, now become King of Austrasia. Brunhilda picked out a favorite, one Protadius, whom she induced Theodoric to make Mayor of the Palace, which meant, of course, that he was to engineer the realm while Theodoric concentrated his serene attention upon an early death to be attained through excesses and indulgence.

Protadius appears to have been of great energy but little discretion. He started in to enrich himself not wisely but too well, and incurred the fierce enmity of noblemen that he tried to despoil, or of others that he surpassed in the arts of aggrandizement. For some purpose not disclosed but probably related to the private hoard he was accumulating, Protadius now brought on a war between Theodoric, the titular degenerate of Burgundy, and Theudebert, titular degenerate of Austrasia. By what means? The simplest. He declared that Theudebert had no right to the kingdom and was no prince royal, but only the son of a liaison between the queen mother and a gardener.[1]

At this both kings put their armies in the field and moved to battle. Some Burgundian nobles urged that their country should not go on with the war. To think that they did this because they disliked slaughter or even because they were impressed with the ignoble nature of the conflict would be relief to the modern mind wandering depressed among all these Neanderthalian insanities. It was no such matter that moved them, but only hatred of Protadius and desire to humiliate him.

The King refused to depart from the counsels of the Mayor, and the armies moved on. They were almost within striking distance when the Burgundian nobles thought the time had come to settle the long account with their detested

[1] Hodgkin, pp. 17-18. He is following Fredegar, the chronicler.

enemy. While one band of them surrounded the King and prevented him from rescuing his favorite, another made after Protadius. At the moment he was sitting in a tent playing checkers with the court physician. Rushing in, the nobles made him a prisoner, declaring it better that one man should perish than that thousands should kill one another.

By some slip or oversight, difficult to understand in view of the customs of the times, they did not at once put him to death, and he managed to get word to the King of what had happened. The King sent an order that he should be released. The messenger changed it into an order that he should be killed. Thereupon the nobles killed him. Having now no mayor, no counselor, and no manager, King Theodoric made peace with King Theudebert, the cause of the quarrel was forgotten, and both armies returned home.[1]

But there was still Brunhilda to be accounted with. Two years later she revenged in characteristic fashion the murder of Protadius; first by cutting off one of the feet of the man that had changed the King's order and then by despoiling him of his possessions. Next she procured the killing of Vulfos, a Burgundian nobleman whom she held responsible for the conspiracy against Protadius, and then turned her attention to more immediate matters.

For many years, the chief of these had been her quarrel with her sister-in-law.

Each queen kept at the court of the other an organization of spies, *agents provocateurs*, assassins and so on, and each hated the other with implacable fury. Brunhilda was by common consent esteemed the fairer, which might have been at another time a sufficient cause of dissension; but here was something that went deeper.

Pictures of life as it was in the childhood of our race. For example, the beginnings of this story. When Sigebert, King

---

[1] This is the story as related by the unknown scribe that continued the *Annals* of Fredegar. He puts the beginning of the trouble in the tenth year of the reign of Theodoric II of Burgundy. Conf. Hodgkin, pp. 17–18.

of Austrasia, had married Brunhilda, Chilperic, King of Neustria, had married the Princess Galswinthe. The brides were sisters, being daughters of Athangild, King of the Visigoths. Before his marriage Chilperic of Neustria had maintained this Fredegonde as his mistress. After his marriage, he continued secretly his relations with her.

Galswinthe discovered the liaison and in wrath started to return to her father's house in Spain. Before she had gone far, she was found dead in bed, having been strangled. Whereupon Chilperic married Fredegonde.[1]

Brunhilda, enraged at the murder of her sister, cried out for war upon the country of the assassin. The two brothers, Sigebert and Chilperic, accordingly went to war, bloody and ruinous, with Burgundy now on one side, now on the other.[2] The Austrasians under Sigebert beat the Neustrians under Chilperic and the Neustrian territories were in a fair way to be overrun and annexed when an assassin in the employ of Fredegonde plunged a poisoned knife into Sigebert's side and he died.

His widow presently consoled herself by marrying a man much younger than herself. Fredegonde's agents perfected their plans to kill him also. But the Queen of Neustria yearned for something more than death to be her rival's portion. She therefore thoughtfully arranged that while the husband was to be killed, the wife must be seized and brought to her — for purposes of torture, no doubt.

Part of this plan showed at first fair promise. Brunhilda was captured and brought a prisoner to Rouen, but there the thing unexpected happened.

King Chilperic had married in his youth a noble lady named Audovera. When he wished to marry Galswinthe, he set a precedent for a famous episode in English history by divorcing Audovera on pretext of some shadowy or spiritual relationship,[3] and shut her into a convent. Her son and the

[1] Guizot, pp. 160–61, following Gregory of Tours.
[2] Dieffenbach and Vogt, p. 264.　　　[3] Guizot, pp. 160–61.

24

King's, one Merovech, was now captain of Rouen. He put all things askew by illustrating the strange infatuation young men sometimes feel for women much older than themselves. He fell violently in love with Brunhilda and organized a conspiracy to free her and restore her to her throne. In this he involved Prætextatus, Bishop of Rouen. Brunhilda was helped to escape and Merovech married her, the Bishop performing the ceremony.[1]

But at this juncture, King Chilperic was hunting in a forest near Paris when he was murdered by a hand unknown but reasonably suspected.[2] The gentle Fredegonde had two sufficient impulses to hate her liege lord. She was enraged with him because he had allowed Brunhilda to escape from her clutches, and she had every reason to believe that a love affair of hers with one of the courtiers had been discovered and was about to be betrayed to the King. Nothing seems lacking to this story except to mention the fact that for the sake of her crimes and those she had instigated her husband to commit he had earned the name of Nero the Second,[3] and that among her accomplishments was believed to be knowledge of a brewage that drove men mad with a desire to kill.[4]

Being now in supreme power and freed from her foolish spouse, she swept swiftly to her revenge upon Merovech and the Bishop. Both were attacked by her trained assassins. Merovech was killed instantly. The good Bishop was struck down before the very altar and while he was performing the sacred offices of the Church. He was fatally wounded, but lingered for three days.

The unspeakable Fredegonde went to see him on his deathbed, probably to gloat over him.

'I hope we shall find the wretch that so foully assaulted thee,' she said with a sweet smile.

The Bishop reared himself on his bed.

'Who is that wretch?' he cried. 'The same that murdered

[1] Michelet, p. 175.   [2] Dieffenbach and Vogt, p. 293.
[3] Michelet, p. 173.   [4] Michelet, p. 173.

25

our King, the same that hath shed a torrent of innocent blood, the same that hath brought manifold horrors upon this kingdom. Thou, thou, blackened with all these iniquities, thou art cursed eternally, and God will revenge my blood upon thy head!'

The curse fell unheeded. Not long after, that she might insure the succession for her own son, Chlothar, she murdered her second stepson, Chlodwig, and then Audovera, the mother of Merovech. How the wretched Audovera had offended was not made clear, but one or two additional murders on her score evidently meant little in Fredegonde's life.[1]

She had a daughter named Rigontha with whom she continually quarreled. Often their differences ended in fisticuffs. Once Fredegonde came upon Rigontha bent over a chest, the contents of which she was exploring. The loving mother threw the lid of the chest down upon her daughter so that it caught her across the neck and held her fast. The Queen then pressed the lid so hard that she was strangling Rigontha until the maidservants ran in and rescued her.

Rigontha was betrothed to the King of the Visigoths and with a rich dowry and many presents started for Spain, her new home. A large body of knights accompanied her as an escort. The first night from home, fifty of the escort stole one hundred of the horses and some of the presents and decamped. The next night others followed this example. When the bride reached Toulouse, she was guarded only by the Duke Desiderius into whose care she had been especially consigned. The Duke heard at Toulouse that Rigontha's father had died. Thereupon he shut the bride into a tower, seized what was left of the wedding presents, and departed.[2] The bride was left to make her way to her husband as best she might. There is a story that the knights that robbed her

---

[1] Dieffenbach and Vogt, pp. 292–94. The scene at the Bishop's deathbed is the subject of one of Alma Tadema's most famous and effective paintings.

[2] Gregory of Tours, cited by J. I. Mombert, *A History of Charles the Great*, p. 62.

QUEEN FREDEGONDE CURSED BY BISHOP PRÆTEXTATUS

By Laurence Alma-Tadema

were acting in behalf of Fredegonde, who in this way recovered the treasure she had expended upon the offspring she hated. But this seems merely fanciful.

Gregory of Tours reports that when she was sending forth the assassins employed to murder her brother-in-law, she gave them this word at parting:

'If you return, count upon my gratitude and rest assured that I will greatly advance you and your children. But if you die in this attempt, depend upon my distributing among the churches rich alms for the salvation of your souls.'

The Kings of Burgundy and Austrasia now made a compact that in the event that either should die without an heir, the other should inherit the vacant throne, and thus the two countries should be united. This inspired Fredegonde with the ambition to obtain the united crown for her son Chlothar, but before she could commit more murders she died — in her bed by some oversight of the avenging deities.

Meantime affairs were not going well with the other queen. At all times the arrogance and bloodthirsty tyranny of the nobles weighed heavily upon the people of all these countries. Brunhilda ventured to oppose the petty despots and strove to beat into them some sense of restraint. The result was a conspiracy against her. There was more than one excuse for it. She had begun with some genuine capacity for government and some sense of its obligations, but her misfortunes developed in her an ungovernable temper and a ferocious resolution.[1] The nobles succeeded in driving her from court. Their triumph was short. After a time she made her way back, took up the office of regent, or something like it, over her grandson, who had now become the titular monarch of Austrasia, and resumed the struggle with the nobles.

In those days, most issues left unsettled by the dagger were determined by poison. Brunhilda made headway against the nobles, even when they burst upon her with civil war, until

[1] Vétault, pp. 38–40. She seems to have tried to teach to her son Childebert the rudiments of good government.

27

the murder of her chief champion, Duke Wintrio. Then she gave up and fled for asylum to Burgundy.

There a feeble-minded son of a feeble-minded father was nominal sovereign. The indomitable nature of Brunhilda's character may be judged from the fact that although she had come as a fugitive fleeing for her life, in a short time she made herself the virtual ruler of the country and so continued for twelve years.[1]

Then she managed to induce Theodoric, the King of Burgundy, to renew the once abandoned war upon Theudebert, King of Austrasia. The Burgundians, aided by Neustrians, defeated the Austrasians in two mighty battles, Toul and Zülpich. Theudebert, King of Austrasia, was captured while in full flight and brought before Brunhilda at Châlons. She had him put to death — her grandson.

Theodoric now gathered the scattered bands of the Austrasians, joined them to his own forces, and planned to move with a new army upon Neustria, when he died suddenly while camped on the Ruhr; means not stated, possibly poison. When the news reached Brunhilda, she determined to carry out his designs, using for figurehead his son and successor.

But there were two influential and sane Austrasians on whom all this long riot of women's intrigues, murder, poisonings, stabbings, plottings, adulteries, and the rest, had made an impression of profound disgust.[2] They felt that government by the dagger had gone far enough. At this juncture, they went over to Neustria and joined the forces of Chlothar, son of Fredegonde, and their nation's enemy.

There was a battle, the forerunner of many throughout history, of Jena and Waterloo, of Sedan and the Marne,

---

[1] Thirteen, according to Hodgkin, p. 21.

[2] Hallam says: 'It is a weary and unprofitable task to follow these changes in detail through scenes of tumult and bloodshed,' and Gibbon observes that it would be difficult to find anywhere more vice and less virtue. The authors of the *Geschichte des Mittelalters* call this chapter in the history of our ancestors one long story of 'cruelty, tyranny, lust, unlimited and passionate hatred, treachery and superstition.'

Neustrians against Austrasians, French against Germans, Latin against Nordics. The Neustrians won, the Austrasians were overwhelmed, and Brunhilda fell at last into the hands of her ancient foes.

To the victory of the Neustrians, the two rebellious Austrasians had contributed their utmost, fighting manfully in the ranks.

The fate of Brunhilda, now the captive of the son of her old rival, is one of the poignant tragedies of history. He dealt with her after the fashion of the times and the instincts of a savage having morals apparently lower than those of the Apache. First he placed her on a camel and paraded her up and down the camp to be jeered at and insulted by the soldiers. Then for three days and with fiendish ingenuity, he tortured her, watching with delight the signs of her sufferings. When his appetite for cruelty had been a little appeased by this spectacle, he had the poor old woman stripped, and bound by her hair, one foot, and one arm at the heels of a wild horse. Then he loosed the horse and Brunhilda was crushed in its flight.[1]

I omit the dreadful story of the murders committed upon the boy grandsons of Queen Clotilde, the slaughter of the little sons of Theodoric II, and other details of life in a human abattoir as led by these people. One turning the blood-soaked pages of their record would wish to do so with tongs, a gloved hand, and handkerchief at the nose.

Yet is it well for us to remind ourselves of such passages in our story. These were our forbears; out of such loins we have sprung. Twelve hundred years — in the life of mankind upon earth it is nothing. Contemplating thus what we were but yesterday, the wonder is not that we are so bad. The great, surpassing, sobering wonder is that we are not worse.

[1] Dieffenbach and Vogt, p. 296; Hodgkin, p. 25.
The story of the two queens has been handled *in extenso* by Michelet in his *Histoire de France*, vol. I, pp. 172–96.

With the overthrow of Austrasia in Chlothar's battles, Celt and Teuton, French and German, Latin and Nordic, were once more bound in an incongruous and intolerable union. Nominally at the head of the state was this monster that had tortured and murdered Brunhilda, but the real rulers were the two Austrasian noblemen that had helped him to win. One of them, Pepin of Landon,[1] was Mayor of the Palace. The other, Arnulf, Pepin's dearest friend, wise counselor, far-seeing coadjutor, was among the most remarkable men in mediæval history and one upon whom we should now fix a deliberate heed.

With him begins a new story in the tangled affairs of the times and one of those compensations of history that are so rare and so grateful.

It is much to be lamented that we know so little of the great and unusual people that, before the first irruptions from the woods, occupied Europe from the Alps to the Rhine and across the English Channel. We may be sure that Cæsar, who defeated them, left in his 'Commentaries' but a sketchy and probably disingenuous account of these Celts or Gauls, for they must have been of great intelligence and character, and were beaten more for lack of cohesion than of capacity. Particularly the branch of them that had settled in Ireland must have advanced auspiciously in culture and civilization. The Phœnician traders that visited them continually had brought them early to a written language; their own genius composed in it histories and poems of priceless value to succeeding generations. At a time when continental Europe dwelt in unutterable darkness, when the putrefaction of the Roman Empire and the raids of the barbarians had erased even the memory of learning, Irishmen were writing epics and developing art. Racial and religious prejudice long

[1] There are three Pepins significant in this history. It is necessary to distinguish among them that confusion may be avoided. This is the earliest of the three. The name 'Pepin of Landon' was never used in his own time, but has been added by the historians to differentiate him from the others.

obscured or perverted these facts; there is no reason now why the world's debt should not be freely acknowledged.[1]

At first the Celts in Ireland were pagans. In the sixth century, Saint Columba followed there as missionary evangelist that Saint Patrick whose peculiarly intelligent and effective career has been justly celebrated ever since, and Ireland not only joined the Christian flock, but for a time in a way we are to see later she led it.

But I speak of a great compensation. Here it is. Saint Patrick made Ireland Christian. In return, Ireland furnished to the Christian religion and civilization in Europe a support of incalculable value to both. The nobles from the woods, so lately and often violently transformed from paganism, were in manners and morals hardly to be distinguished from those that had never abandoned their forefathers' faith. The offices of the Church and its material rewards struck them as a form of the plunder to which they had been accustomed, and strange spectacles and stranger scandals followed when rough and accoutered warriors, lately barbarian, began to demand imperiously the bishoprics and other high stations for themselves and their followers. Often there was no power on the spot strong enough to withstand these, and it is quite possible that throughout Austrasia, at least, Christianity would have been asphyxiated and rapacity would have run at large but for the steady opposition of the popes, supported by a newer and purer view of religion for which an effective and perhaps decisive reënforcement came from Ireland.

'At that time,' says M. Vétault, 'Saint Colomba, estab-

---

[1] Vétault, pp. 31–32.

Charles L. Wells, *The Age of Charlemagne*, pp. 54, 310. 'Ireland had lighted on her shores a lamp of learning and of religious life, destined not to go out until the whole Western world had been illuminated by its brightness and had caught fire from its flame' (page 54).

In the *Historisches Jahrbuch*, vol. 32, 1911, pp. 809–925, is an illuminating article by the learned Dr. Bastgen in which occurs an explicit acknowledgment of the great work of Ireland, and 'its serious and earnest scholarship.' 'Culture found there its most careful nurse,' says Bastgen, and he adds that in more than one way it was the 'insula sanctorum.'

lished with his Irish colony in a rugged defile of the Vosges, at the very gates of that kingdom of Austrasia until that time so inaccessible to the ideas of civilization, attracted and transformed in his monastic school a whole generation of disciples, the élite of the Frankish race. Thus did Ireland repay its debt to Gaul,... thus did the Celtic race, of a genius supple and resourceful, fulfill its destiny.' [1] He goes on to point out the cultural services of Irish scholarship, to which we are to return later. Then he declares emphatically that 'the Irish influence dominates the story of the Carlovingian origins because it is from Ireland, without a doubt, that Arnulf derived his religious convictions and fortitude and he was one of the great turning points on which the fateful story now devolved.'

The background of this remarkable man is not wholly certain, which is natural enough in the muddling times into which he was born, but the dreams, speculations, and inventions about it would fill a book. One of the fantastic quirks of the human mind is a passion to discover for every great man a distinguished, noble, or, if possible, royal ancestry, dead in the teeth of the historic fact that most great men have sprung straight from the soil like weeds or Lincoln. This addiction has had little rest in the case of Arnulf, for whose glory the busy lineage-finders have evolved remarkable things. One pretends that a Gallic ancestor of his in the fifth century, a Tonantius Ferreolus, was a senator in the mixed Gallo-Roman organization that the Cæsars set up in Gaul, and that a grandson of this senator named Amsbert had married the Princess Blithilde, daughter of a King Clothair of the Franks. The father of Arnulf, Arnoald, was alleged to be the fruit of this union, thus neatly providing royal blood, not only for Arnulf, but, what is more important in this narrative, for his descendants. It is lucky that we do not have even to try to believe all the antique dreamers that

[1] Page 32. Conf. Wells, p. 55; C. R. L. Fletcher, *The Making of Western Europe*, p. 156.

have applied their scanty wits to the making of these fables. There is no warrant for the visions of this one, but ample testimony to discredit them. The great man of Austrasia and founder of a great line was born a short distance north of the present city of Nancy and of parents that, if fairly well-to-do, had probably a direct, unmixed, and recent descent from the skin-clad *émigrés* from the wilderness. They owned a piece of land and probably tilled it. 'The Arnulfs were no family of nobles,' says Freytag. 'They drew their origin from farmers in the old Frankland where their fathers had cleft the sod and their mothers had turned the spindle and spun the wool.'[1]

It is to be supposed or believed, nevertheless, that Arnulf had some education in his youth, which must have been obtained of the monks, there being no other sources. No doubt it left upon his mind impressions that guided him all his life. When he was still a lad he obtained a place in the Austrasian court at Metz.[2] There he fell under the instruction of a devout and able officer named Gondulf, who was, so far as we can make out now, the Mayor of the Palace, or something to that effect, and therefore chief engineer of the realm. Before Arnulf was twenty-eight years old he had passed through all the lower ranks of the clergy and was a conspicuous and honored member of the government, wise adviser of the mayor or manikin king (whoever it happened to be), invested with ducal authority, and governor of six counties.

He was not only for the council board; he was a valiant and able soldier. The times did not forbid a priest to wear armor nor yet to marry, for the clergy celibate was of later enforcement in that part of the world.[3] Arnulf was regularly married to a noble lady named Doda by whom he had two

[1] *Karl der Grosse*, p. 13. The notion of a princely descent for this house seems to have originated with Paulus Diaconus (*vide* page 4, Abel's edition). But the worthy Paulus is a fairly poor witness.

[2] Vétault, pp. 46–47; Hodgkin, p. 25.

[3] Gregory VII in the eleventh century made it compulsory, but it had been urged as far back as the fourth century.

33

sons. She now desired to retire from the world and take the veil in a convent. Her husband interposed no objection, but indeed prepared to give to her course the endorsement of imitation. A friend of his, Romaric, was about to enter the cloisters. Arnulf had decided to follow him when he was stopped by an explicit order of the King. Almost at once thereafter he was made Bishop of Metz. He was in his thirtieth year.[1]

Then for a long period, never neglecting his important see, he counseled his bosom friend Pepin of Landon and exercised upon the affairs of the state a great and usually beneficent influence. His was the larger mind, the better discernment; his advice was implicitly followed, say the chroniclers. He seems to have used his powers with a conscience, and strange to say, he tried to prevent war. Once, at least, his guidance saved the realms from the worst of all such upheavals.

King Chlothar, nominal sovereign of united Neustria and Austrasia, had a son, Dagobert, who was allowed to amuse himself with the notion that he strutted with importance in Austrasia. He had gone now to his father's court at Clichy to be married to Gomatrude, the sister of Queen Sichilde, his father's second wife. The marriage was celebrated in the Merovingian manner, everybody becoming uproarious on mead and other strong drink. Dagobert seized the occasion to demand of his father that the lands still withheld from him as King of Austrasia should be given to him.

Chlothar refused them, a furious quarrel ensued, Dagobert went forth, and being supported by his nobles, would have gone instantly to war but for the intervention of Arnulf. The dispute was left to the arbitration of a selected group of good men, mostly bishops (strange to find arbitration playing any part in such an age!) and headed by Arnulf. Fredegar says in his chronicle that it was the saintly character and searching eloquence of Arnulf that restored peace

[1] Vétault, pp. 47-48.

between father and son and forestalled a civil conflict that would have dripped with more slaughterings and echoed with more tortures of more helpless captives. In all these dark and revolting annals, I think this is the only instance of the kind, and clearly justifies the profound reverence that surrounds the great name of Saint Arnulf, Bishop of Metz.[1]

His course and that of Pepin of Landon in supporting the wild tigress Fredegonde against the wild leopardess Brunhilda have been much criticized. One apologist points out that in reality it was not to the Kingdom of Austrasia that these two owed their allegiance, but to Theudebert, King of Burgundy.[2] But the other fact, already mentioned, seems the more important. The restlessly intriguing Brunhilda had been carrying on one of the conflicts between the crown and the nobles that figure so often in mediæval history. Pepin and Arnulf had found her tyranny, with its bloody accompaniments, unendurable.

King Chlothar, the worthless, died (tardily, no doubt, and, by another error of avenging fate, peacefully) and was succeeded by Dagobert, equally worthless, and much more of a manikin. The days of the *fainéants* returned. Arnulf, for all these years helping with wisdom to guide the state, to moderate savageries, and to keep Gaul and Teuton from slaughtering each other, grew weary of public life. Again he longed to retire to the cloister with his friend Romaric.

One day he announced to the poor little King his intention to resign his place and devote the rest of his life to peace and meditation.

The King flew into a violent rage. For himself he knew nothing about the machinery of the state that clacked daily about him and had no notion where he could get another engineer in Arnulf's place. Besides, he had reason to fear that any change might endanger his ease, his meats, his wine, and his women, which bounded his life and monopolized his majestic attention.

[1] Vétault, p. 58.   [2] Hodgkin, p. 24.

'If thou dost,' he shrieked at his chancellor, 'I will cut off the heads of thy two sons.'

'My sons' lives,' replied Arnulf sternly, 'are in the hands of God. Thine own life will be short if thou slayest the innocent.'

The maddened King plucked forth his dagger and rushed upon the priest to kill him. Erect and motionless stood Arnulf. He uttered no word, he raised not a hand. With scornful wrath he gazed upon the King.

'Miserable wretch!' he cried. 'What dost thou? Wouldst thou repay good with evil? Here stand I, ready for death at His will Who gave me life and Who died for me.'

Before this blaze the King faltered, stopped, stared weakly back, and threw away his dagger. Then, the Queen at his side, he collapsed at Arnulf's feet, sobbing and begging forgiveness.[1]

From a man of this iron cast there might come a heroic line. Arnulf had two sons. One of them, the younger, Adelgisel by name, fell naturally and happily in love with Becga, daughter of Arnulf's old-time friend and co-mate in government, Pepin of Landon, Mayor of the Palace. They were married and had a son that in honor of his maternal grandfather they named Pepin. He was the second of the three Pepins pivotal in this story and is historically known as Pepin of Heristal.

Meantime his grandfather, Pepin of Landon, had been affecting history in another way.

For seven years under his mayoralty, Austrasia had peace and prospered, so that one of the innumerable 'golden ages,' created out of the memory or the imagination of a later period, was ascribed to the time of his rule. Then his King removed to Paris and fell upon evil ways, which is to say that he adopted the sodden and stupid life to which so many of his family had been addicted. His nobles prepared to re-

---

[1] Hodgkin, pp. 24–25. Nearly all this information is derived from the *Vita Anulfi* of an unknown writer of about that period. Something is to be had also (with caution) from Paulus Diaconus.

volt against him. Pepin heard of this and hastened to Paris to save him. The nobles seized the peacemaker and were resolved to put him to death. From this fate he was saved, we are assured, miraculously. Any one that in those times escaped a murderous plot laid against him by the noblemen or royalty of his country must have had the same thought — reasonably. He was kept a prisoner eight years. When he was capriciously released, he made his way back to Austrasia. In his absence his son-in-law, Adelgisel, had been Mayor. Pepin now resumed his old place and held it for a year.[1] Then he died.

This was in 640, the same year that saw the passing of Pepin's old friend, Arnulf. Pepin left a son, Grimwald, who did not at once succeed him because the mayoralty was snapped up by one Otten, an obscure officer of the court who suddenly made himself formidable through powerful and un-expected backing. It is likely that some of the nobles had taken good account of Grimwald and concluded that they would fare badly with him in command. He waited on the outside three years. Then Otten was assassinated and Grimwald came into the office.

His function in history was to signalize the poverty of those that have not patience. Before long he undid himself by haste and trying to force the hand of destiny, an error that has tripped many another man of ambition. The puppet King when Grimwald took charge was a foolish prating per-son named Sigebert III. When he died he was succeeded by his son, another Dagobert, who conspicuously reproduced the traits of his father. Mayor Grimwald had grown tired of having these mumbling objects about him, for which, if we may trust every indication in the chronicles, he can easily be acquitted. He arose one day, seized the person of the Dago-bert chatterer, cut off his long hair and long beard (the worshipful emblem of his race and kingship), and sent him to be shut up in a monastery in Ireland.

[1] Vétault, pp. 60–61; Hodgkin, p. 27.

Thereupon he proclaimed his own son King.

But he had far overshot his mark. The Frankish nobles were not ready for this laying of subject hands upon the head anointed even though it was the head of an imbecile. They were perfectly willing to have a king isolated in a farmhouse, but not to have him kicked from his inherited kingdom. Besides, the old tribal instinct of fidelity to the chieftain was strong in their blood as it has continued to be in the blood of some of their descendants. They arose in revolt, hunted Grimwald from the palace, harried him to and fro in the kingdom, and at last captured him.

Then they proved their devotion to other traditions of their kind by sending him a prisoner to Paris, where, loaded with chains, he lay long in a filthy dungeon. At last, in 656, he was brought forth and 'made an end of,' which means that he was killed with fiendish and prolonged tortures.[1] Some of the chroniclers remark that as he had rebelled against the sacred person of a king, it was thought well to make an example of such treason. Ten or twelve centuries later, Europeans found the savage red men of North America doing such things and were shocked and horrified. They had not looked into their own history.

— Force of arms having thus, as often, vindicated divine right, the victors sent to Ireland for the sacred person of their weak-minded King and with much joy restored him to his throne; meaning his farmhouse, meats, wine, and women. Whereupon a new mayor of the palace succeeded to the actual reins of power in Austrasia.

This was Pepin of Heristal, grandson of Arnulf, the saintly Bishop of Metz; grandson also of Pepin of Landon, the wise and stout of heart.

His initiation into the business of the times and the part he was to play therein was fairly grim. While he was still a boy his father had been murdered by a personal enemy. Pepin pursued the murderer and with his own hand struck

[1] Hodgkin, pp. 28–29; Dieffenbach and Vogt, p. 298; Vétault, p. 63.

him dead.[1]   In all the upboiling affairs of the next thirty
years in that part of the world, his was a name of moment,
but like others subsequently of fame he began with a reverse.

The Kingdom of Clovis was still divided, Austrasia and
Neustria had separate governments, French and German
hating each other liberally. In each country the system was
thriving of a king for show and a mayor to rule. Pepin of
Heristal was Mayor and general manager of Austrasia. The
Mayor and general manager of Neustria was a violent person
named Ebroin, a ferocious and restless adventurer whose aim
in life seems to have been to create trouble where none already existed to his advantage. His career, which eclipses
most romance, is probably as good as any other illustration
of the state of the world. He first indents the pages of history
as Mayor of Neustria, but what he had been before that time
is dubious. By a novel departure from prevailing practice,
he was elevated to his place by the vote of the Neustrian
nobles instead of by poison, dagger, or terror, and then
turned against the men that had put him in office. He had
chosen for himself two ambitions, to become enormously
rich and to attain to absolute power. In pursuit of the first
he encountered an able and active prelate named Leodegarius,[2] who was Bishop of Autun. The Bishop objected to
the Ebroin methods of fortune-gathering, headed a force
against him, overthrew him, captured him, shaved his head,
and sent him to retirement in a monastery.

He then seized for himself the reins of power and ruled in
fact though not in name for three years. This was about as
long as any chief lasted in those days. He now became involved in a quarrel with a party at court headed by another
bishop, him of Clermont, was in turn defeated, fled, was
captured and sent to join Ebroin in the monastery.

All this was done under the name and with the sanction of
the dodo King of that time, who was one Childeric. Some-

[1] Vétault, p. 67. He is following the annalist of Metz.
[2] Better known now as Saint Leger, into which form his name finally settled.

39

body now murdered Childeric, which left the Bishop of Clermont powerless at court. In the monastery Bishop Leodegarius and Ebroin, fellow prisoners, ended their strife and arranged a combination in case they could make their escape. They made it in the confusion that followed the killing of the King, and together got into their power the next dodo King, name forgotten and unimportant anyway, for nobody can follow the long dreary succession of superfluous Sigeberts, Childerics, and the rest. With the advantage of the royal pawn, Ebroin succeeded in having himself made again Mayor and started with fresh avidity in pursuit of his ambitions — both of them.

Before long, he quarreled with Leodegarius and blinded him. Four years later he killed him and thenceforth ruled in Neustria unopposed.[1]

Pepin of Heristal, Mayor of Austrasia, learned of all these dark deeds and thought it would be well to rid earth of a monster whose crimes showed black even in that somber age. He therefore joined hands with a noble kinsman named Martin, and the two made war upon Ebroin.

The decisive battle was fought at Laon. It was a terrible affair, long remembered in history. Ebroin crushed the forces of Pepin and Martin, and pursued them for hours, hewing them down as they fled, until the slaughters, if we may believe the chronicles, were appalling.

Pepin got him safely home. Martin took refuge in the walled tower of Laon. Ebroin invited him to come forth. Martin declined. Ebroin said he would guarantee Martin's safety. Martin refused to believe him.

'I will swear,' said Ebroin, 'that if thou wilt come out thou shalt not be harmed.'

'On the bones of the saints?' asked Martin.

'On the bones of the saints,' declared Ebroin. 'Behold, here is the holy casket. Thou shalt see me swear on it that thou shalt abide with me in perfect safety.'

[1] Hodgkin, pp. 31-33.

Whereupon Martin, seeing Ebroin take the oath in this manner, gave himself up with his companions. Ebroin cordially invited his prisoners to come and inspect the sacred casket on which he had sworn. He opened it before their eyes and showed them that it contained nothing. Then on the spot he put them all to death.[1]

Two years later he met his own fate and in a manner appropriate. Among the amusements to which he was partial was the annexing of other persons' property. On one occasion he examined the farm of a nobleman named Ermenfrid, and it seemed fair in his eyes. So he seized it. Count Ermenfrid seems not to have shared the Mayor's views as to what is diverting in life, and resented the spoliation of his property. On Sunday morning the Mayor started from the palace to attend Mass. Ermenfrid lay in wait for him at the door. As Ebroin came out, Ermenfrid plunged a sword through him and escaped.

After Ebroin, the Neustrian or French noblemen chose for mayor one Bechar, who was himself far from being of the wise men of earth, and was appointed to administer the affairs of a king still duller. Pepin of Heristal, Mayor of Austrasia, or Germany, shrewd, ambitious, carefully watching the tides of affairs, thought that now had come the time to set even that unfortunate affair at Laon. Forthwith he summoned his army and marched against Bechar; in those days any one minded to make war stepped out of doors and made it, excuse or no excuse.

The battle was joined at Saint Quentin, long afterward to be famous for other battlings. Pepin hewed the Neustrians, hip and thigh. Bechar, being overtaken, was conveniently assassinated, and thus in the year 687, the empire of Clovis was once more united. Latins and Teutons, French and Germans, acknowledged once more a common allegiance and made out to live together, with Pepin of Heristal as the only mayor, and some puppet, I forget which, as the one king.

[2] Hodgkin, p. 33.

Thus came into almost illimitable power the grandson of Arnulf, that good priest, intrepid leader, wise counselor, famous bishop. Like him, a great man; like him, forerunner of great things to be.

CHAPTER III

THE HAMMER AND THE HAMMERED

YET unlike the good priest and saintly bishop were in one respect Pepin of Heristal and the rest that followed him. In accordance with the prevalent morals of their times, they were of lax views about marital obligations. Thus Pepin of Heristal had one wife by full rank, a noble lady named Plectrudis, and another by brevet named Alphaida. By Plectrudis he had a son named Grimwald and by Alphaida a son named Charles. In his turn Grimwald, the legitimate son, maintained both the full rank and the brevet arrangements. By the full rank wife he had no children; by the other he had a son named Theuwold.[1]

When Pepin of Heristal, after many years of successful management of the turbulent realm, came to die, he summoned to his bedside his son Grimwald to be instructed in the mayoralty business. But Grimwald did not come. At the moment he was on a pilgrimage to the tomb of Saint Lambert. He stepped into a wayside church to say his prayers. While he knelt, a hairy man from the woods, a Frisian, crept up behind him and stabbed him to death.

The causes of this crime are not well disclosed and by some of the chroniclers are deemed inscrutable.[2] Yet the habits of a violent age did not go quite so far as mere homicidal mania. It appears that the incident, so momentous of consequences to us, happened not without an occasion.

Grimwald's pilgrimage was in a way expiatory. A short time before, Lambert, who had been a bishop and a holy man, spoke words in condemnation of Alphaida, the Mayor's mistress. A band of ruffians broke into the Bishop's house and

[1] Hodgkin, pp. 37–38; Dieffenbach and Vogt, p. 299.   [2] Hodgkin, p. 37.

43

slew him at his prayers. The same element, exasperated that the heir apparent should pay public honor to the man they detested, sent the hairy fellow after to wreak their vengeance.[1]

It was now expected that Pepin would name Charles, his illegitimate son, in Grimwald's place, for Charles was well known to be strong, intelligent, and capable. Instead, Pepin astonished everybody and caused endless trouble by naming Theuwold, the illegitimate son of Grimwald.

Theuwold was eight years old and a weakling.

The puppet King at that time was himself but fifteen. What Pepin's selection meant was that a boy of fifteen was to have as guardian, counselor, and ruler a child of eight.

The usual explanation of this performance is that the old man had lost his mind, but as a matter of fact, the theory is hardly necessary. Nothing in these records strikes the investigator as more remarkable than the frequency with which the actors do things strange, unaccountable, unreasonable, and clearly unreasoned.

So Pepin of Heristal, grandson of Arnulf, slept with his fathers and the realm promptly started downhill. Women came again into the story the more to complicate its tangled fortunes. Pepin had ordered that Plectrudis, Theuwold's grandmother, should share with the infant the cares of government. The first thing Plectrudis did was to avenge herself on her old rival, Alphaida, Pepin's concubine, by seizing and imprisoning Alphaida's son Charles.[2]

It is to be noted with emotions of gratitude that she did no more than to imprison him. According to the current code for sovereigns and others, she might have put out his eyes or strangled him. Perhaps she only forgot him in the press of other matters; perhaps she postponed to a more convenient season the pleasure of killing. For the time being, she had elsewhere enough to absorb her attention.

Civil war broke out in her dominions. The nobles, who,

[1] Michelet, vol. I, pp. 225–26.   [2] Hodgkin, p. 38.

having effective armaments in their control, were always looking for a chance to use them, revolted against the rule of an old woman and a little child. Instantly the kingdom cracked along the old line of cleavage, Latin against Teuton, French against German. The nobles of Neustria were the chief rebels. For this reason, the nobles of Austrasia took the other side. Again, as so often before and so often since, the hereditary enemies met in battle, this time not far from Compiègne. The Latins won; the Teutons were utterly routed. Plectrudis and the infant Mayor were besieged in Cologne, the kingdom slipped back readily into the disorder that at all times threatened these states, and in the midst of it Charles, son of Alphaida, managed to make his escape from prison, year of grace 715.[1]

By such fragile hooks hang the tremendous issues of fate. It would have been natural, easy, and in accordance with precedent if this youth had been murdered in prison. It would have been feasible to recapture him on his road to liberty. If either mishap had befallen him Europe, so far as any one now can see, would have been Moslem and Notre Dame cathedral a Mohammedan mosque.

Charles, having broken from his jail, gathered around him a few followers and plunged on his own account into the war that seethed throughout the country. The genius within him woke but slowly. At first he was worsted in the battles he precipitated. It appears that he learned in the sternest but maybe the best of schools; he was tutored by his own defeats. Only a mind capable of great things can be highly distinguished in that hard tuition. From being beaten, he discovered how to beat his enemy and conscientiously bettered the instruction. After four reverses, he began to win, and once started upon that habit, sedulously adhered to it.

Plectrudis has picked out as a mayor of the palace and guardian of the infant ruler a valorous knight named Raginfrid. He musters his forces at Ambléve, year 716. Charles

[1] Hodgkin, p. 38; Dieffenbach and Vogt, p. 299.

45

meets and overwhelms them there. The next year, Raginfrid having organized another army, Charles beats him again. Raginfrid forms an alliance with Eudo, Duke of Aquitania. The allies advance to give battle. Then Eudo is seized with the common malady of the times, which seems to have been a sporadic dementia. For no reason that has been discovered, but certainly not for fear, he suddenly deserts his ally and goes home. Raginfrid is left to fight Charles unaided and suffers his third and last defeat.

Then Charles, the land cleared of his enemies and no one to oppose him, picks out a puppet king of his own and takes over the real control of the kingdom. Once more Austrasians and Neustrians, Germans and French, are united under one government, and Charles, who is a statesman as well as a warrior, begins to put his house in order before the threat of a new and more terrific invasion.

Those singular, able, and fascinating people, the Saracens, afford to the world now much more than its most wonderful example of religious fervor. They are also something of an ethnological mystery. Nothing that equals their rapid ascendancy has been known in human affairs. Mahomet was born in 569. He was forty years old before he began to make known, even to his family, his pretensions to prophecy.[1] The Hegira, from which his followers date everything, was in 622. In the attack upon Medina, 625, he had but three thousand warriors. At that time the Saracens or Arabs were an almost insignificant people, desert dwellers in a desperate land, not taken seriously by the ordered world. One hundred years later, they had conquered northern Africa, Egypt, Syria, Persia, Corsica, Sicily, the whole of Spain, the whole of Portugal, the whole of southern France.[2]

This astonishing advance was accompanied by deeds of

[1] Gibbon, vol. v, chap. L, p. 468.

[2] In the reign of Omar, the second Caliph, from 634 to 644, the forces of Islam are said to have captured or destroyed 36,000 cities, strongholds and castles belonging to their enemies, to have annihilated 4000 churches and temples and built 1400 mosques. Conf. Dieffenbach and Vogt, p. 200.

extraordinary daring, self-sacrifice, and chivalry. Ever since, it has been the alluring field for romantic speculation. The swarthy conquerors were not alone brave and able; occasionally they displayed a moderation and tolerance quite out of keeping with their age.[1]

In 633 their successful armies were advancing toward Damascus. The all but atrophied Eastern Empire at Constantinople came near to simulating a certain animation at the approach of this peril, and sent an army of seventy thousand men to combat the Mohammedans. In the Islam ranks was one young commander of almost abnormal prowess and resolution, whose honored name, Caled, resounds through the drift of Mohammedan romance and song. When he was besought to rest from his tremendous labors in killing infidels, he replied: 'We shall rest in the world to come. He that labors to-day shall rest to-morrow.'

He had a friend and emulator named Derar. When the imperial army of relief was coming close to the Saracen host, Derar, alone and naked, made himself a spy upon the Christians, carried himself almost within their ranks, when discovered fought against thirty, killed or disabled seventeen of them, and returned in safety to the Saracen camp.[2]

Perhaps the problem of the Saracen numbers is adequately solved by the success with which they made converts. In Damascus was a young Christian named Jonas that was in love with a maiden of his own faith. When the imperial forces had been routed and the Saracens began the siege of Damascus, Jonas attempted to flee by night with his lady love to a place of safety. He was discovered and captured, but the maiden escaped. Immediately he professed conversion to Islam, took up the sword in the Saracen army, and became one of its most active and resourceful leaders.

The doom of the city was soon evident. A delegation of one hundred elders, clergymen, and merchants sought the tent of Abu Obeidah, the chief Saracen commander, and

[1] Gibbon, vol. v, chap. L, p. 507.   [2] Gibbon, vol. vi, chap. LI, p. 29.

begged for mercy. He promised that all lives should be spared if the city were surrendered peaceably. They opened one of the gates, and the Saracens began to file in. But at the same moment, unknown to Obeidah, the redoubtable Caled had forced a gate on the other side of the city and was pillaging and slaying. The Christians sought the General, who sternly commanded all slaughter to cease and vigilantly and successfully protected the Christians; so that for years after Damascus had become thoroughly Arab and Mohammedan, twenty thousand Christians dwelt there in peace and the full exercise of their religion.[1]

About four thousand had fled and among these was the maiden beloved of Jonas. When he discovered her escape, he induced Caled to head a detachment and go in pursuit of the fugitives. The chase was led for days and amid wild adventures. At one time the trail was lost. At another, the search was by night and amid tempest through a country all hostile to the pursuers. The fugitives had been advised to make their way toward Constantinople, where the Emperor would protect them. At last the Saracen troops of Caled and Jonas beheld the Christian quarry camped in a valley and rushed upon them. Poorly armed and taken by surprise, they made a feeble resistance and nearly all were slain. Jonas found the object of his love and seized her. She vehemently denounced his apostasy and treachery. He carried her away by force, but when he next came into her presence, she plunged a dagger into her heart.[2]

With the prestige and inspiration of their great success, and with the base of so colossal an empire to rest upon, the Saracens attempted the conquest of the remainder of Europe. In 668 they had besieged Constantinople and been turned back. After they had mastered Spain in 713, they returned to Constantinople and subjected it to a second siege in 716–718. They had 120,000 men and 1600 vessels, probably small. The defenders of the city destroyed the Saracen fleet

[1] Gibbon, vol. vi, chap. li, p. 34.   [2] Gibbon, chap. li, pp. 34–36.

with the substance, long mysterious to the rest of the world, known as Greek fire. The besiegers, being thus cut from connection with their base of supplies, began to starve, when, mercenary and other troops gathering against them, they were driven off.[1]

They had failed for the time being to capture the city, but their audacity in besieging the last of the Cæsars in his own capital had put an end to the dwindling prestige of the Empire and probably induced them to a still more tremendous effort in a new enterprise. Since they could not at the time extend their dominion eastward, they determined to spread it to the north.

That all the hosts engaged in these great movements came from the arid wastes of Arabia is clearly impossible. It is doubtless true, as we have seen, that wherever they went the propaganda of the sword in their hands was swift and effective in the making of many converts. But that large numbers of these should be of the energy, daring, and devotion shown by Jonas is all unlikely, and even if the conquered populations were enslaved instead of being slaughtered, that fact would not account for the great hordes that rushed, oblivious of danger and death, upon the Christian swords: not for that nor for other manifestations of Moslem efficiency. To this day the colossal nature of their work left at Cintra, Toledo, Seville, Granada, and Almeria astonishes all beholders. A handful of invaders could hardly have achieved such enduring monuments, and to hold Spain alone would have required a larger number of fighting men than the whole of Arabia could now furnish.

Year upon year in all the realms of Christendom appeared no power able to cope with these onrushing fanatics. In 720, two years after their repulse at Constantinople, they besieged and captured Narbonne and took over with it the entire province that had been a Frankish possession. The next year they sat down before the important city of Toulouse.

[1] Gibbon, chap. LI, pp. 115–24; Fletcher, pp. 210–11, 214.

Among the many peoples from the woods that hurled themselves upon Romanized Gaul, none appear braver or more respectable than those now called Aquitanians, who settled south of the Loire and seem to have resisted the sloth and corruption that destroyed the Lombards and the Visigoths. They were no friends of the Northern Franks, with whom they carried on aggressive war whenever not engaged in fighting for their own lives against the invading Saracens. When the Mohammedans besieged Toulouse, the leader of the Aquitanians was Eudo, who, despite his eccentric performances with Raginfrid, was resourceful and able. More than one struggle he had maintained against Charles and the Northerners. He now raised an army of valiant warriors, suddenly appeared before Toulouse, and gave to the Saracens their first notable reverse since they had landed on the soil of Western Europe. He drove them away and raised the siege.[1]

The religion of Mahomet, although with a singular power it laid hold upon the imaginations and passions of men, could not change human nature. The riches and the easy conquest of Spain were too much for cupidity and ambition to withstand. At the time of the siege of Toulouse the chief of the Saracen movement was Abderrahman, a commander of the first order. An Arab chief named Munuza thought to supplant him and set up in Spain a principality of his own. He made a promising start; all went well with him. Eudo believed chicanery might be effective against an enemy that arms had usually failed to shake. He made an alliance with Munuza, giving him his daughter Lampegia in marriage; from which we may surmise that the Christian religion had not gone deeply into the Aquitanian consciousness. It appears that Eudo planned to use Munuza as much against the Northern Franks as against the forces of Abderrahman. But the great Saracen chief in one battle overthrew all such hopes. He made swift end of the revolt of Munuza, who was

[1] Hodgkin, p. 40.

50

killed in the fight, and Lampegia, the Christian wife, was added to the Caliph's harem.[1]

Abderrahman went on with his preparations to subdue the remainder of Europe. He must have been of a commanding intellect, for he proceeded with deliberated, unhasting care. While the Saracen influence was being extended, he waited until fully ready for the supreme effort. It came in 732. Then with the enormous host he had gathered and outfitted, he moved north, overcoming every obstacle. Eudo, with all the Aquitanians he could summon, met him at the river Garonne, and was utterly crushed, narrowly escaping with his own life. Within two hundred miles of Paris itself came on the Saracens, and apparently there was nothing to stay them.

That truer Roman Empire, which at all times was more spiritual than physical, more in men's minds than palpable, had never faced a crisis so imminent. It stood at last to be annihilated, with the Christianity it had adopted, with the Western conception of life, with every conspicuous function of organized society as we understand it. The inroads from the North, devastating as they had been, were by comparison of slight havoc for the reason that in the end such conquerors were absorbed and conquered. But the Saracen, having a culture of his own in some ways superior, having no inferiority complex derived from the skin-clad status of a forester, having a religion that he accepted without compromise, was an absorbent and not to be absorbed; and the prospect of his domination in Europe was the prospect of a complete, far-reaching, and enduring revolution.

It tells much of the desperate nature of the crisis faced by Christendom and Europe that Eudo, beaten at the Garonne, was compelled to appeal to Charles, his old-time enemy, then Mayor at Metz.

A long line of military commentators has since tried to reconstruct from the fragmentary records of Christians and Moslems an outline of what followed in the struggle that

[1] Gibbon, chap. XLII, p. 129; Hodgkin, p. 41.

51

meant so much to the world. One odd fact stands out clearly and memorably. The strategy employed by Charles was duplicated twelve hundred years later by Joffre at the battle of the Marne and with the like result. The urgent advice of Charles was that the invading Saracens should be allowed to advance until they were well within the country. Doubtless his thought was that the farther they penetrated, the longer and the more exposed would be their line of communication and the smaller their efficient force at the front, a wisdom that was abundantly justified in 1914. When at last the Christian general was ready to offer his resistance, the invading host was near the city of Tours, which it had already attacked. One may easily judge of the worth of the records upon which we must proceed in these matters when one observes that to this day it is not certain whether Tours was actually captured. But at least it was invested, and Mayor Charles, advancing from the North with all the troops he had been able to summon from all the sources between the Loire and the Rhine, chose for his battle-field a strong position on an open plain between Tours and Poitiers, October, 732.[1]

The battle strength of the Saracens was chiefly in their dashing cavalry and then their trained archers. For six days Abderrahman maneuvered in an attempt to turn the Christian flank. When he discovered this to be impossible, he ordered an attack in front and thereby his own undoing. The Saracens charged with their customary valor; the Franks stood like a wall of iron. The Saracen writers have their own story of what followed. In the midst of the battle, they say, a report was circulated that the camp containing the rich spoils of many campaigns had been attacked and was being plundered, whereupon a large part of the cavalry rode away to protect their pelf. This retrograde movement was taken by the rest of the army for flight and produced the terrible disaster of the day.[2] However this may be, when the failure

[1] Creasy's *Fifteen Decisive Battles*, pp. 157–58.
[2] Creasy, p. 160; Fletcher, p. 218.

of the Saracen attack was apparent, Charles ordered a counter-attack, the Saracens were driven headlong from the field. Abderrahman fell, pierced with a dozen spears, and Christendom was saved.

The troops of Charles pursued, hewing and slaying. That night the Saracens silently abandoned their camp and took refuge in flight, each emir for himself. In truth, they did not stop running until they were once more within reach of the sheltering walls of Avignon.[1] Not again did they attempt the conquest of North Europe and the Koran was not expounded at Oxford to an undergraduate body of the circumcised.[2] The battle of Tours ended with the salvation of Western civilization and the immortal glory of Charles Martel, the terrible Hammer, who had won this day. There is scarcely another of greater moment in history or one more fiercely contested, although we are not obliged to believe the chroniclers that aver the slaughter of 375,000 of the infidels.

Abderrahman lost the conflict, but left a justly celebrated name for military ability as well as for humanity and justice. He was the expression of an unaccountable mass intellect that if it missed universal dominion stamped civilization forever with the science of mathematics. One of the facts about the Saracens that awes the modern reader is the manifold capacities of a people projecting themselves thus across a page of history and then slipping back into eclipse. The beaten remnants of Abderrahman's army were gathered and made a new stand at Avignon. There Charles inflicted upon them another defeat. Again they rallied. In a still greater battle at Narbonne they were a third time undone by the same indomitable leadership. One last stand they made in Provence. The Hammer once more descended and crushed them. With that *débâcle* fell the last chance of a Moslem Empire in Europe.[3]

The might of one man to accomplish world wonders seems

[1] Gibbon, vol. VI, p. 132.   [2] Gibbon's phrase.
[3] Gibbon, chap. LII, p. 132; Einhard, *Life*, p. 10; Hodgkin, p. 44.

more and more doubtful the more we examine history and
consider the equations of time, chance, and conditions. But
if ever one arm and one brain were mighty, it was here.
When one stops to think what would have happened if the
Saracens had come north sixteen years earlier, one may gasp
at the probable sequence.

The Hammer was efficient against others than the hordes
from the south. When he was not fighting them, he was
fighting a strange, supple, restless, and fierce people that inhabited the basin of the Elbe and continually menaced his
northern borders. Saxons, these were called. They were a
division of the woodsmen, but with traits of their own generally unadmired by those that had dealings with them. The
Franks were to have good reason to remember both name and
traits.

As the wars with the Saracens were drawing to an end died
the particular puppet king or *fainéant* in whose forgotten
name The Hammer administered the kingdom. He left no
heir, this stuffed piece of royal stage property, and it appears
that there was not at the time another lay figure available for
the empty place. Till the end of his own life Charles continued to manage the affairs of state in the name of a royalty
that no longer had even the shadow of an existence.[1] It is an
odd commentary on the slow development of intelligence in
the human race that despite the great power, prestige, popularity, and ability of Charles Martel, savior of Europe, he
was compelled to resort to a fiction so absurd and footless.
Yet before we smile with too much complacency over this
evidence of the mediæval stupidity, we might well remember
how closely the spectacle was paralleled in later days and in
what governments of loud *réclame* the puppet king has been
apparently indispensable furniture to the state. What was
the era in which a notable kingdom of Europe was ruled in
the name of a dangerous and imprisoned maniac? Within
the memory of living men, certainly. In still other realms

[1] Hodgkin, pp. 44–45; Dieffenbach and Vogt, p. 300.

54

then as now the mayor steered the ship behind his *fainéant*. Nearly twelve hundred years have passed over the earth since Charles the Hammer did this, and from at least this spiral of our road we can plainly discern, and not far below, the parallel passage of the ancestral footsteps in the year 738.

The personal character of the man that saved Christendom is hard to surmise and impossible now to reconstruct. The chroniclers were too much awed by the imminence of the peril and the providential escape therefrom to draw any picture of the surpassing figure of the times. That he was a military genius of the first order is shown by his career. He was incessantly fighting, and after the reverses of his pupilage and youth, never defeated. And again, it must have been an unusual commander that could overcome a general so skillful and experienced as Abderrahman. As an administrator, he restrained the two hostile elements, Neustrian and Austrasian, French and German, from outbreaks of violence against each other, and caused them to march along together, keeping step for his own sovereignty, a feat of no slight difficulty. He found a disrupted realm and left it fairly or at least nominally united. But he seems to have had little respect for the religion he had rescued from destruction, and he assailed the Church with a scandal that one might think was wholly gratuitous.

After his so many victories, his noblemen that had fought with him demanded rewards for their fidelity and valor. He paid them out of the possessions of the Church, seizing lands and bestowing them as he would,[1] using his absolute power to confer bishoprics and livings, often upon unworthy heads.[2] Toward the end of his life, the Pope, at that time Gregory III, was beginning to be attacked by an enemy that we must deal with at length hereafter. He sent to The Hammer for help. The man that had saved Christianity coldly declined the appeal of its head. True enough, he could not have helped the

[1] Hodgkin, pp. 46–47; Dieffenbach and Vogt, p. 301.
[2] Vétault, p. 91, 'The battle that saved the Church of the Gauls cost it dear.'

55

Pope without antagonizing a former ally and present friend, but the manner of the refusal seemed unnecessarily curt. Finally, he was so little zealous for the Christian faith that (if we can trust the chronicler Hincmar) in the eastern provinces of the Frankish Kingdom, or those nearest to the original woods, the labors of Saint Columba were all erased and the heathen idols returned to displace the Christian altar and crucifix.[1]

He was married twice, having two sons by his first wife and one by his second. A situation was produced in his last days, the most familiar in history, romance, and the drama. His youngest son Grifo, encouraged by his mother, a Bavarian princess named Swanahild, deemed himself unfairly treated, and even in his father's lifetime had attempted a revolt. It is extraordinary how these types recur. Swanahild was another Brunhilda, although not quite a Fredegonde, and once more the serenity of the Franco-Germanic patchwork was disturbed by a scheming, capable woman.

The last days of Charles Martel saw the shaping against him of this powerful conspiracy thus engineered. Hunold, Duke of Aquitaine, and Odillon, Duke of Bavaria, the brother of the Princess Swanahild, were the leaders. They strove to unite against the mighty Mayor elements the most incongruous. Worshipers of Odin from the forests of the North were to fight side by side with Christians from Aquitania and the South. At one time it was even hoped that the Saracens would join the combination, but they were rent with internal dissensions and slowly ebbing from the shores of the Mediterranean back to their native Africa. Swanahild and Grifo gave the rebellion every encouragement; Swanahild is supposed to have been its chief executive. At her instigation and her son's, the Princess Chiltrude, Charles's daughter, fled from her native land to offer her hand to a prince in arms against her own household.[2]

This was the ugly outlook when on October 22, 741, The

[1] Vétault, p. 91.   [2] Vétault, p. 96; Hodgkin, p. 49.

Hammer died. Then it was found that the prophetic Swanahild had but too truly forecast the inheritance. Briefly, the
realm (disguised as two mayoralties) was shared by the
elder sons, Pepin and Carloman. Grifo was turned off with
what might be called a half-loaf, or less. In the center of the
empire, where Neustria and Austrasia met, was to be created
a small state of which Grifo was to be the ruler — buffer
style. But Pepin was to have powerful Neustria and the
West and Carloman was to have powerful Austrasia and the
East, and any one could see that between these upper and
nether millstones the tiny nominal state over which Grifo was
to lord it would be of few days and full of trouble.

The revolt now blazed forth.

There was no king in the Kingdom of the Franks when
The Hammer passed from these stormy scenes. It is to
be supposed that the monarchical theory never looked more
absurd than in his will. He, the bastard and peasant, without any title except that of a head steward, disposed of a
mighty kingdom as if it were a couple of finger rings. Never
was more clearly demonstrated the fact that what governs is
mind and not the stuffed prophets that are called kings. As
chief steward he had created an empire and as chief steward
he gave it away. The bulk to Pepin and Carloman; to Grifo a
territory about as large as a Western county in the United
States and much less important.

By this entrance appeared upon the scene a remarkable
and compelling figure, the third Pepin in these annals, known
as Pepin the Short, a man with the wedge in his hand ready
to overturn old things and bring in new.

But though there was actual and absolute power to be
bequeathed, there was no title to go with it, or none that
meant anything. Beyond a mayor of a royal palace with no
royal palace to be mayor of, nothing could be more absurd
except two mayors in the same predicament. Besides, the
populace, accustomed to a peep-show of kings, was probably
uneasy at the deprivation. It was like the attempt to create

a republic in England nearly a thousand years later. The people wanted their plaything back.

Contrary to current practice and historical precedent, Pepin and Carloman, although brothers, did not quarrel. Indeed, on this one thing they seem to have agreed with astonishing harmony. The plaything king had better be revived, they believed. There were still, at farmhouses and elsewhere, enough of the worthless descendants of the once mighty Clovis family. From among these the brothers picked this Childeric III whom last we saw in the ox-cart jolting down to Soissons. Wherein he possessed eminence more than another nobody knows, but this matter, totally unimportant now, could not have been much more vital then. The main purpose was to have somebody that could be called a king and so satisfy the mindless. The brothers chose this one, sent him to keep his state and his women at his farmhouse, and administered the kingdom between them on a partnership basis and without too much friction.[1]

The partnership was soon dissolved in a way and for reasons that stand alone in history. But for indubitable evidence, the whole thing might be dismissed as mere fiction. The brothers had first to deal with the revolt that Swanahild had stirred up and that was now growing hourly more formidable. Each brother quickly showed his ability and energy. Pepin, moving southward, met and crushed the Aquitanians before they could join with the other divisions of the rebels. Carloman, a capable, restless, savage spirit, drove with relentless fury against the heathen Alemanni in the East. Poor Grifo, his paper domain in the heart of things, his intriguing mother and his flattering sycophants, were soon expunged from the affairs of the empire. The son was shut up in a castle and the mother in a convent.[2] It was while Carloman was combating the Alemanni that he did the thing resulting in the finale of the partnership. He sent word to the chiefs of the wild men drawn up against him, proposing an armistice and

[1] Vétault, p. 95; Hodgkin, p. 49.   [2] Hodgkin, p. 49.

58

a conference. The chiefs came, trusting his mayoral word. Then he surrounded them, disarmed them, and put most of them to death.[1]

The deed was, for the times, not so remarkable as its results. Conscience in the generality of rulers seemed then embryonic, supposititious, or a figure of speech. In Carloman it must have been veritable and stalwart. Suddenly he resigned his share in the government, entered a monastery at Mount Saint Oreste, north of Rome, became a monk, and spent the remainder of his life in repentance, holy meditation, and if we can believe the reports, in the lowliest of offices.[2]

With his place and titles he renounced his name, took another, and calling himself a murderer and the first of sinners, served in the monasteries *incognito* as scullion or other menial. According to the chronicle, which may or may not be authentic, he was accompanied into his seclusion by one faithful squire, who refused to leave him. One day the monastery cook, enraged at some mishap, possibly one that spoiled the broth, struck the eminent scullion in the face. The scullion received the blow with meek submission, deeming it but part of the penance he had incurred by his crime. But a few days later, the blows being repeated, the faithful squire could bear the sight no longer, and rushing in, seized the pestle and battered the cook over the head.

It sounds like something prepared for the melodrama of our worthy grandfathers. At the uproar, the monks come running, much incensed that the quiet of their retreat should be disturbed with an unseemly brawl.

'Why do you strike the harmless cook?' they demand.

'I could no longer endure to witness his cruelty to the best, the noblest, the highest of men, him that for piety lowers himself to serve here as a menial.'

[1] Hodgkin, p. 50.

[2] Einhard, *Life*, p. 10. He professes not to know why Carloman retired. The Continuer of Fredegar (page 18) pleads that the Alemannians had broken the treaty made with them.

59

'Who is this man?'

''Tis Carloman, Duke of Austrasia, your lord and ruler!'

Tableau. The monks fall at the feet of Carloman, begging pardon for their ignorant mistreatment of so great a man. Carloman falls at their feet begging forgiveness for his crime.[1]

Perhaps the instinct of the good story is not so recent as we have believed; perhaps the old monk chronicler had in him the makings of a first-class reporter.

However this may be, Carloman remained in the monasteries, that is clear, and Pepin succeeding him in the control of Austrasia and the East, French and Germans again came together and walked the same road under the same leadership; capable, this time, far-seeing, and with a gift for government as well as for war.

But the capable Pepin wearied, as Grimwald had wearied before him, of the dismal, empty spectacle of a fatuous king that, though able to stand between him and his natural ambition, was incapable of managing aught but his harem and his poor table, and even these not too well. He determined to abolish this part of the peep-show, but remembering what had happened to his predecessor, he had too much wit to tempt that besom of the ox-brained nobles. He would not venture without the sanction of the Church. It was the world's good fortune to have at that time a succession of wise and perceptive statesmen in the Papacy. Pepin sent to Rome a mission that frankly revealed to Pope Zacharias what was at issue, and the futility of the existing system. The Pope had the good sense to see that the power and title should go together and ruled that Pepin should be crowned king.[2]

[1] Hodgkin, pp. 52–53.

[2] There pertains to this incident a curious illustration of the ease with which history is made and its probable longevity if it happens to be made wrongly. According to Erchanbert's *Abriss der Frankengeschicte*, Pope Stephen had come to France to implore the aid of Pepin against Aistulf, King of the Lombards. Pepin demurred.

'I have a master, the King,' said he. 'I know not what he will decide about this matter.'

So the Pope sought the King and repeated his appeal. The King said:

In the city of Soissons, therefore, in this year of 751 with which we started, before the holy Archbishop Saint Boniface, amid the acclamations of the multitude, Pepin the Short was crowned King of the Franks — Pepin, son of the illegitimate Charles Martel, and grandson of a mayor's peasant mistress.[1]

And how about this Childeric III, descendant of the mighty Clovis, rightful heir to the crown that Pepin had seized? Why, the ox-cart reaching Soissons at last from the farmhouse, this Childeric was shorn of his long reddish hair and his long reddish beard and led thence into a monastery and oblivion.

So vanished one line of kings and began another. What vanished had come to be of not the least importance to mankind, except possibly a few cooks, concubines, and meat butchers. What displaced it had consequences that not only changed the status of the human pawns, so long pushed hither and drawn thither in these carnificial games, but bred an influence that ramified to every corner whither civilization penetrated, to change the trend of affairs and

'Seest thou not, O Pope, that I do not possess the dignity and power of the kingly office?'

'Truly,' said the Pope, 'that is right and just because thou art not worthy of such honor.'

Then turning to Pepin, he said:

'In the name of the blessed Saint Peter, I command thee to shear this thing and send him into a cloister. Wherefore cumbers he the earth? He is of no use to himself or others.'

Whereupon he was shorn and sent to a monastery.

Then the Pope said to Pepin:

'Thee hath the Lord and the power of Saint Peter chosen to be prince and king over the Franks,' and soon thereafter made he him to be king. (Abel's edition, 90–91.)

All this is mere fantasy. The Pope was not Stephen. It was Zacharias and he was in Rome when Pepin was crowned. The visit of Pope Stephen (II) to Frankland came later.

Nearly all the histories, including the gravest authorities, have the date of the crowning wrong, giving it as 752.

[1] Dieffenbach and Vogt, pp. 302–03; Einhard, *Life*, p. 11; Einhard, *Annals*, p. 45; Continuer of Fredegar, p. 19. This annalist says that the elevation of Pepin to the throne was by the choice of the assembled Frankish nobles and therefore sanctioned by ancient tribal customs.

Capefigue, pp. 116, 146–47; Fletcher, p. 126.

61

the ways of men's lives, upon which to this day it is potent.

But this aside, there had been immediate and priceless gains. The anointed head had been discrowned, the right of succession had been shaken, the subject had become master, a precedent had been established against the fable that any divinity hedged about a king, and the grim, glowering world was eased thereat.

CHAPTER IV

ENTER THE LOMBARDS — AND ONE OTHER

As kings go and considering the time in which he lived, Pepin the Short, son of The Hammer, grandson of a mayor's mistress, was a good king. He managed well the conglomerate realm that he had first compacted and then seized; under him French and Germans went along without turbulence. He showed that hereditary enemies can live in peace and forget the ancestral quarrel when they have a substantial reason to forget. Some features of the Pepin régime seem too good to be discarded. He was the first ruler of the age to surmise, however vaguely, that there might be other employment for rulers than to drive their subject peoples up to the battle line and have them killed. About war, he seems not to have been wholly insane nor to have craved it incessantly, like the others of his hard-driving guild; but when moved to fight he fought as one worthy of such an ancestry, worthy to be of the Arnulfings, worthy to hark back to the stalwart Bishop of Metz.

Two campaigns of his, fought in Italy, covered his name with glory and had momentous consequences for Europe. To understand both campaigns and consequences we shall do well to take time enough to see what Italy was in those days and what it meant to the rulers of Frankland.

Approximately at the period when the Franks with other men from the woods were pressing down upon the Rhine Basin and Central Europe, and again at a later period, they were passed in the migration by a certain tribe of kinsmen of theirs that having conspicuously long beards were called Lombards.[1] It is to be hoped that contemporaneous chron-

[1] However, this origin of the name, while generally accepted, is far from certain. Some maintain that it was derived from their long pikes or partisans or halberds

icling has done the Lombards a gross injustice; otherwise we should have to think of them as of all the barbarians that issued from the woods almost the worst. Certainly they aroused for a time an unparalleled terror. Their long wild beards and long hair, their strange attire, strange weapons, and fierce scowls seemed to the peaceful plainsmen not less than a portent. They shaved the backs of their heads and allowed their hair to grow in wild, tangled locks and masses over their eyes and waving upon their shoulders — a sight to terrify the sane in any age or country.[1]

Perhaps it was from these adornments as much as from their native traits that their ill repute arose. All barbarians were bad; some were worse than others, is the thought of the chroniclers. Many of these authorities, being at the time unacquainted with the Saxons, gave the palm for evil to the Lombards. Cruelty, rapacity, duplicity, stubborn adherence to idolatry, were among the traits alleged of them that made them disliked. Whether the old chroniclers that affirm this reputation were moved only by malice or prejudice may be surmised from one incident, which, as it is the basis of one of Swinburne's strongest but least known dramas, may have an unusual interest for us.

The Lombards were still domiciled in their native forest wilds. Their first appearance in history had been between the Elbe and the Oder, where they became noted for their ferocity and their own assertions about themselves that they had the heads of dogs and were accustomed to drink the blood of their adversaries.[2] They were a comparatively small tribe, but made up for lack of numbers by a conspicuous success in battle, so that in the fourth century they were well known to the emperors and reasonably feared. By this time, they had moved southward to the basin of the Danube. A prince of a neighboring tribe having come to visit the royal

and others that it came from the long frontier of their old home — 'langge Borde.' But conf. Dieffenbach and Vogt, pp. 122–23.

[1] Dieffenbach and Vogt, p. 123.   [2] Gibbon, chap. XLII, p. 443.

court, if it can be called such, of the Lombards, proved smaller in stature than was deemed comely in the youth of his period, and, besides, used some words of which the Lombardian princess disapproved. She had him put to death in her presence.

Lombardians had served as mercenaries in the army of Rome. Returning they brought such reports of the beauty, fertility, and mild climate of Italy as aroused the cupidity of fellow tribesmen. They resolved to move into and possess so fair a homestead.

But first they had some affairs to settle in their own domain. On their eastern frontier they were already being pressed by the Avars, an extraordinary tribe of Tartars of whom we shall hear more, and on another side they were bordered by the Gepidæ, a division like their own of the great Germanic race of woodsmen. With the Gepidæ, who were as proud, able, restless, and bloodthirsty as Lombards or any others, wild or tame, they were often at war.

The heir apparent of the Lombards was a young man named Alboin, son of King Audoin, who seems to have expressed handsomely in his own person and career the traits of his people. He had killed the heir apparent of the Gepidæ, a youth of his own age, and on the basis of that feat claimed a place at the tribe's banquet table. His royal father declined to grant this honor until he should have won his arms by a deed of conspicuous daring. Alboin chose as his test of courage to visit the royal court of the Gepidæ, where, despite his coming red-handed from the slaying of the King's eldest son, he was entertained as a royal guest, for such were the inviolable laws of hospitality in the woods. He was even allowed to sit in the chair of the dead prince, the chair that he himself had made vacant, and to see the grief of the heartbroken old father.

King Cunimund had a daughter named Rosamund whose extreme beauty excited the desires of Alboin. He had with him forty ready warriors, all young like himself. By savage

65

custom the Gepidæ were obliged to give a banquet in his honor, when the hostile tribesmen fell to exchanging coarse insults. At an intolerable remark by Alboin, the Gepidæ sprang to their feet with drawn swords and would have slain their visitors in the banquet hall but for the King's strenuous interference. He thrust himself between the combatants and sternly reminded his followers of the sacred duties of hospitality. Then to atone for the incivility shown to his guests he presented Alboin with the blood-stained suit of armor his son had worn when Alboin slew him.

With this dreadful trophy Alboin returned in safety home and was immediately admitted to the banquet seat and acclaimed with extraordinary enthusiasm as the hope of the nation.[1]

He was contracted in marriage to a Roman princess, but so great was his passion for Rosamund that he broke this engagement. When his overtures for marriage had been scornfully rejected by the Gepidæ, he succeeded in seizing by force the woman he desired. War instantly followed, in which the Gepidæ were supported by the Romans. Therefore they routed the Lombards and rescued the princess.

The fierce resolution of Alboin was nothing daunted by this reverse. He went to the Tartar Avars and on hard terms bought their support. Lombards and Avars together were too powerful for the Gepidæ. Cunimund made a terrific defense but was defeated. Alboin killed him on the battle-field, cut off his head, and had the skull fashioned into a drinking-cup. Then he once more secured possession of Rosamund and compelled her to marry him, the murderer of her father and brother.

Meantime the Lombards, pressed upon by the Avars and again inflamed with reports of the attractions of the Italian plains, abandoned their home in the forests, crossed the Julian Alps, and poured down upon the fertile lands below. And now could be seen in its perfection the work of the in-

[1] Dieffenbach and Vogt, p. 123; Gibbon, chap. xlv, pp. 97-98.

fluences that had ruined Rome and undermined the Republic. The Italians had been emasculated by two deadly conditions, slavery and imperialism, through the luxury, sloth, and degeneracy these always produce. Instead of making a stand against the handful of barbarians whom their forefathers would have annihilated at a blow, they fled in terror, and being caught, supinely surrendered their country and their freedom for the bare privilege of being allowed to live. Upon their cowardice Alboin erected at Pavia the structure of the Kingdom of the Lombards in Italy.

From such an easy conquest his people pressed on until they had occupied all of northern Italy between Piedmont and Venice, and southward had menaced the cities that were appendages of Rome itself. All this time Rosamund had moved with her husband, as Queen of the Lombards and partaker of their successes. But the instinct of the savage in her had never ceased to contemplate revenge. The climax came one night at Verona. To celebrate his entry into that city Alboin gave a feast to his officers. In his joy he became drunken and called for the skull of Cunimund from which he drank and compelled Rosamund to drink.[1] She had a lover, the King's armor-bearer, whom she induced to assist her in her plans. By a stratagem like that used by Mariana in 'Measure for Measure' and against Bertram in 'All's Well that Ends Well,' she got into her power a stalwart Lombardian champion named Peredeus, who awoke in the royal bed to discover that either he must be put shamefully to death or help to assassinate his master.

At the noonday meal Alboin again drank too much wine.

[1] Thus Gibbon, followed by Swinburne. But there is a different version of the story in which the aged King of the Gepidæ is named Turisund, and Cunimund or Kunimund is his son. It is the son that is killed in battle and from whose skull Rosamund is compelled to drink. Conf. Dieffenbach and Vogt (pp. 124-25), who in the main follow Paulus Diaconus.

For a specimen of the drama, take the lines Rosamund speaks when alone after the banquet, beginning

I am yet alive to question if I live
And wonder what may ever bid me die, etc.　　　Act II.

67

His wife wooed him to sleep in her lap. Then she fastened his sword to its scabbard so it could not be drawn and opened the door to his murderers. Alboin tried to defend himself with a stool, his sword being useless, and was beaten to death, the implacable Rosamund smiling as he lay on the floor breathing his last.

It was characteristic of the emotional, unreasoning people among whom she lived that at the news of the assassination the Lombard chiefs fled in terror and she was able to assemble around her a band of surviving Gepidæ and to proclaim herself the ruler of the country. After a time courage revived in the chiefs and they returned to demand vengeance for the death of their King. Rosamund with her armor-bearer lover fled laden with spoils to the Exarch at Ravenna. He was instantly fascinated by her beauty and she viewed his suit with favor. To rid herself of Helmichis, the lover that had fled with her, she gave him a dose of poison. He detected the nature of the drink after he had swallowed it and with his dagger compelled her to swallow what was left in the glass, so that they died together and the Dark Ages were lighted up for us with a perfectly typical story.[1]

I may add, as a further illustration of the times and manners, that when the Gepidæ and Lombards were at war, previous to the intervention of the Avars, an army of each approached the other to do battle. While they were drawn up in hostile array facing each other and ready to strike the first blow, a sudden hysterical panic seized upon both forces and they fled in opposite directions without raising a sword, leaving the King of the Gepidæ and the King of the Lombards on their respective battle lines looking foolishly at each other without a soldier to command.[2] If they had had any sense of humor they would have made peace on the spot. But a sense of humor was always lacking in our ancestors of the forests.

[1] Dieffenbach and Vogt, p. 125; Gibbon, chap. XLV, pp. 105-07.
[2] Gibbon, chap. XLII, p. 444.

A successor to the bloody-minded Alboin was easily had, doubtless as bloody-minded as he. The Lombards dug themselves in across northern Italy and to the southward established the powerful Lombard states of Spoleto and Benevento outstretched down the peninsula. Their capital continued to be at Pavia, but each of their provinces had its own head, who sometimes paid little heed to the word issuing from royalty, sometimes none at all. Henceforth, for two hundred years the Lombard was inextricably mixed in all the affairs of Italy and the Papacy.

Rudimentary civilization is better than none, but sometimes of unequal results. The Lombards, coming into contact with the culture that persisted in northern Italy, and affected, no doubt, by a softer and sunnier climate, lost something of their original ferocity, but while they became less fierce they were more crafty and no less cruel. Either so, or again report has done them grievous wrong.

At the time Pepin was crowned and Childeric III was shunted into the monastery, the reigning King of the Lombards was one Aistulf. He cherished an ambition to extend the Lombard rule over the whole of Italy [1] and this led him into collision with Pope Stephen II, a pontiff of great ability and force of character.

In Italy at that time existed a governmental anomaly. Twenty-two cities and towns midmost of the country were nominally the possession of the ancient and slowly mortifying Empire of the East. Therefore they were supposed to be governed from Constantinople.[2] They had been left over thus on Italy's doorstep when the original Roman Empire was divided between East and West. As a matter of fact, they were ruled at Ravenna by this officer called the Exarch, who had as little as possible to do with the intrigues of the East and usually sought the Pope for guidance.

King Aistulf now looked upon these possessions and found them likely to be useful to him in his progress toward im-

[1] Vétault, p. 118. [2] Hodgkin, pp. 59–60.

perialism. Therefore, without more ado, he seized them, including Ravenna, and threatened the Holy Father in Rome itself.

It was the fashion of the times. To seize what one was strong enough to seize and to keep what one was strong enough to keep was the substance of international ethics.

The Exarch appealed to Pope Stephen, who went in person to ask Aistulf to give up his plunder. Aistulf roughly refused.[1]

The Pope was old and infirm. Yet he endured the rigors and terrors of the Alpine passes that he might in person lay his cause before Pepin and implore help.[2] The *démarche* was remarkable in itself. It was suddenly made more remarkable by a dramatic episode.

Carloman, King Pepin's brother, he that goaded by his conscience had renounced the world and sovereignty for a monk's cell and holy meditation, left the monastery where for years he had buried himself, and without warning appeared before his brother to plead against the Pope. What induced him to this step is a matter of endless surmise among the old writers. It has been asserted that he came at the instigation of some of the higher clergy that were hostile to Stephen.[3] What seems a likelier diagnosis is that it was merely another illustration of a prevalent and possibly infectious lunacy. To do things on impulse alone was the commonest way of doing them, whether by high or low.

In any event, the mission was futile. Pepin listened coldly to the eloquent pleas of his brother, kneeling before him. Then he curtly announced his purpose to undertake the enterprise.

He seems to have deemed one fraternal outbreak of this kind enough. Carloman was not allowed to return to Italy, but was shut into a monastery near at hand where he could be observed and do no more harm. Not long afterward he

[1] Hodgkin, pp. 72–73.   [2] Vétault, p. 123.
[3] Paulus Diaconus, Abel's edition, p. 21.

died. The conjunction starts a reasonable suspicion; persons that interfered with the schemes of the powerful were commonly of short life thereafter. Yet it is resolutely asserted that Carloman was not murdered, which indicates on Pepin's part either a singular desire for novelty or a capable censorship of the means of information.

Pepin sent an embassy to demand of Aistulf the restoration of the seized territory and a pledge that he would refrain from again annoying the Pope. Aistulf scoffed at the request. There passed other unfruitful messages between the two rulers, for Pepin was in no hurry with his invasion. He made his advance in the late summer, crossed the Alps by way of Mont Cenis, and gave Aistulf battle on the plains of Lombardy. The Lombards were overwhelmingly beaten. Aistulf was shut up in Pavia, where he presently surrendered, giving his pledge to restore the cites he had seized, to cease to annoy the Holy Father, and to pay to Pepin indemnity and annual tribute.[1]

'The faith of the kings!' says the old writer, scornfully. Within eighteen months this one had broken all the terms of his capitulation and was besieging the Pope in Rome.

Pepin again swept down with his army from France, inflicted a crushing defeat upon the Lombards, captured Aistulf, and compelled him to keep his engagements. The twenty-two towns and cities were surrendered, not to the dry-rotted Empire of the East, but to the Papacy.[2]

There they remained for the next eleven hundred years and created in their turn one of the most interesting chapters of modern history. For these twenty-two towns and cities became now the basis of the Papal States, so long an independent sovereignty, and of that Temporal Power of the Pope once so poignantly debated. It was these Papal States that Victor Emmanuel annexed out of hand in 1870, and the Tem-

---

[1] Einhard, p. 13; Fredegar (continuation), pp. 21–22; Fletcher, p. 231.

[2] Vétault, pp. 118–21; Dieffenbach and Vogt, p. 311; Hodgkin (pp. 60–68), who discusses at length and ably the origin of the Pope's claim and of Peter's Patrimony.

poral Power faded with them only to be restored in 1929 by Benito Mussolini, through a strange revolution of destiny become the Mayor of the modern Italian Palace.

The visit of Pope Stephen to France had one other aspect of surpassing interest to us that observe these events and still inherit their consequences. Lest Aistulf should withdraw the consent he had given for the Pope's visit to Frankland and, pursuing him with horsemen and chariots, seize him before he could pass the frontier, the Pope had gone in haste and rested not. His route was by the Great Saint Bernard Pass in the dead of winter, a journey full of peril and vicissitude for the young and hardy and almost unthinkable for an old man in ill health. Yet he escaped the snowdrifts and avalanches, endured the exposure and hardship, and issued at Saint Maurice, in the Rhone Valley, where he came to rest in a monastery.[1] He had traveled so quickly that the deputation sent by Pepin [2] to meet and greet him had not yet arrived, and he pressed on toward Pepin's capital, then at Thionville. When the delegation met him, it was headed by a youth of twelve years, tall for his age, singularly good-looking, and of a frank and engaging manner. He was the eldest son of King Pepin — by name, Prince Charles.[3]

And thus does history introduce upon its stage the colossal figure of the remaker of Europe, the founder of the modern state, and the father of modern democracy, Charles of the Franks, destined to be King, Emperor, and Charlemagne.

[1] Vétault, p. 121.   [2] Mombert, p. 40.

[3] Dr. Hodgkin (page 69) repeats the error that the meeting took place at Saint Maurice. It was another Pope and another Prince Charles that years after met at this place on quite a different occasion. (Einhard, *Annals*, p.104.) The present Prince Charles started from the King's villa near Vitry-le-François and had proceeded about ninety miles when he met the impatient Pope advancing at a rate of speed that seems to have astonished the Franks as much as it disconcerted their plans. (Vétault, p. 121.)

CHAPTER V

THE STAGE UPON WHICH HE MOVED

HE was born on April 2, 742,[1] when Pepin his father was but mayor of a fabled palace. His mother, Bertha or Bertrade, known as Bertha of the Big Foot, daughter of the Neustrian Count of Laon, seems to have been of unusual strength of character and abundance of wisdom. For years she exercised over her two sons a powerful and usually a most beneficent influence. Charles, the elder, is said to have been born out of wedlock, a circumstance that occasioned then but little remark or none, it was so common. Nobody knows his birthplace. Aachen, Ingelheim, Carlstadt, Salzburg, Constance, Liège, and Paris are among the cities that contend for the honor, one on apparently as good ground as another.[2] His father was at the moment engaged in suppressing the Aquitanians, and as his mother was of Neustria it is only fair to assume that whatever the birthplace it was within Neustrian territory.[3]

All the researches have failed to obtain definite information about his education. Einhard, his secretary in the after time, and then his laurel-wreathing biographer, was never able to find anybody that knew anything concerning his early years [4] except that he had lessons from his mother; chiefly, it appears, in piety. Nevertheless, he had for his times an education and must have had some schooling. It is certain that

---

[1] Or 747, according to some chroniclers; *vide* Dieffenbach and Vogt, p. 323, but this date is not so well supported.

[2] Vétault, p. 100. The Germans stand out for Aachen; *vide* Dieffenbach and Vogt, as above.

The question has been exhaustively examined by M. Th. Carleté, who holds in favor of Quierzy as the birthplace. *Vide* his *Où est né Charlemagne?* in *Le Comité Archéologique et Historique de Noyon*, vol. VII, pp. 91–107.

[3] Vétault, p. 100.   [4] *Life*, p. 12.

he could read and almost certain he could write.[1] His mother had great faith in him: otherwise he was an all unknown quantity when on September 24, 768, his father Pepin died at Paris of dropsy, and he was summoned to power.[2]

The last years of King Pepin's life had been full of trouble. In those times, to build a kingdom from an aggregation of small states was in itself no great difficulty, requiring chiefly an iron will, an indurated conscience, and a sufficiency of henchmen ready to be pushed up to the slaughter line. But to keep the state intact after it had been formed was a colossal task and almost invariably disastrous. Each of the minor states, dukedoms, principalities, counties, and land patches of which it had been welded had its little sovereign or head that, lacking rational employment, gave himself chiefly to three supreme objects, plotting, pillaging, and fighting. In all of these territories was almost always revolt, potential or actual. The centrifugal force was forever greater than the cohesive.

Among the kingdoms, sub-kingdoms, near-kingdoms, and miniature counties that were embraced in the domain of the Franks was, lying to the southward, this Aquitania that has so often recurred in this story. Again we may regret that we know so little about the Aquitanians, for even the boundaries of their country are uncertain;[3] but roughly, one may say they lived between the Loire and the Mediterranean.

We have seen how Duke Eudo attempted to cast off the Frankish yoke and was by the Saracen advance changed into a suppliant for the help of Charles Martel, whom he had hoped to overthrow. Eudo was succeeded by his son Hunold,[4] who inherited all of his father's hatred of the Frankish domination and at least all of his father's fondness for intrigue. To further his end of freedom, he made a treaty of alliance and

[1] An amusing debate on this matter will be dealt with later.
[2] Einhard, *Annals*, p. 54; the Continuer of Fredegar, pp. 33-34.
[3] Hallam, chap. 1, Part 1; Einhard, *Annals*, p. 55.
[4] Einhard, *Annals*, p. 55.

mutual support with Aistulf, before the King of Lombardy had been chastised by the Frankish army, and from this agreement both parties to it seem to have imagined vain things.

What Hunold might have accomplished with his machinations is a matter for surmise. In 744 they were overturned by one of those incidents priceless to the investigator because of their luminous quality. Hunold had a brother, one Hatto. The quarrels of eminent brothers are of all themes of trouble in the Dark and Middle Ages the most prolific. No generation was without at least one conspicuous instance of brother seeking to slay brother. By a repetition of one of royalty's most persistent blunders, Eudo had divided the authority of the realm between his two sons, or left it so indefinite that Hatto believed he was entitled to a part of it. In the struggle that immediately broke out between them, Hatto fell into his brother's hands. Hunold had Hatto's eyes put out and cast him into a prison. Then, with that strange access of remorse that we have seen in the case of Carloman and remarked as typical of the emotional, impulsive, and unreasoning man of the times, Hunold resigned the duchy to his son Waifar and shut himself up in a monastery to do penance for his crime.[1]

Waifar proved a foe of indubitable courage and ability. His resources were small compared with those of Pepin; yet repeatedly he outmaneuvered the Frankish hosts and for seven years kept them incessantly on the move against him. The full story is one of the lost chapters of history. About all we know of it is through the writers paid to extol Pepin, but even from these appears ground to believe that the Aquitanians had a good cause and fought for it manfully. In his later campaigns, Pepin took with him his elder son Charles, thus by actual experience to be schooled in the business of kingship. As here exhibited before his eyes, it must have seemed to consist of fighting and lying, or countering lies.

The style of warfare waged at last by Waifar was chiefly

[1] Hodgkin, p. 80.

guerilla, but carried on with skill and persistence. For a long time his scattered bands, concealed in caves and woods, defied the King's authority. At last their leader was captured and Pepin manifested his loyalty to the spirit of his age by putting to death so gallant an adversary.[1]

It was Aquitania's revolt that encouraged Aistulf's obstinacy; that and the course of Bavaria, another sector of King Pepin's realm that for the same reason gave him trouble. Its head was an ambitious young man named Tassilo, who was descended from Charles Martel and had Pepin for an uncle. With all his nobles he had most solemnly sworn fealty and obedience to the Frankish State, and all of them went forth determined to violate the oath at the first opportunity. Their chance came while Pepin was pursuing the Aquitanians in the South. Tassilo, in accordance with the terms of his oath, had been summoned to assist with his troops in suppressing the revolt. He came, looked for a time on the struggle, and then with all his forces deserted, alleging that he was ill. When he was safely beyond the reach of Pepin, he made no secret of the fact that he had renounced his allegiance to the Frankish crown and regarded himself as an independent sovereign in all ways equal to his uncle.[2]

Pepin allowed him to retire to Bavaria, doubtless intending chastisement as soon as he should be free from his entanglements in Aquitania and Italy. He died before he could deal with the Bavarian problem, and for the next twenty years Tassilo was a persisting source of trouble to his successor.

Pepin survived his victim Waifar but a few weeks. Besides his son Charles, who had accompanied him in his Aquitanian campaigns, there was his second son, another Carloman, then aged seventeen. Between them he divided the sovereignty, repeating the error that had rent so many other

---

[1] Hodgkin, p. 81; Dieffenbach and Vogt, p. 313; Einhard, *Life*, p. 11. The Continuer of Fredegar says at page 33 that Waifar was murdered by his own people but with Pepin's connivance.

[2] Hodgkin, pp. 128–29; Einhard, *Annals*, p. 45.

76

domains. So far as territory was concerned, if that could be said to be divided at all, the separation followed unusual lines. The natural boundaries between Neustria and Austrasia, Frenchmen and Germans, were ignored; each brother received a part of each of the old contending regions. In the main, Charles had the westerly provinces and Carloman the more easterly, but the dividing line was so irregular that while Charles held court at Paris, Carloman held his at Soissons. Charles received a part of western Germany; Carloman held Alsace, Burgundy, Provence, and a part of Aquitania.[1]

After the manner of royal brotherhood, Charles and Carloman hated each other cordially. Out of this condition would in the course of nature have arisen civil war with much killing of men that had nothing to do with the quarrel, but in this instance Fate interposed beneficently. A new insurrection blazed out in Aquitania. Hunold, the old father of Waifar, after twenty years of seclusion and penance in the monastery of Rhé, must have deemed his crimes atoned for. He now issued from his cloister cell, proclaimed a war in revenge for the death of his son, and saw thousands flocking to his standard. The forest idea of an oath of allegiance was that it endured, if at all, for no more than the lifetime of the lord to whom it was given. In the view of the Aquitanians, the death of Pepin released them from all obligation to his successor, and they came forth to fight once more for their independence.

Charles, undertaking to suppress the revolt, called upon Carloman for help. Carloman took command of a body of troops, and met his brother in the field.[2] They had an interview, after which Carloman withdrew with his forces, and

[1] The historians and commentators have taken widely differing views of this division. Dieffenbach and Vogt, p. 323; Hodgkin, p. 83; Einhard, *Life*, p. 11. Mombert (page 53) thinks Pepin had striven to do away with nationalistic lines. Einhard, *Annals*, p. 55.

[2] Vétault, pp. 162–63.

Charles was left to finish the war alone.[1] In this, his first campaign, he revealed the peculiarity of his tactics as commander for which he was afterwards so famous. He made a swift march, appeared with a handful of troops unexpectedly before the Aquitanian army, crushed it in one battle and ended the war.

Hunold, old and dispirited, fled to the Basques, where he took refuge. Charles demanded from Lupus, the Basque chief, the surrender of the fugitive. Lupus complied, and the war was over.[2]

Not without an incident that humane and discerning men, if such there were, must have hailed with grateful hearts. Pepin the father, making a captive of Waifar the son, had put him to death. Charles the son, making captive of Hunold the father, shut him up for a short time and then gave him his liberty.[3] He was more merciful to the traitor than the traitor had been to his own brother. A new day had begun in that part of the world, and this was the first sign of it.

The disaffection of Carloman was probably a matter that his brother reserved to deal with when the proper time should come.[4] His resentment was forestalled. Carloman died on December 4, 771, after he had reigned three years and when he was but twenty. It appears he died of natural causes, a fact to be noted.[5] He left a widow and two infant sons. The widow gave eloquent testimony to the realities of the age in which she lived by fleeing precipitately in the middle of winter over the Alpine passes into Italy. She had rather trust the cruel avalanches than her brother-in-law.[6] When the

[1] Einhard, *Life*, p. 12.

[2] Vétault, pp. 162–63; Hodgkin, p. 86; Einhard, *Annals* (Abel's edition) pp. 55–56.

[3] This fact, which has escaped the attention of many historians, is to be found in Vétault, p. 192.

[4] 'He endured his brother's hatred and envy with such patience as seemed wonderful. He never allowed himself to be moved to anger about such matters.' Thus the adulating Einhard, *Life*, p. 27. We can believe it if we wish.

[5] Mombert, p. 42.

[6] Einhard, *Life*, pp. 11–12; Einhard, *Annals*, p. 56.

78

brother-in-law heard this, he shrugged his shoulders, and observed only that the flight was superfluous.[1] Some years passed before men, grasping what this meant, saw that the terrified widow had known the spirit of the times better than she had known Charles of the Franks. Nowhere else would she have been safer than in his house. She made her way to Pavia, where she took refuge with Desiderius (or Didier), who had been Aistulf's constable and next succeeded him as King.[2]

Charles was now invested or invested himself with his brother's share of the Frankish kingship. Many writers have conscientiously denounced him for this as an act of usurpation, maintaining that the elder of the two puling infants left by Carloman should have been crowned in his place. It takes some fervency of loyalty to the monarchical myth to furbish forth such a position. We need not join the Charlemagne claques of history to see that it is but foolishness. In the first place, there was no sacred right of succession involved.[3] Pepin had taken the kingdom by main strength and left it with the same warranty. Next, it cannot be pretended that Carloman inherited a distinct sovereignty over any clearly defined part of the territory, but half the sovereignty of the whole, being a political more than a geographical division. Finally and enough, what would have been the result in that day of chronic unrest, with insurrection as the chief business of half the dukes, counts, and chieftains, if there had been an attempt to erect a separate kingdom and put a baby on its throne? It was with the consent of some, at least, of the nobles that had followed Carloman, and with the unreserved approval of the hierarchy, that the entire state was placed in the hands of Charles. One would find it hard to see

[1] Hodgkin, p. 89; Vétault, p. 187.

[2] Mombert, p. 49.

[3] Einhard, *Life*, p. 12. He says the accession of Charles to the entire kingdom was by the unanimous choice of the Frankish nobles, including many that had been of Carloman's court.

Capefigue, p. 151.

79

how they could have done anything else unless they wanted the return of chaos. The Frankish domain was once more united under one head. French and Germans kept the peace, acknowledged one ruler, and men could hear other things than the rattling of sabers.

The state of society the young King now essayed to dominate was the most peculiar of which we have record.

The Roman Empire at the time of its greatest expansion included all of modern France, the Rhinelands, southern and southwestern Germany, over which it had spread a certain culture with a fairly definite system of government and economics. When the barbarians invaded and finally possessed this territory, they brought no culture and scarcely any conception of life other than to fight, to hunt, and to feed. By the time they had mastered the last of the moldering Roman structure and had adopted the Christian religion, they had incorporated themselves with the peoples dwelling in the conquered regions. There now grew up a new composite civilization, so to call it, that usually combined the worst features of the barbarian and of the old Roman State. In this the condition of the generality of mankind was infinitely more deplorable than it had been before; for we are not to forget that the veritable ideas of progress effectual upon Europe and America were not brought out of the Nordic forests. Mostly they came from the shores of the Ægean, Adriatic, and Mediterranean, and survived despite, and not by reason of, the influx from the North.

Under the invaders, a new economic system grew up. The land was owned by the nobles that had been evolved from the system of tribal chiefs prevailing in the woods, and these alone had any opportunity for culture, leisure, or sufficiency. For the owners, the land was tilled by subjugated hordes that were either slaves in name as in fact, or by so-called freemen that were bound to render to their lords military service and annual labor.

The nobles, possessing the land in a primitive age, held

CHARLEMAGNE'S CORONATION CHAIR
Now in the Cathedral at Aachen

over the masses all sources of supply and of life, as in an industrial age owners of factories hold over their workers a similiar predominance. In the days of Childeric III, these landed noblemen were of an almost inconceivable ignorance. Such learning as still survived was virtually confined to the monasteries and possessed by the monks. In later times men have been pleased to say harsh things about the monastic orders. Whatever may be urged against them is insignificant compared with the priceless service they performed to learning and civilization. In the Egyptian darkness that settled over Europe from the fifth to the ninth century, the light was kept burning in the monasteries and only there. We observe to-day in museums parchment volumes illumined with skill and patient care and great beauty. We are too likely to forget that these ancient parchment books were most often classical texts that but for the loyal scholarship of the monks would have perished from the earth. In hundreds of bare stone cells sat roughly clad priests and friars, heads bent over frames, pen or brush in hand, patiently copying the works of antiquity and blessing posterity with inestimable boons.[1]

Elsewhere was no literature, art, common education, or a sense of the amenities of life. Of all the princes, dukes, princelings, and chieftains, great and small, that owed allegiance to Pepin, King of the Franks, it is likely that not more than two or three could write their names or read the decrees and treaties they signed with crosses. Clerks or monks must be employed to read to them the letters and commands of their royal master and to compose as well as transcribe the replies.

In all ways, the eclipse of the refinements of human existence was beyond modern imagination. Even the rudimentary sense of the beautiful seemed to have been lost, and there was almost no life better than the life of a sty. The wealthiest, the most powerful nobles were rammish clowns of un-

---

[1] *Vide* Dieffenbach and Vogt, pp. 320–21, for a good summary of these activities; for their immense value to the world, conf. Hodgkin, pp. 235–36.

mentionable personal habits. In the common orders, the glory of the human mind seemed gone out forever and the race to have plunged back into the morasses of the Stone Age. What were called cities were collections of filthy huts, threaded by narrow and filthy lanes and dwelt in by wretched creatures with matted hair and brutish looks. Even the dwellers in castles and palaces, as is plainly demonstrated now by certain remains, led life in ways that we should deem impossible. In all of what is now Germany, outside of the few Roman settlements, was then not so much as one town.[1] Elsewhere in what were called capital cities, like Soissons and Paris, wolves from the near-by forests ranged the streets at night and no man ventured forth unarmed.

The fine arts had perished. The magnificent development of the Augustan Age seemed to have been all spent and vain. Men almost forgot how to sing the simplest airs. As late as 740, when the Emperor Copronymus sent an organ as a gift to King Pepin, it was regarded as a mystery, being the first ever seen or heard of in all Frankland.[2]

Agriculture was in a condition of unbelievable crudity. Horticulture was unknown. That agriculture survived at all is another of the inextinguishable debts the world owes to the monks. Around every monastery was a glebe of cultivated land, where with patient labor and gratuitous care grains and edible plants were grown that were unknown elsewhere and would otherwise have ceased to exist.[3]

The most ordinary arts of life were lost. Men forgot for a time how to forge iron, for instance, and it was to obtain the iron clamps holding the stones together that noble monuments of antiquity like the Roman Coliseum were wrecked. Even the simple art of making brick was lost.[4] Except in the churches, there was little glass. It is probable that in all of

[1] Hallam, chap. IX, Part I.

[2] Mombert, p. 50; also at page 55. The whole of his chapter III, dealing with this subject, is especially profitable.

[3] Hallam, chap. IX, Part I.   [4] Hallam, chap. IX, p. 538.

Pepin's domain when he came to rule there was scarcely a dwelling with a glazed window. There was no paper, and the conquest of Egypt by the Saracens cut off the supply of papyrus. No material existed for the making of books but parchment or vellum and the high cost of this material helped to extinguish learning.[1]

To the state of the masses under this dispensation, there is no modern analogue except among those dreadful creatures that hive upon the social stratum next below the pariahs of India. The nobles, being ignorant and having no conception of life beyond robbing and eating, were blandly accustomed to view the lower orders as a form of beast like horses except that they went upon two feet instead of four. The rule of the nobles over their subjects was absolutism untempered by assassination or anything else. Each in his own domain, large or small, was monarch. Upon the people dwelling under his yoke he had the power of life and death and all else. In any detail of their most intimate lives, he could interfere. Nothing they had or used or wore or made could they call their own. Ownership of the land conferred rank, power, ownership of all that was upon the land, biped or quadruped, and the title to land lay in the swiftest seizure and the more tenacious grasp.

Beyond the will of the sovereign was virtually nothing that could be called a recognizable law, but there were certain admitted customs, most of which made against the lowly and for the benefit of the noble landowner. Thus murder was atoned for by paying money on a scale of prices adjusted according to the social position of the person murdered. For the killing of one of high degree, the price was six hundred solidi, or about two thousand dollars. For an average person in the middle class, a subaltern officer, or a tax collector, two hundred solidi; for a peasant, should indeed his master make any fuss about him, forty-five solidi — say, a hundred and forty dollars. These payments were exacted by the local sovereign

[1] Hallam, chap. IX, p. 640.

and did not obviate the inconveniences arising from private revenge, which might always be invoked on the same terms.

The sovereign was court, judge, and jury; he heard complaints and made awards according to his own royal and meandering fancy. In what may be called, if we wish, the administration of justice, all the worst superstitions of barbarism were rampant, and a man proved that he was not guilty of the theft whereof he was accused by plunging his arm in boiling water, handling a piece of red-hot iron, floating in the river, or eating a piece of consecrated bread. Even the wisest and best of men believed in these childish fooleries after it had become fairly well known that criminals had discovered ways of making their flesh immune against burning or boiling.[1]

The huts of the common people consisted of one room without windows. Chimneys were unknown even in the most elaborate palaces. A hole in the roof allowed the smoke from the fire to escape.[2] Beds were possessed only by the wealthy; a nobleman was deemed extravagantly rich if he owned so many as three.[3] Men wore clothes made of leather unlined, and customarily wore one suit until it fell to pieces.

The local nobleman, lord, duke, or what not had upon him one restraining influence and none other, whether of human or divine origin. Tribute he must pay and homage with promise of obedience to his overlord, whoever that might be, because his overlord, being able to muster the greater number of spearmen, might in consequence become disagreeable. This aside, he could kill anybody, maim anybody, rob anybody that happened to be weaker than he, and of these privileges he generally and liberally availed himself; sometimes at tariff rates before given, more often scot-free. It appears that none of the overlords at the top, none of the nobles on the successive steps of the throne, none of the retainers under the nobles, ever thought of the generality of people as in any way different from cattle. They were perfectly honest

[1] Hallam, chap. IX, p. 487.   [2] *Ibid.*, pp. 540–41.   [3] *Ibid.*, p. 543.

and sincere in this view, just as in later ages the fortunate were sincere in their contempt for the poor and the hand workers. God had ordained the nobles to rule, the human cattle to be ruled. In these two great fundamental facts the nobles saw all the requisites of a perfect blessed and enduring state of society [1] — so far as in sober moments they saw anything.

At intervals, following an ancient custom of the woods, the overlord would summon to his capital a council of his subordinate chieftains. He might hear their opinions about the policy of the realm, but he commonly did as he pleased. In case of war each was obligated to come with a certain number of soldiers. As there was no surgery, men wounded in battle usually died of their wounds; and from all that can be learned now, the commissariat was something to marvel at.

Slavery existed everywhere. Persons captured in battle, unless they were of rank, or could ransom themselves, were deemed the slaves of the conqueror. If he did not need them himself, he could always find a ready purchaser among the Saracens. 'Britons never will be slaves,' says the old song. They have been, however. Slavery existed in all parts of the Anglo-Saxon kingdom, as elsewhere, and it is odd to observe that the earliest recorded protest against the traffic seems to have come from Irish sources.[2]

It was a kingdom thus based, peopled, and mannered that Charles, in his twenty-sixth year, had come to rule. The disorders that were inherent in such a state fell early upon him, but not altogether by his own fault. It was to be his fate throughout his life to have his affairs darkened, or more rarely brightened, by the influence of some woman. At first it was his mother, Bertrade, the Queen Dowager Bertha of the Big Foot. Often in the earlier acts of this drama we saw the stage crossed by a woman of the one type, sinister, designing, restless, intriguing, domineering, usually unscrupulous, sometimes depraved, but invariably affecting in some

[1] Hallam, chap. IX, Part I, p. 499.   [2] *Ibid.*, p. 507.

85

way the course of history. Bertrade abounded in virtues
and good works; yet she was more or less of the domineering
order, and her ministration along the familiar lines began
early.

The manner of it involves a story instructive, momentous
in its historical significance, and illuminating the eternal persistence of the lure of accumulated wealth.

The city of Rome was conceived of as a republic, of which
the Pope was the temporal as well as the spiritual head. At
that time he was chosen by the suffrages of the people at
large. The possessions of the Holy See were extensive.[1]
After the addition of the twenty-two cities they became of an
imposing size. In 767, the health of the Pontiff, Paul I, was
manifestly failing, and a band of wretched conspirators
undertook to gain, by one of the most audacious stratagems
in history, the control of these great possessions.

The chiefs of this conspiracy were three brothers of ancient
family and great power in their native Tuscany. One of
them, Toto, was the Duke of Népi; the others were named
Passivus and Pascalis.[2] Their military following was large
and devoted. With the aid of it they planned to elevate to
the Papacy a fourth brother, one Constantin. The impu-
dence of this proposal belongs to the phenomena of the age.
Constantin was a layman; he had never taken even the
initiate of the holy orders.

Scarcely had Pope Paul breathed his last when the conspirators at the head of their soldiery entered the city, held a
conventicle at the house of the Duke of Népi, declared Constantin to have been elected Pope, and, overawing the populace, installed him in the Palace of the Lateran. The next
day they passed him at a bound through the degrees of sub-
deacon, deacon, and priest. Then at the point of the pike
they compelled the people to take the oath of fidelity to their
candidate, and on the following Sunday at Saint Peter's,
protected by their military power, they crowned him.

[1] Hodgkin, p. 63.　　　[2] Vétault, p. 165.

But the city, although overawed by the soldiers, seethed with indignation at this sacrilegious performance. Two men, father and son, Christopher the one and Sergius the other, undertook to rescue Rome and Christendom from degradation. Their thought was to appeal to the King of the Lombards, holding court at Pavia, but the order had gone forth that no one should leave Rome except by permission of the conspirators, whose armed satellites guarded every gate. To make their escape, Christopher and Sergius pretended that they had determined to take holy orders and wished to enter the monastery of Spoleto. The purpose to take holy orders was one that no power dared to circumvent. Nevertheless, the suspicions of the conspirators were aroused that two men, father and son, and of such prominence, should at the same time be seized with this desire. Instead of granting a permit to depart, they sent for the Abbot of Spoleto, delivered the two candidates into his hands, and ordered him to see that they were conveyed safely to the monastery.

As soon as they were well outside of Roman territory, Christopher and Sergius managed to elude their guard and got to a Lombard nobleman named Theodice. He took them and their story to King Desiderius.[1]

The wily Desiderius, although willing for his own purposes to mix in the affairs of Rome, did not quite dare openly to espouse the cause of regularity, but sent his petitioners to a powerful Lombard clergyman named Valdipert, with the notion that Valdipert would probably head a movement of rescue which, if it failed, the King could easily disavow.

For thirteen months the false Pope reigned at Rome, held in his place by the army of the conspirators. He even had the hardihood to write to King Pepin two letters reminding him of the alliance between the Holy See and the Kingdom of the Franks, and soliciting support in the difficult position in which he found himself, the conspirators meantime enriching themselves with the papal possessions. At last the volunteer

[1] Vétault, p. 166.

army of liberation raised by Christopher and Sergius with the aid of Valdipert was ready to move. It approached Rome, assaulted and carried one of the gates, entered the city, and engaged in a hand-to-hand struggle in the streets. The Duke of Népi was killed, and after hours of combat, the soldiers of the conspirators were beaten and dispersed. Then the false Pope was seized and on July 28, 768, was cast into a prison cell.

Valdipert, the Lombard, now attempted to serve the interests of his King by securing the election of a pope friendly to Desiderius, a monk named Philip. The wise Christopher and Sergius had no idea of being used as tools for any faction. Monk Philip had been brought out of his cell to be crowned. They sent him back to his cloisters and insisted upon a free election in the accustomed manner and upon which they purposed to exercise no influence. The result of the election was the choice of Stephen III, who was crowned Pope on August 8, 768.

But for those thirteen months anarchy and crime had ruled at Rome. Order was not reëstablished without a terrible struggle. The conspirators were still strong and were supported by bandits and desperadoes. Rapine and murder ran unchecked through the city. Fighting raged in the streets attended with scenes of incredible cruelty on both sides. Passivus, the Bishop Theodore, the Tribune Gacilis, and strange to say, Valdipert, who had helped to overthrow these men, having been captured by different bands, their tongues and eyes were torn out and they were left to perish miserably in the kennels. Constantin himself was dragged from his prison cell and narrowly rescued from death after he had been blinded.[1]

In this emergency, seeing no hope of subduing the lawless elements, Stephen III determined to appeal to the King of the Franks, titular protector of Rome, most faithful of the sons of the Church. He chose for his envoy Sergius, who had

[1] Vétault, p. 169.

been so efficient in the revolt against Constantin. Sergius reached the Frankish court just after Pepin had died and the dual thrones had been mounted by Charles and Carloman.

One thing that Stephen wished was that the King of the Franks should send a delegation to Rome of his most eminent prelates to take part in a conference on the state of Christendom. Charles, Carloman, and Bertrade, who was active in all matters of state, welcomed this invitation and sent the Archbishops of Reims, Sens, Tours, Mayence, and others as Frankish representatives. It was at this conference that, in view of the dreadful experiences of the last year and a half, the manner of electing the Pope was changed. The electoral right was now restricted to the clergy of Rome and eligibility to the Papacy was, in the end, limited to members of the College of Cardinals.[1]

It was thus that history was made. But the next consequence of the conspiracy was more spectacular. King Desiderius thought he saw in the disordered state of Rome the opportunity he desired for profitable interference, and he presented to the Pope a claim for the payment of the Lombard forces that had taken part in the overthrow of the conspirators. Inasmuch as these forces were volunteer and not national, the claim, which in any event would have been untenable, became preposterous. When the Pope refused to entertain it, the King revenged himself by seizing papal lands and other property existing in the Lombard dominions.

Two years of protest and negotiation followed, when Desiderius, declaring that he wished to make a pilgrimage to Rome to visit the tombs of the Apostles, proposed a personal interview with the Pope. When this came about, Stephen approved himself of a firm courage. He yielded nothing, either to the blandishments or the threats of the King, standing immovably for the restoration of the lands Desiderius had taken and for the performance of the Lombard undertakings toward the Holy See.[2]

[1] Vétault, p. 170.   [2] Vétault, p. 171.

There was in Rome at that time a strong faction of Lombard mercenaries and supporters headed by one Paul Afiara. As soon as it was evident that the King had failed to win his point in the conference, Afiara raised a mob of desperate men and attacked the dwelling of Christopher and Sergius, determined to kill them. Friends helped them to escape, although with great difficulty, to the Palace of the Lateran, where they took refuge. But the Lombard partisans did not hesitate to invade the papal residence and to threaten the Pope himself. With heroic calm Stephen met and cowed them, but they remained nevertheless in possession of the palace.

The next day they escorted the Pope to Saint Peter's, where another conference was to be held. Once inside, Desiderius had the doors locked, and then, ceasing to pretend, he loosed upon the Pope a torrent of threats and abuse and thought to terrify him into submission.

Christopher and Sergius had gathered a body of their adherents and were preparing a forcible rescue, when two bishops appeared bearing what purported to be an order of the Pope commanding them to lay aside their arms and present themselves at once at the Vatican, or, failing to do so, to enter upon a monastic life as a penalty for the breach of the law they were about to commit. On receipt of this letter, which was a forgery by Desiderius, the forces of Christopher and Sergius dispersed, and the two chiefs, after some hesitation, determined to present themselves at the Basilica.

As soon as they arrived there, Desiderius had them arrested as prisoners of war. The Pope, anxious to save their lives, begged them to enter a monastery. Desiderius agreed to allow them to do this, and the father and son were received among the clergy. But Desiderius was none the less determined upon his revenge. One of his agents conveyed to them ostensibly secret information that a certain door of the monastery was left unlocked at night and could easily be passed. They purposed to take advantage of this for an exit, but at nightfall partisans of the King entered by the same door, seized the father and son on the pretense that they had attempted to escape, put out their eyes, and cast them into a dungeon. The father died at the end of three days; the son survived some years, but never regained his liberty.[1]

Holding the Pope a virtual prisoner and administering the Papal States in his name, Desiderius now dispatched to Charles what purported to be a letter from Stephen III commending Desiderius as his true and faithful friend and denouncing Christopher and Sergius as tyrants that, aided by an agent of Carloman, had tried to imprison and then to assassinate the Pope. This devilish forgery was designed to forestall any appeal to Charles in behalf of Stephen; also to further the dissensions that Desiderius knew were arising between Charles and his brother.

It was at this point that Queen Bertrade, usually so sane, seemed to lose her wits with the rest. Suddenly she appeared with a project to end all strife and unite the Lombard and Frankish Kingdoms in indissoluble ties. By the look of it, this, too, must have been an invention of Desiderius, but the historians have never definitely settled it upon his head. Bertrade had been visiting at his court;[2] she was always partial to him, and it may be that nothing more than a natural bent toward intrigue and a woman's obsession about matchmaking was the origin of her dazing performance. She now proposed that Charles should marry Desiderata, the daughter of King Desiderius, and that the Princess Gisla, Charles's sister, should be given in marriage to Prince Adelghis, Desiderius's eldest son. If the marriage with Charles was not possible, she was willing to substitute Carloman.

She seems to have believed herself a negotiator of rare gifts. After his estrangement with Charles, Carloman had withdrawn to his own dominions and gone his way alone. Bertrade now visited him and arranged a truce between the

[1] Vétault, p. 172.   [2] Einhard, *Annals*, p. 56.

91

brothers. She next went to the court of Tassilo, Duke of
Bavaria, who for years had been an unwilling vassal of the
Frankish establishment, and induced him to assume a front
of amity and obedience. So far all seemed to prosper, but in
the end her diplomacy went to wreck in the respect where she
had set most store by it. Pope Stephen, learning of the contemplated union between the Frankish and Lombard houses,
managed to get to the two Kings an extraordinary letter in
which he denounced in terms that are almost savage the
whole plan and revealed something of his complaints against
Desiderius. The proposed union he called 'a diabolical inspiration.' It would not be a marriage, but an association
most degrading. He ended the letter, which he said was
watered with his tears, by exhorting each king by the holiest
tokens, not to entertain any proposal of a marriage with
Desiderata, and not to allow his sister Gisla to be married
to Adelghis.[1]

In the mean time Charles had sent an embassy to Desiderius that had demanded the restoration of the seized papal
property, and succeeded in rescuing some of it, so that the relations between the Papacy and the King of the Lombards
were not so perilous as before. Despite the letter of the Pope,
which one might have expected to restrain him, Charles now
prepared to follow his mother's wishes and marry the Lombard maiden. If it was to be either of the brothers, it must be
he, for whereas he had only a mistress, Carloman had a wife
by full rank, the Gerberga whom we have already recorded
for her adventure through the Alps.

It is to be noted thus early in the narrative, what will appear only too plainly as we proceed, that Charles's view concerning the marriage relation had the looseness traditional in
his family. The mistress with whom he was now living was
an excellent Frankish woman named Himiltrude, by whom
he had a son.[2] He put her away and married Desiderata.
But the rest of the scheme failed at the start. The Princess

[1] Dieffenbach and Vogt, pp. 175–76; Einhard, *Life*, p. 28.   [2] Vétault, p. 18.

Gisla refused to be married to Adelghis. Neither command nor entreaty could move her, and rather than endure a worse fate, she fled to a convent, no doubt to escape the strenuous Bertrade. Incidentally, though she could hardly have known it, she had escaped at the same time union with one that was shortly to be proved among the most contemptible of mankind.

One year of the company of the gentle but dull Desiderata sufficed Charles. She was an invalid, she was unlikely to bear children, she seems to have been hardly more than half-witted, and in any case she was without a quality that fitted her to be the consort and companion of one of unresting mind and mounting ambition. With small ceremony he packed the lady home,[1] where she arrived before the widow of Carloman and her children found the same refuge at the Lombardian court.

In Desiderata's case, the insult was aggravated (to the feminine sensibility) by the fact that upon securing his divorce Charles immediately married a beautiful Alemannian on whom his eyes had long been set.[2] The times were of an easy judgment about all such matters, but this performance struck the common opinion as over-raw and was sternly condemned by Queen Mother Bertrade.[3] She had reason; all her matchmaking and diplomacy had come down about her head. For the only time in her life she and her elder son had a serious difference.

One other critic was outspoken. A schoolmate of Charles in the old palatine days and his close friend afterward was Adalhard, the son of Bernard, bastard son of Charles Martel, and therefore a cousin of the King. He occupied at the court a place of trust and confidence. When Desiderata arrived and

[1] Einhard (page 27) says she was sent home, 'men know not for what reason.' The lady left so little mark upon history that even her name is uncertain. Desiderata she is called as a matter of convenience and on the sole authority of one writer. Others think her name was Adalperga. *Vide* Abel's edition of Einhard, footnote at page 27.

[2] Vétault, p. 185.   [3] Einhard, *Life*, p. 28.

had been married, Adalhard took the oath of fidelity to her as his sovereign. When Charles sent her home and chose another spouse, the eloquent young monk condemned the King's course as essentially bigamous, declared he would never serve the new Queen, quit the palace, turned his back on a world where such things were possible, and entered a monastery.[1] For a life of piety and self-sacrifice he was afterward canonized.

The relations between Charles, King of the Franks, and Desiderius were thus strained and menacing when there arose another source of trouble.

As so often happens in history, the two countries were destined to a grapple and the immediate cause of strife was not really material. There came on now a new quarrel between King Desiderius and the Pope, a quarrel concerning lands, cities, and other matters, but chiefly concerning lands. I should point out here that throughout the Dark and Middle Ages the possession of land, even of small areas of land, was held to be of such supreme importance, that nations were often involved in long and bloody wars and thousands of persons were slain in a quarrel about a bit of earth that might not now be deemed worth a lawsuit. The reason for this extraordinary avidity was that the land being in those days the sole source of subsistence and wealth, the fortunate lived by exploiting the tillers of it, just as in later times they lived by exploiting industry or transportation. Therefore the ownership of land was the necessary machinery for the accumulating of wealth, and the means by which land was obtained by and for the benefit of the fortunate often afford us, as we review the ancient spirals, a curious parallel to other economic exploitations in later years. Perhaps there is no lesson of history surer than the long endurance of the methods by which exploitation thrives. The names of these methods undergo many changes; the spirit, purpose, and result seem much the same, no matter in what age or country.

[1] Vétault, p. 184.

CHAPTER VI

THE FIGHT IN THE MOUNTAINS

KING DESIDERIUS and the Papacy were in this state of armed truce when on February 1, 772, Stephen III died and was succeeded by one of the great figures of mediæval history, a statesman of courage and prescience and a stalwart soldier of civilization, Hadrian or Adrian I.[1]

The King, who was unaware of the character of the new Pontiff, continued his policy of oppression. He desired to extend his domain by adding the territories bestowed on the Pope by Pepin, but even more he yearned to humiliate and outmaneuver Charles, King of the Franks, whom he hated with a consuming hatred, notable even for times expert in hating. More than one reason animated him. There was the natural jealousy of adjacent monarchs, and there rankled in him the old defeats inflicted by Pepin on the forces of Aistulf. These might have been motives enough, but to them had lately been added the insult of the unceremonious bundling home of the dull, gentle Desiderata. Still other incentives came into play. The Kingdom of the Lombards and the Kingdom of the Franks were like democracy and monarchy: the two could not co-exist. Pavia had long been the resort and refuge of all persons that had, or thought they had, a grievance against the Frankish domination. We have seen how Gerberga, widow of Carloman, ostentatiously fled thither with her two sons. Hunold, the old Duke of Aquitania, whose life Charles had spared, went there to plot against him.[2] Recalcitrants from the outlying provinces flocked there for comfort and support. From all these,

[1] Einhard, *Annals*, p. 57.
[2] Gaillard, *Histoire de Charlemagne* (second edition), p. 235.

95

Desiderius had gathered a contemptuous opinion of the King of the Franks and rated the new Pope no better.

One aim of his policy, if he was to obtain the lands he desired, must be to keep Charles from interfering in the affairs of Italy [1] lest there should be another invasion of Frankish hosts. Cunning naturally suggested the stirring up of trouble in Frankland, and the handy means to make trouble there were offered by the two sons of Carloman. Desiderius espoused their cause and made to the Pope the extraordinary demand that he should recognize one of these children as rightful King of Neustria and the other as rightful King of Austrasia.

The Pope, with reasonable indignation, refused to be any part of this amiable design.

Desiderius now had recourse to the strategy he had found effective with Pope Stephen. He proposed a personal interview at which all the differences with the Holy See could be ironed out. There is every reason to believe that he had planned, through his agent, Paul Afiarta, to seize the Pope and to keep him a prisoner until he should consent to recognize the sons of Carloman, still using as a basis for his claim to the lands the unpaid bill for the auxiliaries of Christopher and Sergius. Afiarta himself admitted that this was the intention.[2] To support the claim for the auxiliaries, an alleged treaty was produced by which the justice of the claim was acknowledged.

But Sergius was still alive and a competent witness to the fact that the alleged treaty must be a forgery and fraud. Afiarta either strangled Sergius with his own hands or had him killed by one of his mercenaries.

When word of this crime came to Pope Hadrian, he ordered the arrest of the murderer. Afiarta fled to Ravenna. The Pope ordered that he should be sent to Rome for trial. Instead, the Archbishop of Ravenna tried him on the spot,

---

[1] Vétault, p. 192; Hodgkin, pp. 90–91; Dieffenbach and Vogt, p. 328.

[2] Vétault, pp. 193–94.

found him guilty, and put him to death. Now and then, in the weird desolation of murder, rapine, and cruelty that the times present, appears a soul singularly given to mercy and justice. Hadrian was one of these. When he heard of the condemnation of Afiarta, he sent a swift express with orders to prevent the execution of the sentence and to substitute perpetual banishment for the death penalty. The well-meant intervention arrived too late. The criminal had been beheaded. Then the Pope addressed to the Archbishop a letter of severe condemnation in which occurred these words:

'You must remain, before your conscience and God, responsible for this man's death. As he had shown a sincere repentance, you should have taken thought of his soul and given him an opportunity to make his peace with God.' [1]

The pretended claim of Carloman's sons having failed, Desiderius fell back upon the unpaid bill for the auxiliaries, which there was now no one to disprove. As an alleged indemnity he seized three cities of the papal territory, Ferrara, Coarcchio, and Faenza, and threatened Ravenna.

Since the extinction of the shadowy authority of the Exarch, in the name of the Eastern Emperor nominal ruler of the twenty-two towns, Ravenna had been one of the chief possessions of the Papacy. The aggression of Desiderius was mere banditry, but he felt compelled to allege a pretext. Life in the Dark Ages needs all the palliating circumstances that can be named in its favor. Let us then make the best of this fact, that when a potentate went forth to seize and annex, he might say other things in behalf of his performances, but he did not customarily allege that he was acting for the glory of God and the spread of civilization; at least he laid not upon his soul the burden of a greasy hypocrisy. Imperialism was then merely plain imperialism and was not undertaken to teach subject peoples self-government or to introduce the wearing of trousers. The Kingdom of the Lombards was beginning to decay at heart. King Desiderius

[1] Hodgkin, p. 92.

believed the cure to be an extension of territory and went forth to obtain it — on the basis of his claim for debt.

He now renewed to the Pope the proposal of a personal interview. Hadrian properly declined to risk his life in such a meeting unless he had first a trustworthy assurance of the return of the seized papal property.

'If he will not make this restitution first,' he said to the Lombard deputation, 'he shall never see my face. I will send to him delegates into whose hands he is to place the cities and fortresses belonging to the Holy See. When he has effected this restitution, I will meet him any place he may designate.'

The King received this delegation with a torrent of imprecations [1] and threats, declaring openly his purpose to go to Rome and compel the Pope to accede to his wishes. His army was already prepared for the invasion. He led it in person accompanied by his son Adelghis and the widow and sons of Carloman. Thus accoutered, he moved upon the gates of Rome.

The capable and unterrified Hadrian threw up fortifications around the city and prepared to defend it by force of arms. But first he had recourse to the less material mode of warfare. He made known that upon the first Lombard to make a forward and hostile movement he would pronounce the doom of excommunication.[2]

Neither Desiderius nor his soldiers cared to incur this penalty. The Lombards abandoned the attack upon Rome, but they continued to hold the Pope's towns they had seized and to threaten Ravenna.

In this emergency, Pope Hadrian determined to appeal to Charles, son of the Pepin that had saved Pope Stephen, grandson of The Hammer that had saved Christendom. Every pass through the mountains was held by the Lombards, who had probably foreseen some such embassy. Hadrian's plucky messenger was not thus to be balked. He

[1] Vétault, p. 195. He is following the account given by Anastasius.
[2] Mombert, p. 89.

made his way by sea to Marseilles, and thence northward by devious routes as he could until he reached Metz.[1] It was in the fall of the year; Charles was enjoying his annual hunting expedition in Lorraine, and the messenger must seek him in the woods.

The appeal of the Pope awoke in him a mixed reaction. Although he attained afterward to a rank among the military geniuses of the world and was deemed fit to stand by Cæsar and Napoleon,[2] he was, for his times, strangely abhorrent of war. When he could, he strove to avoid it and fought only when there seemed no escape from fighting. In this instance, on the other hand, he was the heir of Pepin and Charles Martel, he was the putative if not the nominated defender of the Holy See, he was a sincere and zealous churchman, he revered the sanctity and authority of the successors of Saint Peter, to one of them he owed his crown. Moreover, he had a certain official duty to perform. Stephen had made him the Patrician of Rome, filling the office created by Alaric. It meant now that he was the responsible military ruler of the city.

In this conflict of impulsions, he adopted a course that, if he had never done anything else, would have been enough to stamp him as an innovator and original genius. Taking all things into consideration, it was a course so singular that his contemporaries must have learned of it with gasping amazement. He proposed a peaceful settlement instead of war, which was remarkable enough, but he proposed himself to finance the adjustment, which was unheard of. He knew well enough that no Lombardian army could stand against his trained Frankish legions. He knew that the sure result of a victory would be an extension of Frankish territory. If he were looking for more empire, he could hardly expect anywhere in the world a better opportunity ready to his hand. No other man in his position has been willing to let such a

[1] Vétault, p. 209; Einhard, *Annals*, pp. 57–58.
[2] Hippolyte Castille, *Parallèle entre César, Charlemagne et Napoléon.* Paris, 1858.

99

CHARLEMAGNE, FIRST OF THE MODERNS

chance slip. Instead of pressing forward to take it, he sent off an embassy to Desiderius inviting him to make peace and offering him 14,000 gold sous to give up his claim against the papal cities.[1] It was a sum equal to about $252,000, but of ten times the present purchasing power of that amount.

Desiderius, who must have been madder than usual, scornfully rejected this offer, although it probably exceeded all of his claims for his fabulous auxiliaries. Reluctantly Charles proclaimed the war, and ordered the gathering of his forces at Geneva.

This meant, virtually, all the men in Frankland capable of bearing arms. The nobles came on horseback, supported by their faithful retainers, fully armed, and the peasants trudged in on foot with what weapons they could best manage. Deficiency in their equipment made not so much difference as one might imagine, since it was certain in those days that on the other side would be another detachment similarly accoutered and these Things, being only Things, might as well beat one another to death with flails as in any other way. Few of the Things in either army knew why they were dragged from their homes and set up to be shot full of arrows or mauled to death by other Things. The pleasure of their lords and masters was that they should be made worms' meat and more than that they knew not.

Ostensibly, the pleasure of their lords in this respect was not extended upon them without a loophole of escape. Should there be one among them that strongly objected to the worms' meat process, he could purchase exemption from service and danger by the paying of two hundred and twenty-five dollars. But this apparently merciful provision was for the vast masses of mankind only a bitter irony. Scarcely any one below the status of a thieving count, robber baron, highwayman, noble pickpocket, or other captain of industry of those times ever in his life saw so much money. Reforms in the social state were just beginning to be conceived. They

[1] Vétault, p. 210.

100

had a long way to go before they could reach and affect anything connected with the war game.

But the forces gathered at Geneva, Charles at their head.[1] The most interesting features of the mobilization, which were the sheltering, feeding, and drilling of so great a host, the chronicles neglect. Admitting the wants of the warriors of that time to have been of the simplest, yet to provide them must have demanded an organization greater and more skillfully directed than we are likely to ascribe to an age so disjointed and haphazard.

The one thing that is apparent in all the accounts is the commander. It was his first campaign; he revealed in it the highest qualities of a general. He had foreseen every move and provided for every contingency. It is said that on July 12, 1918, Marshal Foch knew that the Germans would start an offensive at midnight on the 14th, that it would fail, and that a few months thereafter the war would come to an end in the Argonne. Perhaps the difference between the successful and the unsuccessful commander has something to do with this power to foresee and to anticipate. It appears that Charles had already thought out for himself the substance of those military tactics that caused him eleven hundred years later to be studied by Napoleon. It was to strike swiftly before the enemy could expect an impending blow, and then to strike again while the enemy was trying to recover from the first assault. Vétault says that he made of war a systematic and exact science, 'for he saw as if by inspiration the points to attack, and descended upon them with blows sudden and decisive, moving great masses of men with a precision and rapidity that still astonish us, surrounded as we are by the marvelous inventions that have multiplied tenfold the means of action and the tactical resources of war.'[2]

Quickly he gathered his great host, quickly he prepared it, and moved with it southward. Following a plan that after-

[1] Einhard, *Annals*, p. 58.   [2] Page 165.

ward he saw tested on many a hard-fought and hard-won field, he divided his forces. Part, commanded by his uncle, Count Bernard, moved on Italy by way of the pass that has ever since borne the name of the count's patron saint.[1] The main body under his own command he led by way of Mont Cenis.[2]

King Desiderius had been amply warned of the coming of the Northern armies. He determined not to repeat the blunders that had been the ruin of Aistulf when Pepin was allowed to pour his troops unopposed through the narrow Alpine clefts. With the flower of the Lombard warriors he entrenched himself at Susa, the key to the southern end of the pass, and he sent his son, Prince Adelghis, whom Princess Gisla had scorned as a husband, to blockade the way through the mountains.

The Franks moved on and entered the defiles and gorges of Mont Cenis. It was a winding, dark, and perilous road, for it clung often between a torrent on one side and a precipice on the other. In many places a small force, well posted, intelligently directed, might hold back a multitude. Avalanches overhung and menaced the invaders. Most of the Franks had never before seen a mountain at close range nor dreamed of such prodigious surroundings. Their path filled them with unspeakable terrors. They were over the summit of the pass and had begun the descent when they found the road blocked and held by the Lombards, posted in an apparently impregnable position.

For the first time Charles was confronted with an emergency that tested all his resources and was pivotal to his career. Apparently he could not advance; assuredly he could not retreat without such humiliation and loss of prestige as would endanger his throne. For reënforcements or help outside of himself was no chance. He tried to force the Lombard

[1] It had previously been known as Jupitersberg.

[2] Wolfram von den Steinen, *Karl der Grosse, Leben und Briefe*, p. 13; Hodgkin, p. 93, *et seq.*; Vétault, p. 241, *et seq.*; Dieffenbach and Vogt, p. 328.

entrenchments; every attack was driven back. To pass the barrier before him seemed beyond human strength or persistence. According to the tradition, which may be the skirt of truth, or only the filigree stitched thereon, he sat down to study the situation, while his troops continued to hurl themselves upon the Lombard fortifications and to be repulsed like sea waves from a rock.

At last he had an inspiration to a desperate venture. Scanning the grim peaks about him, he thought he perceived a route through which a small body of troops might creep unobserved and turn the enemy's position. What he needed was a leader that knew enough of mountaineering to find the way, and this was the more difficult because Charles's forces were plainsmen. But they brought to his tent one night a native of the mountains, a minstrel, a wandering singer whose business was to amuse.[1] Charles, looking attentively upon this visitor, as was his wont with all men he encountered, thought he saw in him the qualities of resolution and candor. The peril involved was great. A treacherous stranger might betray all to the Lombards; but with the intuitive judgment of men and character that was one of the sources of his success, Charles decided to take the risk.

Before dawn, the detachment set forth under the sole guidance of this minstrel. That day the attack was renewed upon the front with the usual vigor and the usual result. The attention of the Lombards was fixed upon the repelling of these assaults.

Suddenly, just before noon, there was a wild yell in the heart of the pass, and a body of Franks leaped as if out of the side of the mountain upon the Lombard flank. At the same moment Charles urged forward a new assault upon the front. The Lombards, thus assailed on two sides and taken all by surprise, broke from their fortifications and fled in wild disorder, leaving all their baggage and throwing away their arms as they ran. Down the pass they sped, pursued by the

[1] Mombert, p. 91. The path was afterward called 'The Way of the Franks.'

whole Frankish army. The slaughter was great, the defeat overwhelming.[1]

Before the last of the terror-stricken survivors had issued from the mouth of the pass, King Desiderius in Susa had word of the disaster. Without a moment's delay he abandoned the defenses he had created against this powerful foe and fled along the road to Pavia.[2]

Panic fell upon the countryside. By the Lombards the advancing Franks were regarded with such superstitious terror as their own forefathers had inspired in the degenerate Romans. There never was a more striking instance of the compensating balances of history. It was now the enervated Lombards that deemed their visitors to be strange, superhuman, irresistible creatures from a new world. Desiderius shut himself in Pavia. Adelghis, the unlucky commander at the pass of Mont Cenis, never checked his headlong flight until he was safe in Verona. All other opposition ceased. With that one victory, Lombardy lay virtually at the conqueror's feet.

Charles moved swiftly on, receiving the submission of city after city. At last he was before the gates of Pavia, where Desiderius cowered. He laid out the siege, ordered the trenches, encompassed the city, and prepared to wait until it should fall into his hands. His forces had been augmented by the arrival of the division under his uncle that had traversed the Saint Bernard. There was nothing now in that part of the world that could stand against him.[3]

The Monk of Saint Gall enlivens his account of these matters with an incident. He says that the day Charles arrived before Pavia, King Desiderius and Duke Otker

[1] Von den Steinen cites an old chronicler who avers that the minstrel's reward was ample. He had stipulated that everything should be his as far as he could make his horn be heard. He got him to the top of a mountain and blew. Then he descended and asked every one he met if one had heard his horn. If the answer was 'yes,' the minstrel said: 'Then you belong to me' (page 13).

[2] Capefigue, vol. I, p. 177; Einhard, p. 14.

[3] Capefigue, *Charlemagne* (Paris, 1842), vol. I, p. 167. He points out that one element in the quick success of Charles was the superiority of the Northern horses.

mounted one of the towers of the city wall to watch the on-coming hosts. First, says the monk, appeared engines of war that Darius and Cæsar would have envied.

'Is Charles in that great crowd?' asked the King.

'Not yet,' said the Duke.

There came next the ordered ranks of soldiery, gathered from every part of the kingdom.

'Surely here comes Charles,' said the King.

'Not yet, not yet,' said the Duke.

The King was greatly troubled. He said:

'What can we do if he comes with forces even greater than these?'

'You cannot understand what Charles is like until he shall appear before you,' said Otker. 'As to what will come upon us then, I do not know.'

While they exchanged these reflections came the royal guard, which, according to this chronicler, never knew repose.

King Desiderius was stupefied.

'Surely that is Charles,' said he.

'Not yet,' said Otker.

Next defiled before them a brilliant cortège of bishops, abbots, clergy of the court chapel, and then the nobles. At this the unfortunate Desiderius could no longer endure the spectacle, and already felt the chill of death creeping upon him. He burst into sobs and murmured painfully:

'Let us descend! Let us conceal ourselves in the bowels of the earth, far from the sight and fury of so terrible an enemy!'

Otker, who was also trembling, for he knew well the for-midable power of Charles, having lived near him in better times, said:

'When you shall see the full company bristling with lances like a harvest field, when the waves of the Po and the Tessin reflect nothing but the glitter of the arms of his men, when they shall throw around these ramparts new torrents of men covered with iron, then you will understand that Charles is approaching.'

They had scarcely said these words when suddenly a dark cloud seemed to fall around them; one would have said that a tempest, unchained by Boreas himself, had obscured the light of heaven. As King Charles advanced, the glitter of the encircling swords threw upon the city a day more sinister than night itself. Charles was soon seen, a giant clad in iron; on his head an iron helmet, iron gauntlets on his hands, his breast and shoulders enveloped in an iron cuirass. His left hand brandished an iron lance while the right was stretched forth holding the iron of his invincible sword. Even his horse had the color and the strength of iron. Iron covered the roads and the plain; everywhere the rays of the sun fell upon the flash of iron. From the city arose a confused clamor of 'What masses of iron, alas! What masses of iron!'

'King!' cried Otker to his host, 'there is the man that your eyes have so long looked for!' and saying these words, he fell in a faint.[1]

Thus proceeds the worthy Monk. We may regret that in his day were no newspapers, since he seems to have possessed qualities that would have made him invaluable for the front page.

Leaving his uncle to manage the siege, Charles led a division of the army toward Verona. But the Prince Adelghis had no taste for further controversies with the terrible Franks. Alone he deserted his followers, stole from Verona by night, and, after wanderings and adventures that long surrounded his name with an unwarranted halo of romance, reached Constantinople, where he sought protection at the court of the Emperor of the East. The widow and sons of Carloman had left Pavia and taken asylum at Verona. They were in the city when it fell into the hands of Charles. The records do not tell what became of them. An effort has been made to identify one of the sons in Saint Siacre, who

[1] Monk of Saint Gall, pp. 74–77. A French version may be found in Vétault, pp. 212–13. The monk says that Duke Otker had been at the court of Charles and had fled thence to escape his displeasure. As a matter of fact, Otker was one of the nobles that accompanied the widow of Carloman in her flight.

was first a monk of Saint Pons in Nice and afterward bishop of that city.[1] Although accepted by some historians, the story has no good foundation. The one thing that seems fairly certain about these captives is that they suffered nothing at the hands of the victor.[2]

The day of the wild horse and the slow torture seems to have passed when he arrived.

The conqueror returned to Pavia, noted the satisfactory progress of the siege, and in his tent among the trenches celebrated Christmas; for all his life he was a devout and careful observer of religious ceremonies and festivals. His plan was to reduce Pavia by starvation, since the walls were too strong to be taken by assault and Desiderius refused to surrender. Why he held out is a mystery, supposing him to have been not wholly insane. There was no possible source from which he could hope for the least help, and delay meant only prolonged suffering and the useless sacrifice of his subjects. It was as sensible as most other things done by kings in those days. Since he was so obdurate and the siege was likely to be so drawn out, Charles determined to realize an old dream by visiting Rome.[3]

To Europe, to civilization, to the people of his day, to us in our own, and to all the millions that have dwelt in Europe between his day and ours, the consequences of that resolve were of great importance, though it seemed at the moment to be no more than a holiday jaunt — of spectacular proportions. No King of the Franks, no Mayor of a Neustrian or Austrasian Palace, no ruler of French or Germans, had ever paid such a visit or thought of it, most of these persons being chiefly concerned about fighting, except when their attention was taken up with their dull feasts or their women. But Charles was different from these. He had been, for his times,

[1] Vétault, p. 216 (footnote).

[2] 'He was known as the mildest of kings and in no other German hero the virtues of moderation, justice, and mercy so inborn as in him.' Von den Steinen, p. 20; Hodgkin, p. 95.

[3] Hodgkin, p. 95; Vétault, pp. 216-17.

well educated; he knew two languages well and had a tolerable acquaintance with a third.[1] Above all, he cherished a genuine and almost passionate love for learning, for he had gathered enough of knowledge to glimpse the benefits that might come from gathering more.

From certain remarks of his in later life, one may see clearly that he was ashamed of the barbarous ignorance of his court and his people, for scarcely any one outside of the priestly orders could be said to have so much as a vestige of culture. He was ashamed, too, of the blankly barren showing of his people in the arts of life. He knew that in architecture, music, letters, and all the gentler and nobler pursuits, the more fortunate inhabitants of the Italian peninsula put to ineffable shame the rude and raw immigrants that he commanded. He had often heard of the culture of which Rome was at once the guardian and exponent. He determined to gratify two desires, both strongly appealing to the better side of his nature — to visit the Holy Father of his Church and make observation of the learning he hoped to introduce in his own country.

If anything can now be surmised with assurance about the operations of his original and powerful intellect, it is that he had perceived another fatal flaw in the condition of the regions he ruled. Among them all was no welfare except for the handful of nobles. The rest were fast bound in misery and iron, desperately poor, brutally ignorant. The notions he had gained from his favorite authors were all against any such scheme of life. His own natural instincts of good will toward all rejected it. The peasant in him instructed him otherwise.[2] He had always been of a studious habit; despite his cheerful countenance and a sanguine disposition, he preferred serious things.

The bent of his mind is better shown by incidents than by a hazardous attempt to project oneself into his thinkings. In his age it was the universal custom for kings, nobles, and the

[1] Einhard, *Life*, p. 34.   [2] Freytag, *Karl der Grosse*, p. 7.

powerful to be entertained at dinner by coarse jesters, fools, acrobats, and tumblers. Charles would have none of these. Daily at his table were read to him the works of historians and philosophers.[1] He had rather discuss a page of Livy than hear bawdry, or sit bolus-eyed to watch jugglers swallow knives or gymnasts that could walk on their hands. This in such an age, before all else uncouth, we should deem no more than another fable if it were not so well upheld. And yet one may offer as a concession to the times and the power of environment that next to studious pursuits and theological discussions, this man liked hunting.[2] So strangely blended in him were the civilized and the savage impulses. He would relish a good sermon and doubtless be uplifted and bettered by it and then go out and run a deer to its death. And with more reason, he was proud of the fact that he was accounted the best swimmer of his day.[3]

His addiction to learning was nothing in the way of whim and we may dismiss at once the notion that it was some form of play acting. The man was incapable of posing. Macaulay remarks that something of the charlatan and the fakir persists in men the world has elected to call great, and cites as an illustration the sorry theatrics with which Chatham on his crutches used to enter the House of Commons.[4] Charles of the Franks has been scrutinized from every angle by hostile eyes keen to detect faults, and while enough of others have been laid bare, no one has detected in him a trace of the mountebank. His feeling about the darkness wherein his people dwelt must have been genuine and strong, for he had been but a short time King when he began to make quest about Europe for scholars and teachers, and the first of his purposes in now visiting Rome seems to have been to observe diligently the true state of education in the city that, despite

[1] Einhard, *Life*, p. 33.
[2] *Ibid.*, p. 32.
[3] Dr. Albert Huyskens, *Karl der Grosse und seine lieblingspfalz Aachen*, p. 10.
[4] Essay on Francis Thackeray's *Life of William Pitt*.

so many vicissitudes and so much of brutal strife around it, remained the capital of civilization.

But the fact that he had sent for the scholars and teachers to adorn his court is the first great fact that marks him out as different from his times, a phenomenon, almost a prodigy. Other rulers in his position had sent for and gathered about them first of all men of brawn, archers, noted warriors, men distinguished for much killing. Either so or, in gentler and sweeter moments, behold the monarch grinning at fools and applauding wrestlers. If not fools, then ladies more renowned for beauty than for virtue. This was the first ruler since the coming of barbarism that had cared anything about an intellectual diversion. In its own way, the fact was almost as momentous to Europe as the battle of Tours. It signaled the beginning of the return of civilization — after a long détour.

But now Charles was marching toward Rome, goal of his dreams. At a distance of thirty miles, the officers of the city came forth to greet him with elaborate ceremonies; the enthusiastic pomp and fervor of the welcome at the city gates must have suggested a triumph like that of a returning and victorious consul in the days of Roman grandeur. Pope Hadrian had good cause to be grateful to this valiant and faithful son of the Church. Charles, on his politic side, knew well enough how helpful the Holy See might be to him in the difficult task he had set for himself in the North. But he bore himself now like one unwilling to assume the stage center. At the gate of the city he dismounted and walked the rest of the way to the Church of Saint Peter, not the present magnificent pile of Bramante and Michael Angelo, but that earlier basilica that for architecture and size must have been the wonder of the mediæval world.

The Pope met him at the top of the steps; the two warmly embraced, and hand in hand they visited the tomb of Saint Peter.[1] They seem to have formed at once a personal friendship reasonably founded; they had similar views and tastes.

[1] Hodgkin, p. 96.

Charles talked long and often with the Holy Father, not alone about political matters, but theology and scholarship. Easter Sunday came and was celebrated in a great banquet. Charles entered and worshiped in the most famous churches of Rome.

His visit gave rise to a dispute that lasted among historians and writers for hundreds of years, and is not yet stilled. According to one chronicler, Charles thought so highly of Hadrian that he bestowed upon him a deed, not only of the twenty-two cities that formed the Papal States, but to an immense possession in addition to these, comprising virtually the whole of Italy aside from Tuscany, Piedmont, and Naples.[1] The deed, if it ever existed, was never carried out, and, again, if it existed, included a vast territory that was not Charles's to give away. But the weight of later opinion is that the document was all imaginary.[2] What he did beyond doubt was to confirm the papal title to the twenty-two cities, or those states that continued to obey the Pope as temporal as well as spiritual ruler until the days of United Italy.

The commander-in-chief now went back to the trenches before Pavia, and the siege continued. The result was a foregone conclusion. The inhabitants were starving. Nobody but the foolish Desiderius wished the hopeless struggle to continue. In June of that year, 774, Charles (being then thirty-two and having reigned six years) received the surrender of the city[3] and celebrated the end of his successful campaign. The Pavians had suffered much from famine and disease; the capitulation was a benefice. Short work was made of its details. Desiderius was at once deposed, Charles was crowned in his stead as King of the Lombards, all the Lombard cities acknowledged his rule, the royal treasure passed into his hands. One of the apparently indestructible fictions of history has made him to be crowned with the famous iron crown of the Lombards. The fact that the iron

[1] Hodgkin, pp. 97-99.
[2] *Ibid.*, p. 99; Gaillard, p. 276.   [3] Einhard, *Annals*, p. 59.

crown of the Lombards was not used until six hundred years later is powerless against this pleasant invention.[1]

A few years before, the fallen King would have been put to death. A century before, he would have been tortured. Without joining in the adulators' chorus, we can compare the treatment of Desiderius with the treatment of Waifar and discern with another sigh of relief the certainty of better things.[2] Desiderius was not blinded, shot full of arrows, nor tied to a wild horse. With the others of the royal family he was escorted over the Alps, where he entered a monastery and spent the rest of his life in the offices of a monk. We noted in a previous chapter that when paganism fell down, there came, however slowly, the beginnings of conscience as a factor in the affairs of state. Its manifestations in a people emotional and neurotic were sometimes of an astonishing nature. After a career so varied, so active, and so full of ill deeds, Desiderius recorded that he found in the sacerdotal duties the greatest happiness of his life. Nothing could induce him to return to the world he had so profitably left behind him.[3]

The women of the family seem to have become nuns. The ancient chroniclers, who sometimes slipped in their reporting, omitted to say whether the gentle but dull Desiderata, the discarded wife of Charles, was among these, or what became of the widow of Carloman. Prince Adelghis, being at the court of the Emperor of the East, escaped the cloister or other obscuration. He was destined to appear there in some adventures not exactly edifying, but not again as claimant to his father's lost crown. The old house of Lombardy had fallen forever; the fierce and all-conquering horde that had sped along the plains of northern Italy was become a sign of contempt instead of terror. To such ends had gone the aims

[1] Mombert, pp. 99–100; Wells, p. 198.

[2] Mombert (at page 98) cites a Lombard historian that said: 'he [Charles] exhibited the rare example of tempering his victory with clemency.'

[3] Vétault, p. 212.

of Alboin and the crimes of Rosamund. Fewer than two hundred years of soft skies and genial sunshine had wrought this change, and the conquerors of one century were the conquered of another. With the Lombards as with the rest of the barbarians, they did not master Rome but were mastered by it. The spiritual dominion of the Mediterranean, little disturbed by epochal upheavals in the political and social state, kept its course through the world as it has until this day.

Lombardy was not in reality united with Frankland.[1] Charles, becoming King of the Lombards, ruled over his new territories with the authority of an absolute monarch. 'Rex Francorum et Langobardorum.'[2]

One vestige of the once mighty Lombard Kingdom was left intact. Far to the south, the Duke of Benevento refused to acknowledge the Frankish sovereignty, proclaimed his independence, and made his capital an asylum for all the malcontents and conspirators of Italy that had a grudge against Pope or King. Charles might have marched then to reduce this recalcitrant; he was stayed by disturbing news from the North and called to a scene of action that for many years to come demanded his best attention. He had reason afterward to regret that he left the Beneventan gad-fly behind him.[3]

[1] Einhard, *Annals*, p. 60; Mombert, p. 99.
[2] Hodgkin, p. 102; Gaillard, p. 281.   [3] Vétault, pp. 222–23.

CHAPTER VII

EDUCATION AND DEMOCRACY

It was in the North that he went to the greatest testing of his fortitude and constancy, but before we come to that story of crux, we ought to deal with some momentous results, direct and indirect, of his visit to Rome.

Much more than a new title and a halo of new glory he carried home with him across the Alps. War-lord, ruthless on the battle-field, unturnable in resolution, he cherished still for learning, art, and the softer aspects of civilized life this peculiar veneration, which, as it was gratuitous and indomitable, must have been native. In Rome, while he had gratified this curious side of his nature, he had strengthened it. In this respect he looks different from the general run of conquerors, empire-builders, and military heroes. The purpose to wedge culture into the ways of his half-baked people was straight against precedent. It could add nothing to his territories, power, or renown. Seemingly out of sheer faith and zeal he absorbed himself in it. He came back now with manifestly a new impetus to this task.[1] Afterward it was throughout many and diverse adventures the most consistent policy of his government. As a German history declares, all his life he had rather honor a good student than a good field marshal.[2]

One reason why he had wished to visit Rome was to see for himself the memorials of its old-time culture. He could not go far along that road without being once more impressed with the difference between the state of the Franks and that of the Romans.[3] Crude and bleak as were the conditions left

---

[1] Wells, p. 323.   [2] Dieffenbach and Vogt, p. 348.

[3] 'He found learning all forgotten in his entire kingdom.' Monk of Saint Gall, p. 3.

in Rome after the tidal waves of Vandals and the like, they were infinitely better than the best that were known on the other side of the Alps. In Rome was a sense of art, a sense for the beautiful, and a taste for some measure of intellectual pleasures, and he might have commented to himself upon the everlasting persistence of the mysterious old Latin spirit, since it had survived four centuries of the corrodings of imperialism, four more of the sabots of the wild men, and was still cogent and victorious.

His virtuous resolves [1] he did not forget, strange to say, even in the wild campaigns with the Northerners into which he was next catapulted. Before long Fate put into his hands the means to make good his project and, according to tradition, it was from Ireland that the first help came.

One day he heard strange news in his palace. A trading vessel, merchandising from the British Islands, had put down at one of his seaport towns two Irishmen,[2] who, although they appeared to be salesmen, were crying unheard-of wares.

Up and down they went in the streets of the town where they had landed, saying:

'If any man has desire for knowledge, let him come here and acquire it, for we have it for sale.'

When this was reported to Charles, he sent in haste for the two men and had them brought before him. Was it true, he asked, as he had heard, that they had knowledge to sell?

'Indeed we have, O King,' said the strangers, 'and are ready to part with it to whomsoever in the name of the Lord shall truly demand it.'

The King asked at what price they held these wares. They said:

'We demand no price, but ask only this that we may have a place of shelter and those things that man on this pilgrimage cannot renounce, which are food and clothing.' [3]

[1] Wells, p. 323.

[2] 'Two Scots out of Hibernia,' is the reading of the text, but, as is well known, Ireland was in those days invariably deemed by the annalists to be a part of Scotia.

[3] Monk of Saint Gall, p. 4.

115

For a time he kept both at his court and set them at work to give instruction. Before long he sent one to Italy to the monastery of Saint Augustine at Pavia, to collect books and manuscripts. The other, Clement,[1] he is said to have retained to kindle the first light in the darkness, plant the first oasis in the desert.

It was the first genuine public school in France, in Europe, or in the modern world.

All the battles he fought in all his career amounted to little or nothing by the side of this momentous event. Whether he took Saragossa or Saragossa took him, or each did take the other, the world speedily forgot and now cares not a rush. But for what came of the little school started by the itinerants of learning it gives daily thanks. The whole system of free public education as we know it has grown by slow degrees from that tiny and unregarded planting.[2]

There had been schools before that day. Some of the monasteries, some of the cathedrals, maintained instructors and had pupils. For a time it was even contended that a kind of court school had existed in the palace of King Pepin the Short. But the monastery and cathedral schools taught chiefly candidates for the priesthood; all that later investigation has been able to make of King Pepin's effort is a tutor maintained to teach the royal children. To the people in the mass and to the less fortunate was accessible not one agency of education.[3]

'The pursuit of knowledge for its own sake,' says the scholar that has delved the deepest into these mysteries, 'the disinterested devotion of the intellectual powers to philosophy and speculation, was no longer recognized as commend-

---

[1] The name is open to gravest doubt. The Monk probably confounded this missionary of learning with the celebrated Clement of a later day. Professor Halphen, in his *Etudes Critiques sur l'Histoire de Charlemagne*, pp. 129, 130, is disposed to reject the Monk's story.

[2] Einhard, *Life*, p. 35.

[3] Monk of Saint Gall, p. 4; Hallam, chap. IX, pp. 602–03.

116

able or even permissible.'[1] While Austrasian and Neustrian, Frank and Gallo-Roman, contended for power, letters had undergone a progressive paralysis. In the dreary line of Clovian kings and *fainéants* had appeared but one, a certain Chilperic, that had so much as thought of the subject.[2] And now it was touched to life again, not by scholar in tippet and gown, but a soldier, with sword in hand and panting from the fray.

'And while under the Merovingians,' says Dr. Mullinger, 'learning almost ceased to exist, the circumstances of the time were such that it may be doubted whether it would ever have revived without some potent external impulse.'[3]

The potent external impulse was now supplied by this robust man with a squeaking voice that not only commanded the revival but took part in it. He established the school,[4] he sent his own children to it, he ordered the children of the courtiers to attend it. These things were natural. What completes the story with a touch of drama is that he entered the school himself, sat book in hand, and as a pupil drank from the stream of knowledge.[5]

Something else bulks less in the striking picture, but infinitely more to us. It is the great fact that the doors of his schools stood wide open to all. Boys of the lowliest birth were admitted to it. The King expressly stipulated that the children of the poorest should have equal rights with the children of the most fortunate. The Annalist says so, and says it with an emphasis that for once carries some conviction. 'There all that felt the desire for learning could come freely and assemble.'[6] Inside those precincts, all looked alike.

It was as if he took captive in his hand the spirit of the times and compelled it to return to the learning it had forsaken. A prospering school at the capital did not appease his

---

[1] J. Bass Mullinger, *The Schools of Charlemagne*, p. 32.
[2] *Ibid.*, p. 37.
[3] Page 37.   [4] Einhard, *Life*, p. 35.
[5] Mullinger, p. 65.   [6] Monk of Saint Gall, p. 4.

ambition. Eventually, as we shall see, he must have similar schools elsewhere in his kingdom with the same rules about the open door. Self-appointed Secretary of Education, Head Superintendent or what else, he went about the country looking narrowly after these institutions he had founded and tautening them to his own ideas of order, seemliness, and efficiency. For this reason, they lived and died not, and we see that this was really an unusual person.

Other cultural interests had a share in the profit of his pilgrimages. He had been an attentive observer of Roman architecture and resolved to introduce that also among his own people. He brought down from Frankland a native architect and ordered him to take lessons from a Roman master. He carried away with him models of pillars, capitals, friezes, façades, plans for buildings. These were not of the order of spoils kings of his day were wont to esteem and annex. We might do well to underscore the fact. In the way of cherished trophy, from the skull of Cunimund to a model of the Basilica of Saint Peter's — it is a long gap to cover in two hundred years. Surely those that decry or deny progress must have read history with their eyes but not their minds. The difference between 574 and 774 was the difference between a black sea at midnight without a single light and a coast with a lighthouse and soon to be charted, buoyed, and beaconed.

The architecture he brought from Italy he used in a new palace destined to a peculiar place in history. We may run ahead of chronology to show the connection. Years after that first visit to Rome, ten years after, perhaps, he determined to establish a new and permanent capital for his dominions.[1] The old system of governing from three or four cities and shifting the headquarters of government whimsically from one to another was picturesque and gratified local pride, but it was clumsy and costly. For his site he chose

[1] Dr. Albert Huyskens, *Karl der Grosse und seine lieblingspfalz Aachen*, pp. 11–13. The new palace at Aachen was completed for the celebration of Easter, 788.

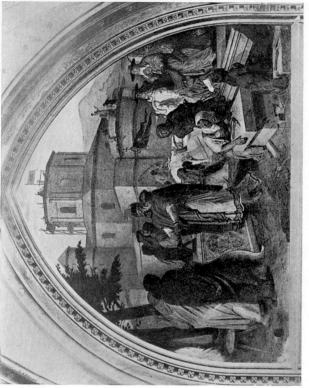

THE BUILDING OF THE CATHEDRAL
Mural painting by Rethel in the Rathaus, Aachen

what is now Aix-la-Chapelle, or Aachen, the *Aquae Granni* of the Latins. Even in those days its thermal springs were widely known for health-restoring qualities, and the wise old Romans, who seldom overlooked anything of this kind, had established baths there. It was in Austrasian territory, but among the advantages of the new order was this, that now the jealousies and strifes between Austrasians and Neustrians, the division that had caused so much bloodshed and misery, seemed laid aside. Men heard little of Austrasian or Neustrian, but only of Franks. What under Pepin had looked like a mere truce between French and Germans began to wear the appearance of an obsolete quarrel. In this notable taming of the savage breast, the ancestry of Charles may have had a share; half Neustrian he was, half Austrasian. Besides, he seems to have been broad enough to view these divisions as unimportant in view of the things he wanted to do, which in itself amounted to another innovation.

The city he largely rebuilt after his own plans. It was afterward his chief residence; from it he ruled Lombardy and Bavaria as he ruled Austrasia. In the end his buildings came to be destroyed in a new eruption of Northern barbarism, but the fame of them lingered in the human mind, and judging by their remains they must have been of a rather imposing size and a stately but unadorned design.

His new Aachen he planned to make not only the seat of government, but the capital of that learning into which he had breathed life after it had seemed but dead.

Either he was the instrument, rough-hewn but thorough-going, of a directing Providence or he had behind his buckler and corselet something like the discerning soul of a prophet. It sounds improbable now, but is still true that so far as intentions could go he was a reformer of extraordinary virility and oddly modern convictions. He wanted everything to be better, not only education but everything else — including music. At the cost of misadventures to be told later, while he strove to bring in education, improve laws, and soften manners, he now undertook to improve the singing in the churches.

What this must have been before his time and throughout that part of the war-mad world is a fearful suggestion. An age that had lost most other arts and even the memory of them must have been in a parlous state about its music. Part of the business of this inexorable and irrepressible apostle was to visit the churches and listen to the chorals. When he found the choirs singing off the key, he publicly rebuked them and put them right — thus beautifully adding example to precept.

Besides all this, which is enough to set him forth to our wondering attention and honest applause, he served us well by multiplying the number of classical texts and sagas, whether sacred or profane, then extant in his kingdom, understanding how little chance there was to spread the knowledge of books unless he had books from which to spread it. In those days, of course, the only way a book could be published,[1] or had, was by copying it with a pen. The scholarship of all succeeding ages owes to this big-boned, iron-muscled, hard-hitting fighting man a singular indebtedness. But for his care scores of invaluable texts would have been lost to us. He employed copyists and clerks to duplicate these treasures and so preserved and transmitted them, and he made of the library his father Pepin had started the most valuable collection then on the Continent.

We can smile at the extravagance of his age and the next that tried to make a kind of demigod of this piece of valiant dust, and still admit certain evidences of versatility. While he was establishing schools, gathering scholars, collecting manuscripts, and changing the music of his day, he was often planning, directing, and occasionally leading the wars that kept a circle of foes from strangling him and his empire. And at all times he must be administering the affairs of a composite state made up of so many incongruous peoples of so

[1] Hallam, chap. IX, p. 482.

120

many different origins that the mind wearies to keep track of them.

Before his time they had never mingled — oil and water. Each division or province or conquered state had its prince or princelet — vain, proud, restless, irascible, and more or less insane. No one had ever kept order among these fantastic chieftains, excepting only Clovis. He inspired them with a restraining terror, chiefly of assassination; but even the fierce, fiery Clovis left them unchanged in the obdurate will to mischief. Pepin, the father of Charles, was an able and clear-sighted ruler, but for the last nine years of his life he was trying to suppress one revolt after another. Charles the Hammer was hardly less than a genius, but most of his life was spent in warfare. The best that could be said of the Kingdom of the Franks under Pepin was that it was a kind of chained-in chaos; if a score of nobles with the instincts of the wolf-den were not trying to murder one another, the only reason was the lack of means or opportunity. Yet now these irreducible and hostile elements seemed to coöperate without serious friction; Lombards in Italy, energetic Gauls in Neustria, fanatical Gepidæ in the Danube Basin, Burgundians, Alemannians in Switzerland, Frisians, Aquitanians, Ligurians, Ripuarians — they all managed to live together under one generalship.

These are the facts; they seem to cause the embroideries of the adulators to look rather foolish. No other man in history has suffered more from the laurel-wreathers than Charlemagne. When they are done with their libations, this remains clear to the thinking mind that he was confronted with a greatly tangled problem in government and solved it. For the most part he kept peace in his vast caldron of a kingdom, and yet it does not appear that he kept it by means of the iron heel, the bared dagger, or the fear of the poison jar.

One significant fact about his administration is that he could leave his country whenever he wished and his people did not rush upon one another at the turning of his back. Enemies outside his borders might rejoice at his absence and run over the frontier line sword in hand, but the people inside kept the wonted pace. Four times he went to his beloved Rome, and returned in peace; the second time bearing those architectural trophies of which he was so proud. What it was in his system of government that succeeded so well we may surmise if we take a closer look at it.

Traditionally, the headship of the Frankish Kingdom was an absolute despotism, hampered by nothing on earth but the chances of revolt. Once a year took place this assembly of the nobles. Up to the time of Charles it was a decorative but not an important body. The King or Chief announced to it what peoples he hoped next to rob and the assembled noblemen signified their applause by clashing their shields and grunting.[1] The King or Chief was the source of all authority in the realm or gau, canton or district. If it could be said to have laws, they were of his making. If they could be said to be enforced, he did the enforcing.

This was the government in theory and in practice. The jealousy of the small princes was not usually directed against the things the King decreed or did, but against his existence. Nothing resembling the modern scheme of responsible control existed in the length and breadth of the King's dominion; no vehicle of criticism, no avenue of protest except by force, no means by which the thought of the people, if they had any, could be expressed; no idea anywhere that such a thought might be worth the expressing. The purpose of government was to maintain a fighting machine by which the King's enemies might be subdued and their lands confiscated; and a tax-gathering machine by which the lords of the manor might live at ease. Government was rule by the tribal chieftain of the forests, enlarged in an attempt to fit a larger theater. The Chief had favorites about him and parasites and tax-eaters. He had no ministers, and if he were not of

[1] Vétault, p. 407.

the order of *fainéants*, he usually had no designated counselors.

Upon this anarchy the son of Pepin entered with an enormous prestige and therefore an enormous power. It appears that if he had willed he might have ruled Frankland and Italy as Chosroes ruled Persia. The first thing that makes him remarkable to the modern inquirer is that he did not will to rule in this manner, but introduced the seed of a conception of government new to the world in which he moved.

It consisted of the notion that the first object of government is the welfare of all the people governed.

He had an advantage about this that essentially, in his psychology, manners, sympathies, and to a certain extent in his blood and descent, he was a peasant.[1] He was the first European monarch to feel that the peasants were human beings and worth thinking about when it came to lawmaking.[2] His true historical portrait is that of a big, hard-working, serious-minded countryman, going head down and hard set upon a task as he understood it. He was to manage the government, not alone for his own glory, but for the good of the nation and the furthering of the Christian religion. Nowhere has been found any sign that he was deluded into fantasy concerning his own surpassing greatness or the belief that his mission on earth was merely to spread an empire. He was called a military genius, but the flaws in his make-up happened not to include bald militarism.

Before his time the welfare of the people had meant the welfare of the King, the nobles, and the powerful; with sincerity it was believed that those of humbler rank, having no minds and probably no souls, were sufficiently cared for if their betters were prosperous. Everywhere the powerful made laws, or what passed for laws, and established customs for their own sole advantage; everywhere the toilers main-

[1] Freytag, p. 7. 'The ideal incarnation of a German peasant of the olden time.'
[2] Hodgkin, pp. 242–43.

tained themselves as best they could on the scraps, remnants, and gnawed bones of the governmental feast. The mission of this man seems to have been to weaken these prerogatives and undermine these notions by extending for the first time to the people at the bottom some part of the care and protecting power of government at the top.[1]

Even casually, one can see in him the most democratic monarch that up to that time had appeared in Europe.[2] When we say this we do not say enough. In some aspects of his career he was the only monarch that broadly practiced democracy. Instead of confiding in and drawing his support from the class of noble parasites that always hang about the steps of a throne, he seemed to have an innate contempt for all such creatures. He knew men, he recognized swiftly the qualities he sought, and in the choice of his lieutenants he showed the real bent of his real mind by picking merit from any walk of life wherein merit might appear.[3] For the first time since the barbarian night had settled upon Europe, a man born into a low caste, or the lowest, had a fair chance to distinguish himself. Opportunity was no longer the sole and exclusive possession of those that custom had been pleased to call nobly born.[4] Worth became for the time being the chief qualification for advancement.[5]

The nobles fumed and complained because he continually added to their number men that had been meanly born. He seems to have cared little for criticism. Possibly he suspected or surmised a truth a thousand years before the world discovered it, that power, ability, invention, initiative, and progress come from the common mass of mankind, and the least useful members of any society are most often those that have the greatest inheritance of wealth and station. He

[1] Hodgkin, p. 24; Dieffenbach and Vogt, p. 406.

[2] Einhard, *Life*, p. 32; Vétault, p. 409.

[3] Hodgkin, p. 245.   [4] Monk of Saint Gall, p. 17.

[5] 'He did his utmost to discover and promote men of promise. A chronicler remarks with amazement that even the serfs of the royal demesne were sometimes singled out to be his counts.' Davis, p. 60.

created throughout his realm positions of administrative responsibility.[1] To the men that filled these and so stood at the head of provinces and local divisions of the state, he looked for the enforcement of his ideas, and to such a position he did not hesitate to raise any man, freeman, noble, serf, that had shown capacity, fitness, and character.

It is not easy to limit the value to Europe of this innovation coming at such a time. Magna Charta secured to the landowners and the fortunate a barrier against the encroachment of kings; beyond that it was a gesture. But the substance of the thought or impulse back of the policy of Charles was much more. It was the germ of a republic. Crude, minute, remote, primitive, imperfect, a long time sterile, it was still the germ of the modern republic. Centuries had to pass before it flowered and then not always evenly or perfectly; yet all the time it was the germ of the modern republic. The idea of opportunity as independent of inheritance and material possessions was in his innovations. After centuries in which it seemed dead and forgotten it came to life again when the discontent of enslaved populations and the rebirth of democratic ideals led at last to such democratic achievements as the beginning of the general franchise, responsible government, and the annihilation of the monarchical theory.

Democracy not being an acquired taste with this man it was probably nothing he had reasoned much about; still less was it anything he could use to his own benefit. All his ostensible interests and the interests of his class lay the other way. Democracy was something in his blood and his bones. He was always the most approachable of monarchs; any one could address him. When he held the annual Mayfield [2] or assembly, he went about talking in the most unassuming way with men of all conditions, and particularly informing himself about the state of the common people in every part of his dominions. The chroniclers say that he despised all forms of

[1] Hodgkin, p.245.   [2] Dieffenbach and Vogt, p. 348.

display. Habitually he dressed in the simple and ancient garb of his nation,[1] high boots, hose, a plain belted tunic, and a square mantle usually of blue. The efforts of courtiers to adorn themselves with costly or brightly colored garments he sternly rebuked. He was fond of rebuking; it was his apostleship in reform. Pride, idleness, arrogance, and vanity were sins for his lashing. If he had not been a good soldier he would have been one of the world's notable preachers.

As he moved about the country to observe for himself the actual conditions he must deal with and to take note of those schools of his, he seems to have thought he could teach to the nobles the beginnings of his own doctrine of opportunity for worth. The Monk of Saint Gall has a flowery dream of one such visit. He says that returning victorious from one of his wars, Charles inspected a school and found that the boys of the so-called lower classes had far outstripped in learning the sons of noblemen, whose compositions are said to have been 'tepid and absolutely idiotic.' Thereupon (having, no doubt, some memories about the Scriptural sheep and goats) he set all the poor boys on his right hand and the rich idlers on his left and after praising the industrious students on his right he turned to the others and said:

'You young nobles, you dainty and beautiful youths, who have presumed upon your birth and your possessions to despise my orders and have taken no care for my renown, you have neglected the study of literature while you have given yourselves over to luxury and idleness, or to games and foolish athletics. By the King of Heaven, I care nothing for your noble birth and your handsome faces, let others prize them as they may. Know this for certain, that unless you give earnest heed to your studies, and recover the ground lost by your negligence, you shall never receive any favor at the hand of King Charles.' [2]

[1] Einhard, *Life*, pp. 31–32; Monk of Saint Gall, p. 44.

[2] Monk of Saint Gall, pp. 5–6. Professor Halphen discredits the story, saying that it is a mere paraphrase of the Scriptural assertion that the first shall be last and the last first.

MODEL OF CHARLEMAGNE'S CATHEDRAL AND PALACE AT AACHEN

Reconstructed by Professor Bachkremer and Dr. Huyskens (Curtius, sculptor) from the ancient remains and records. Now in the Rathaus, Aachen.

Whether he actually said this to the pupils no one knows, but justly he might have said something of the kind to his noblemen, for it was in accordance with his general policy.

After his passing there came a reversion, as is usual after a forward step, and the tyrannical counts seemed more powerful and more arrogant than ever. But in politics the usual formula runs the other way; reaction is never quite equal to action. A standard had been set up, or an example or a precedent, to which, when the reactionary tide had ebbed, men turned, more or less automatically. As the hero of two nations, France and Germany, Charlemagne's immense popularity helped to revive the movement he had founded. Men felt, without reasoning much about it, that if this was what he believed in it must be good. Even the mass of fiction and legend that sprang up about him contributed something to the same end. Views of the value of Charlemagne's work must always differ according to the differing conceptions of the value to mankind of an enlarged democracy. Sometimes, also, they differ in accordance with racial prejudices and impulses. If there had been no Charlemagne the peasant would nevertheless have been emancipated. If there had been no Magellan the world would have been circumnavigated. Without Charlemagne there would have come schools and a system of instruction. Yet he remains historically the pioneer of modern democracy and modern education, as Magellan of circumnavigation. Slowly the once submissive peasants began to absorb the notion that perhaps they might be more than Things. With succeeding centuries that notion spread until the classes that had been governed and exploited began to demand a share in the government, the demand that has not since ceased to be heard.

CHAPTER VIII

THE SAXON IN HIS HOME

THE world has long forgotten the names of the peoples among whom Charles of the Franks tried to introduce order, method, and these beginnings of democracy, as it has forgotten the complexities of the problem offered by that seething, incongruous mass of primitive men and minds. What, for instance, can seem stranger now than that there should have been dwelling, wedged into the heart of the European and Caucasian continent, a great nation of pure Mongols, with yellow skins, black hair twisted into pigtails, flat faces, and alien ways, and that this nation should have been an active element in the troubles indefatigably besetting this man? And yet, so startling a fact is but one illustration of the changes through which Europe has passed, of the tumultuous migrations that since the days of Augustus had shifted so many peoples, of old social landmarks all erased, and finally of the materials out of which a new method of organized government was next to be formed.

Outside the circle of the Roman influence, which still managed in some wonderful way to preserve the seeds and even some of the ideals of the old culture, there was a ring of peoples that the Franks and Romans called at first barbarians and then heathen, all pressing heavily upon the outposts of civilization. On the east were the Avars, the pigtailed Mongolians I have just mentioned; north of the Avars were the Bohemians; then the Sorbs, Wends, and other Slav peoples; then the Saxons, and beyond them the Danes and other Scandinavians, all fierce, war-loving, economically disadvantaged, and at some time irrupting upon the Franks. But of all these none for capacity and gifts in trouble-making equaled the Saxons.

128

Directly to the north and northeast of the Frankish Kingdom of Charles was their habitat, embracing what is now Holstein, Hanover, Brunswick, and Westphalia,[1] and not much of what is now Saxony. Some of them had conquered and were then ruling England. The rest had a rude and loose confederation that extended from the Elbe almost to the Rhine. They were Teutons of the fiercest breed and among the stubbornest people that ever lived; heathen, having a strange religion to which they were fanatically devoted; in a crude way farmers and graziers; but always warriors and having in warfare disagreeable traits. They played the war game after methods of their own, never acknowledged defeat, and never by any chance kept faith with anybody.

The old chroniclers, who held them in no partiality, made much and probably too much of their first entries in history, signaled by two incidents. According to such authority, they drew their name from a word in their language that meant cutlass, this being their choice among weapons. Originally from Scandinavia,[2] a band of them was hired to fight in the army of Alexander. After completing this service they were adventuring homeward upon the river Elbe when they came in their boats to a piece of the littoral that seemed good in their eyes. They landed and, with their cutlasses well concealed in their robes, proposed to the inhabitants a treaty of peace and amity. While this was under discussion, they suddenly drew their weapons and slew the men they were treating with. After that they took possession of the country and established it as their home.[3]

The other incident happened, we are told, about the year of grace 570. A band of Saxons accompanied the Lombards when they descended upon Italy. In the course of time they started homeward, being soundly beaten on the way. Auvergne was on their line of march, where they were warmly received because they seemed to be well supplied with pieces

[1] Mombert, p. 101; Davis, p. 8; Fletcher, p. 242.
[2] Capefigue, p. 197.   [3] Vétault, pp. 197-98.

of gold which they dispensed without parsimony. When they had departed, it was found that their money was nothing but copper, 'which,' says Gregory of Tours, 'they had managed to color, I know not by what process.' [1]

When we have taken of this part of our ancestry as favorable a view as is possible, giving weight to their valor, warlike prowess, and sturdy virtues of fidelity to chief, roof-tree, clan and the rest, the fact still protrudes upon us that they must have been singularly undesirable people for a close acquaintance. They had no idea of life except to fight, to feed, to steal, and to sleep. To acquire by peaceful means whatever could be had by rapine was accounted shameful among them, and until a youth had shown by some act of bloodshed the possession of the traits deemed admirable, he was condemned to the lowest steps of their social ladder. It would be pleasant if we could really believe the fiction that from these hairy nomads and their colleagues came the modern ideas of liberty and progress [2]— that Swinburne was right when he visioned freedom as sleeping armed beside their 'forest-hidden fountains.' But the fact seems to be that the idea of liberty inherent among these people was the idea of tribal independence and that our modern conception of individual human dignity as the basis for another kind of freedom had other sources. Of their tribal independence they were exceedingly jealous; within the tribe they submitted to an absolutism on the part of their chieftains that seems to us now hardly less than degrading.

Otherwise than by freebooting they lived by the chase and upon their herds. Agriculture they despised except so far as it was necessary to supply the deficiencies of hunting. Youths that had not yet won to the order of merit did the work that was not done by that other inferior element of the population, the women. [3] 'The warrior divided his time between sloth and orgies. Gambling carried to the point of a frenzy,

---

[1] Vétault, p. 198; Fletcher, p. 143.
[2] Michelet, pp. 135–36.   [3] Vétault, p. 199.

the grossest pleasures of the table, the transports or the torpor of drunkenness, were their only distractions, followed by long hours of brutal slumber or a reverie morose and stupid at the bottom of a smoky hut.'[1] Their life was purely animal, 'without other education than the development of the instincts of nature, where the spirit was scarcely conscious of its own existence, where the unnatural stupefaction of the moral sentiments and the atrophy of the intellectual faculties left the field free to the fury of the passions and the suggestions of a monstrous ignorance.'[2]

On the whole, one might say that they had some of the worst characteristics of the North American Indian with none of his redeeming qualities.

Their religion was a debased form of the old Scandinavian worship of Odin and Thor. Its emblem was a tree, the holy world-sustaining ash tree, called the Yggdrasil or Irminsul. It does not appear that the faith they professed had moral tenets beyond the overcoming of one's enemies, the observance of tribal loyalty, and the acquiring of much booty. Even so it was stained with horrible human sacrifices. Oxanam, in his 'Christian Civilization Among the Franks,' maintains that they did worse things, and evidence is plain enough that there was at least a cult among them that practiced cannibalism. The central point of their worshiping was a sacred grove where stood a stone column that had been fashioned into an image of the Yggdrasil. It was here that they performed their human sacrifices, usually, though not always, of captives taken in war.

Charles had been but three years a king when trouble began with these people. Of all his traits, a resolute devotion to his religion was most prominent;[3] all his life he was fond of sending Christian missionaries to unconverted peoples. The Saxons deranged his plans not only by slaughtering his missionaries, but because they were industrious border raiders,

[1] Vétault, p. 199.
[2] Ibid.; Michelet, pp. 130–45.   [3] Hodgkin, p. 106.

131

ruffians, bandits, and thieves,[1] which upset the agriculture he
was bent upon Installing. Hence, in 772, just before he was
called upon to rescue the Papacy from the clutches of Desiderius, he had come to the conclusion that one of his missions
was to abolish the Saxon heresy and with the sword to force
upon these obstinate pagans the Christianity they refused to
receive from peaceful evangelists.

A singular incident precipitated the war. Christian missionaries had penetrated Saxon England long before they had
attempted the Saxony of the main land, and had been notably successful in mastering the savage intellect. Christianized
Saxons from England now attempted to introduce the new
faith to their European relatives.[2] In the spring of 772 the
pagan ceremonies were in progress at the holy grove when of
a sudden there arose a voice making protest and proclaiming
the God of the Christians. It was that of Saint Libuin, a
disciple of Saint Boniface, who had come from England as a
missionary.[3]

The whole assembly scowled upon him with astonishment and wrath. But he continued unafraid and gave
them warning, according to his biographer, that unless they
turned from their heathen idolatry, the King of Heaven had
commanded a neighboring prince, strong, wise, indefatigable,
to inflict a terrible punishment upon them. He would come
like a torrent, invade their country, lay it waste with fire and
sword, and carry off their wives and children to slavery.

With cries of rage the crowd sprang upon the intruder and
a hundred cutlasses were at his breast when one of the elders
of the tribe stopped them. 'We have often received the ambassadors of neighboring peoples,' he said, 'of the Danes, the
Slavs, the Frisians, listened to them peaceably and sent them
away with presents. This man says he is an ambassador from

---

[1] Hodgkin, p. 106; Einhard, *Life*, pp. 14–15; 'no war the Franks fought equaled
this for length of time it lasted, for bitterness and for the efforts it demanded.'
[2] Hodgkin, p. 107.
[3] Vétault, pp. 206–07; Capefigue, pp. 199–200.

God. Why do you repulse him and seek to murder him? Fear
the anger of the power that has sent him.'

The Saxons listened and allowed the courageous Libuin to
depart in peace. But the fanatical spirit of the tribe was
aroused. Warriors, to show how little they cared for the
wrath with which they had been threatened, and to avenge
the escape of their visitor, followed him to a small mission he
had erected near their confines but within Frankish territory.
There they burned the mission houses and put all the Christians to the sword.[1]

Charles was at the moment celebrating Easter at the ancient home of his ancestor, Pepin of Heristal. The report that
came to him there of the massacre of Saint Libuin and his
little company determined him to a course he must have long
contemplated. He assembled his army at Worms and at its
head entered the Saxon territory bent on punition.

It is to be supposed that he had little notion of the size of
the task he had undertaken.[2] The Saxons usually mustered
inferior numbers, they were split into tribes, they had little
power of united effort, the bonds of their confederation were
flimsy ties, against trained legions they had little military
skill. But they offset these defects with great mobility and
swiftness of movement, intimate knowledge of the morasses
of the wilderness, and a peculiar elasticity of spirit by virtue
of which they were never broken however much they were
beaten. Besides all which, they had a faith in themselves
and their own great superiority to all else in the living world.
Hence they were almost indomitable.

In his operations in Saxony that year of 772 Charles knew
nothing but successes. He drove the Saxons before him, he
captured Eresburg,[3] their holy grove and chief citadel, he destroyed the image of the great tree, the Irminsul, sacred in

[1] Mombert (page 105) takes a different view of this incident.
[2] Einhard, *Life*, p. 15.
[3] Einhard, *Annals*, pp. 57, 59.
'The Franks were the inheritors of the military science and prowess of the
Romans.' Capefigue, p. 198.

their worship. In large numbers they surrendered to him, accepted his terms of peace, gave him their pledges of good conduct, delivered into his hands twelve hostages as their guarantees of good faith. As indemnity for the assault on Saint Libuin's mission, he carried away from their sacred grove an accumulation of treasure that had been deposited there by generations of worshipers. Thus laden back to Italy went he, convinced that he had pacified Saxony and started it upon the road to Christian salvation, for among his terms had he not included safety and protection for the missionaries?

So far all was well. He had been called into Italy by his troubles with Desiderius, and scarcely two years later, 774, while he was all intent upon his operations in the South, out blazed in revolt the entire Saxon nation. Without the least regard to treaty, promises, hostages, or aught else,[1] they moved across the border (at a point near Darmstadt) and penetrated the Frankish territory, burning, killing, and stealing as they went. They recaptured their ancient fortress of Eresburg, which had been among the trophies of Charles's expedition; they destroyed churches and scattered monks, drove back the guards and menaced Frankish cities.

The military tactics that Charles introduced and developed came now into play. The point in his performance that Napoleon studied and the world still wonders at was his ability, marvelous considering the country and the times, to move rapidly and to strike unexpectedly. Winter was close at hand, military operations were deemed for the rest of that year impossible. Charles turned swiftly from Italy, shot through the Alps, summoned his forces at Mainz, and before the snows began he had driven the Saxons like dead leaves before the wind. In many engagements he had beaten them, nowhere had they made a successful stand, and he returned to winter quarters again laden with spoils.[2]

With the dawn of spring he resumed the war. He harried the country from end to end, scattering his enemies, reëstab-

---

[1] Einhard, *Life*, p. 15; Einhard, *Annals*, p. 63.   [2] Einhard, *Annals*, p. 64.

THE DESTRUCTION OF THE IRMINSUL, SACRED IMAGE
OF THE SAXONS

Mural painting by Rethel in the Rathaus, Aachen

lishing his posts, verifying the prophecy of Saint Libuin. The missions were restored, the work of proselyting was resumed. But he might have said as Napoleon said on a like occasion that he could not be everywhere. While he was moving toward the northeast, winning daily victories, he left behind him an important division of his army to guard his lines of communication. The Frankish soldiers, having found the Saxons but poor opponents in the field, and believing the war at an end, were lolling at ease. No enemies were in sight, the countryside was peaceful. All discipline was relaxed. On a warm sunny afternoon the camp lay mostly asleep while a company of troopers took out horses for forage.[1] A band of Saxons, watching from the hills, stole down and mingled with the horses on their return, about nine o'clock at night. With their cutlasses on their backs, with their strong hands grasping each a horse's mane, they came along in the herd unseen, unsuspected, until they had entered the camp.

Then with savage yells they whipped out their swords and fell upon the sleeping soldiers.

The Franks, unarmed and taken unawares, were at a disadvantage. A desperate battle ensued, the masses of unarmed Franks striving to get at their weapons, the Saxons driving them back with slaughter, the few armed Franks attacking the enemy from the other side. Under such unequal conditions the courage of the Franks was put to a heavy test, for most of them were fighting with their bare hands. The real result is to this day beyond finding out. The Franks were not annihilated; the Saxons retired. From this it has been supposed or divined that the hard-fighting Franks won back their camp and routed their foes. But an enigmatical sentence in the 'Royal Annals,' which provide us with our chief knowledge about these things, would justify one in a totally different conclusion. It says that the enemy 'retired in accordance with the clauses of the pact that, because of the difficulties of the situation, had been concluded with them.'

[1] Einhard, *Annals*, pp. 61-62.

This looks like no Frankish victory.[1] 'In accordance with the pact made with them' — it has a sinister sound. The world must have thought so. In that battle the Frankish cause and arms suffered a loss of prestige something like that Cornwallis suffered at the battle of Guilford Court House.

Charles, enraged at this reverse and its grave reflection upon his military establishment, came tearing back, trapped the Saxons while they were still exultantly feasting, and scattered them to the four winds. But the incident remained and still remains one of the curiosities of military history. A certain Homeric touch about it fascinates the imagination. That picture of the savage, bare-armed warriors borne along half-hidden in the manes of the horses of their enemies, the picture of the sudden assault in the heart of the sleeping camp — it is unforgettable. Better than many words, it tells us how the Saxons made war and what these people were that the Franks had undertaken to subdue.

The net results of the operations of the year of 775 were that the Saxons were beaten everywhere, made a new submission, agreed to a new treaty, swore to a new set of oaths, furnished new promises, surrendered new hostages. Charles turned southward to his winter quarters. The frost was scarcely out of the rivers the next spring before the Saxons had broken all their treaties, violated all their oaths, disregarded all their promises, and were again in open revolt. Charles made one swift move and caught them in a hopeless position on the river Lippe.

This time the Saxons professed their willingness not only to swear allegiance to the Frankish Kingdom, but to become Christians. Thousands upon thousands of them were accordingly baptized and received into the Church.[2] But

> The spot it takes not off the panther's skin,
> Nor shall an Ethiop's stain be bleached with it.

Professing Christianity or heathenism, the Saxon was a

[1] Halphen, *La Conquête de la Saxe*, pp. 150–51.
[2] Hodgkin, p. 110; Einhard, *Annals*, p. 61; Halphen, p. 151.

measureless liar, incorrigible, constitutional, subtle, wily. Two years after the baptism in the Lippe, that is to say, in 778, Charles started upon that campaign in Spain the fortunes of which we are yet to tell, and had hardly crossed the Pyrenees before the whole structure of his Saxon administration crumbled at an outbreak of the national spirit directed by the genius of one man.

This was Widukind, or Wittekind, the great hero of Saxon history and romance, whose deeds have been celebrated in a body of legend and lyric eloquence not inferior to any other of its times. Beyond doubt he was a remarkable person; in him appeared an epitome of the craft, ingenuity, adroitness, and conquering spirit of his nation. He was by birth of the Westphalians, a chieftain or leader that had attained to some note when one of the early successes of Charles drove him over the border to the court of his brother-in-law, Sigfrid, King of Denmark, where he found refuge. The southern activities of the Franks lured him back to Saxony in 778, and the instant he appeared the insurrection flamed. As to a destined deliverer all Saxons gathered to his standard. For once it looked as if the old tribal differences were to be sunk in one cause of national independence. Oaths, treaties, promises, baptisms, hostages, were forgotten. With a great army Widukind marched to the assault of Karlstadt, the chief fort that Charles had built to maintain Frankish supremacy in Saxony. It surrendered, and Widukind destroyed it.

Next the Frankish garrison of Eresburg was closely besieged, while the main body of Saxons, pressing on, entered Hesse, put the inhabitants to the sword, burned the villages, ravaged both banks of the Rhine. They captured Cologne itself and burned there a Christian church. They spread devastation and terror along the border and seemed to threaten even cities at the heart of the kingdom.

Before Charles could return from Spain, the winter had set in, and for the time being he could do no more than to perfect his plans to retrieve these disasters. With the coming of

137

spring he put his army in motion, made one of his marvelous quick marches, and suddenly struck the Saxons in their strong fortification far up the Lippe. His towering form dominated every conflict. In other instances he might make the plans, arrange the strategy, and leave the execution to his generals. On this occasion he charged at the head of his troops.

The Saxons, cheered on by Widukind, doubtless fought as well as they could, but small was their chance against such a foe and small at any time in open field maneuvers. All their science of war lay in ambuscades and surprises. The well-trained Franks cut their lines to pieces and sent them flying. Widukind made his escape from a disastrous day. Such of his people as he had left behind him surrendered, taking the usual oaths and giving the usual pledges. The Franks over-ran the country as far as the Weser, built new forts, established new posts. Once more the stubborn and subtle people were overawed and compelled to accept a peace and a ruler they equally detested.

At the first opportunity Charles turned his attention to the establishing of a stable government for the Saxon territory and one likely to avoid these costly, troublesome revolts. About such things he had one notion that amounted to a sweeping innovation. In his time and for centuries afterward the custom of the conqueror was to impose upon the conquered the full weight of the victor's yoke, keeping them in order by daily reminding them of their lowly and hopeless estate. Charlemagne's plan, which he did not always adhere to, sought to rule the people he defeated by placing over them governors taken from among themselves and of their own habits and psychology. On this occasion he chose many Saxon leaders, made them counts, and elevated them to commanding positions in the new government, giving them authority to administer justice, levy taxes, organize the country's defense, and represent him in the manner of the Frankish counts in his own country. The curious will notice

138

a rather interesting resemblance to the policy that in modern times has been so successful in the colonies of France. Elsewhere it had been equally successful with the Franks. The men selected for government usually proved faithful to their duties and learned, perhaps for the first time, the responsibilities of authority and the nature of an oath. In the end it might have been as successful with the Saxons if a singular reversion to barbarism had not for a time overturned it.

But for the present it promised well and the outlook was alluring. The church organization was restored and extended, the churches were rebuilt, more Saxons professed conversion, Charles made rich presents to all the chiefs that embraced Christianity. He never suspected the sneer of future generations that he had proselyted with bribes where he could not convince with the sword. Probably he would not have believed prophecy if it had revealed such comment.[1]

But in this instance the policy of friendly assimilation had no chance to approve itself. Having done a wise thing, Charles of the Franks must now perform spectacularly in the ranks of folly. The spirit of the age that he was usually to defy and reverse seemed to assert itself upon him in that peculiar manifestation in which even slow-pulsed and reasoning men went hand in hand with madness. Scarcely had the beneficent arrangement of native rulers begun to function when out came the famous Saxon Capitularies of 781–2 to undo the good and open another Pandora's box of troubles.

It was a new set of laws, almost unprecedented for severity and wholly wonderful for untimeliness. From some source must have come a prompting that a people unsubdued by other means could be awed by a roll of parchment. The new laws established the death penalty for an astonishing list of offenses, including many that were not really crimes, but only violations of custom or religious tenets. Thus whosoever, not being aged or infirm, should eat flesh in Lent, whosoever should through dissimulation avoid Christian baptism, who-

[1] Mombert, p. 112.

soever should practice the rite of burning the bodies of the dead, whosoever should break into a church and steal anything thence, was to be put to death. Other provisions farther illuminate the age. It was deemed necessary to prohibit cannibalism on pain of death, to insist that Christian churches should have greater honor than had been paid to heathen temples, and that the right of sanctuary in a church should not be violated.

A diet of all the chieftains sanctioned the decree.[1]

From this mainly savage code some of the virulence was drawn by a provision at the end that in all cases of capital crimes secretly committed, if the wrong-doer voluntarily sought a priest and made confession of his offense his life should be spared.

But even so potent an amelioration did not make the thing workable. Commentators have usually ascribed to it the next uprising of the Saxons. This is fallacious for the obvious reason that the Saxons uprose anyway as soon as Charles was out of the country and would have done so if the criminal code had been softer than Malaga raisins. The next year showed the tough and elastic Saxon spirit in its most familiar aspect. Perhaps we need not wonder if from the events that now fell in Charles concluded that no treaty, no promise, and no pledge would ever be observed by such a people.[2] No sooner was his back turned upon Saxony as he went to other problems of his realm than reënter Widukind from the other side. It was the signal for a fresh and still more threatening revolt. Thousands of Saxons that had sworn allegiance and had been baptized abandoned their new religion with their new sovereign and flocked to the native leader. He seems to have determined to make this the crucial effort of his campaigning. Not only the Saxons were mustered, but from be-

[1] Mombert, pp. 115–16.

[2] 'Nul pouvoir central n'y représentait les intérêts généraux et n'y person nifiat cette sorte de conscience morale d'un peuple, à laquelle incombent l'initiative et la responsabilité des conventions internationales.' Vétault, pp. 225–26. One is irresistibly reminded of the famous passage in Burke's speech about Hyder Ali.

yond the borders he drew to his ranks a great horde of fierce
Slavs, and with this force he began to move southward.

On the way he afforded a significant indication of the essential state of the peoples that had felt drawn to him as toward a natural exponent and leader. His practice wherever
he went was to put to death with horrible tortures every
Saxon convert that falling into his hands refused to renounce
Christianity. But a fanatical urge of religion more than
aught else was the spring of all these battlings. It would be
pleasant if possible to conceive of a people making a heroic
struggle for independence, but the fact is only too apparent
that the savage hatred of the Saxons toward the Franks was
a matter of religion and not a devotion to freedom.[1]

At first Widukind went from success to success. The small
Frankish forces that had been left to guard a region apparently pacified retreated hastily before his great army, the
missionaries fled, the churches were burned, the forts seized.

He even showed qualities as a field commander, this Widukind, helped by dissensions and disorders in the ranks of his
enemies.

In the absence of Charles, the chief command of the Frankish forces devolved upon Count Theodoric, an able general
and related by blood to the King. He had been instructed to
enlist as he went along converted Saxons that had professed
a willingness to fight for their new faith. Being disappointed
in this, he still pressed to the northward, with what regular
troops he had, and found Widukind strongly entrenched on
the slopes of a hill called Süntel, near Minden, on the Weser.

Theodoric divided his army into three commands, each entrusted to a Frankish general, and laid out a plan by which
the assault was to be delayed until all the forces were so disposed that the advance could be made in unison. The sub-
commanders were jealous of Theodoric.[2] Being sure that an
easy victory was about to be won, they determined not to

[1] Hallam, chap. 1, Part 1; Hodgkin, p. 112.
[2] Hodgkin, pp. 114–15; Vétault, p. 279; Einhard, *Annals*, p. 69; Halphen, p. 166.

allow him to have the glory of it. Without waiting for the signal they rushed upon Widukind's lines.

But the Saxons did not run, as had been expected. Instead, they stood stubbornly to their trenches. The Franks, aroused to their customary valor by this resistance, made a desperate charge. While they were thus engaged, Widukind sent a part of his troops around the Frankish flank, encircled it, and had the assailants at his mercy.

When the Franks too late realized their fatal blunder, they made superhuman efforts to retrieve it. Two of the jealous leaders, the Counts Adelgis and Geilon, threw their lives away at the head of their troops. A small force succeeded in hewing out its escape, but the defeat was catastrophic and the losses heavy.[1]

Theodoric mustered the shattered remnant of his army and led it away in retreat. The Saxons did not pursue him; they were too busy gathering spoils and obliterating the traces of the religion they abhorred.

Charles was in the South when he heard of the disaster of Süntel, and moved as might have been expected to revenge it. But when, by forced marches over hard roads, he had reached the Weser, the summer was over, Widukind and his followers had vanished into the Northern woods; there was no sign of an enemy to oppose or to punish. Peace and quiet reigned upon the land. All the visible Saxons professed to church and crown an inviolate loyalty. For the recent disturbance, they said, but one man was to blame. He was Widukind.

Charles summoned an assembly of the Saxons at Verden.[2] He reminded them of the promises they had made, the compacts they had subscribed, the faith they had professed. Five years before at Paderborn they had put into his hands as a guarantee of their honest intent not only their goods and private possessions, and not only their country, but their lives. He called upon them, that they might save their for-

---

[1] Vétault, pp. 279–80; von den Steinen, p. 20; Einhard, *Annals*, pp. 69–71.
[2] Mombert, p. 118.

feit, to deliver to him the companions of Widukind, the men that had burned the churches and killed the missionaries.

The Saxons replied that these, too — wretched men! — had concealed themselves none knew where. Then the King insisted that the culprits should be found and sternly he rejected farther excuse or paltering. Then were brought before him forty-five hundred men, some of them chieftains, who were declared to be the persons that had participated in the rising. Charles looked upon them and stained his career with its darkest blot. He ordered the entire forty-five hundred to be put to death, and we are told that they were beheaded by his soldiers.[1]

For this act of frightful severity he has ever since been censured. The very patience, tolerance, and generosity that had marked his usual policy and made him the bright exception in an age of cruelty caused this relapse into savagery to seem the more conspicuous and the stranger. Such things in a Clovis or a Childeric would have seemed but the fashion of the times. Of the man that spared Hunold, Desiderius, and hundreds of others his predecessors would have slain, better things were to be expected.[2] For eleven hundred years the panegyrists have exhausted ingenuity in his excuse. It has been urged that the Saxons had pledged their lives when last they had promised obedience and order; that they had so often violated their treaties the patience of Charles was naturally exhausted; that the men he put to death were still smeared from the torturing and slaying of priests, missionaries, women, children; that they had been tried according to their own native customs and condemned; that since they

[1] Hodgkin, p. 116; Einhard, *Life*, pp. 17 and 31; Einhard, *Annals*, p. 78; von den Steinen, pp. 20–21; Capefigue, p. 216.

Nearly all historians and commentators have accepted the number, forty-five hundred as correct. It rests upon one line in Einhard, and Fletcher points out its improbability (page 244). Forty-five hundred beheadings would be at the rate of three a minute for twenty-four hours.

[2] 'It formed a lamentable contrast to all the rest of his political career, for there never was a conqueror that showed so solicitous a regard for the people he conquered or was so respectful of their rights and customs.' Vétault, p. 284.

had sworn allegiance and had violated their oaths, they were guilty of high treason, in all ages among all peoples punishable with death. When all this has been urged, the ugly fact remains. It was, as M. Vétault points out, too much and too essentially like a slaughter of prisoners.[1]

In trying to account for so strange a deed, one fact has been overlooked. The habit of expecting — and demanding — the one-piece man is among the dearest and least reasonable delusions of the human race. Charles of the Franks may well be believed to have been by far the most enlightened and merciful ruler of his times.[2] But how many removes was even Charles of the Franks from the woods and the stone hatchet? Education, reflection, and his religion had chastened and mollified the spirit of the wild man, but not so that a reversion was impossible. The instinct that moved Widukind to kill priests and torture converts was still rudimentary in the King of the Franks. Under common conditions it lay latent in him; when he was stirred by savagery he responded in kind.

Still another reflection belongs to this, the one great flaw in the Charlemagne repute. There are in the world those that maintain man to have made no progress, but to be essentially the same in thought, spirit, and deed as when he came forth from the caves. It is odd that believers in this fantasy have never bolstered their untenable faith by citing the apt parallel offered here. Truly in this instance the spiral seems to return upon itself unchanged and unexalted. The wholesale executions upon the Aller occurred in 782. One thousand and seventy-five years later, on the other side of the globe, a subjugated people that had taken no oath, violated no pledge, traversed no faith, arose against their alien possessors. When that revolt had been subdued, it was punished with death penalties as severe as those that have made Verden a historical sign of gloom. Persons familiar with what happened at the Alumbagh after the Indian revolt of 1857 will think that

[1] Page 284.   [2] Von den Steinen, p. 20.

144

English writers, at least, may not with justice condemn Charlemagne.[1] Yet so strange are the possibilities of racial self-deception that it is from the pens of English writers that he has been most severely denounced. Sixty years after the Alumbagh the parallel was rather more than repeated in the dreadful day of Amritsar, though it is to be doubted if even that black horror would modify the views of the English critics that with detestation look upon Verden.[2]

One other theory offered to explain Charlemagne's course here ought to be noticed. He was at that time acquainted with a woman named Fastrada, known to have been scheming and alleged to have been of a ruthless and cruel disposition. It has been surmised that it was upon the suggestion of Fastrada that he proceeded to make of the Saxons a memorable example of vengeance. Whether this was indeed her work or was not, one thing is certain. Before long this woman was casting a dark shadow upon his life and urging him along ways much more alien to his spirit than to hers.

But whatever excuse or palliation the massacre may have had in the savage code of retribution or in the machinations of rulers, assuredly it had none in wise policy. As policy it was but another inexplicable blunder in one that should have known better. Swiftly fell in the evil results. At the news of that terrible day on the Aller, almost the whole Saxon nation rose as one man, mad for vengeance. All oaths, treaties, pledges, all bonds of allegiance, all obligations of religion, all tribal jealousies were thrown to the winds. Faithless as the Saxons had always been to others, they kept faith with themselves. The house reared by so many years of labor fell at a touch. Charles must begin again the conquest of Saxony.

A unanimous cry went up from the people for the return of

[1] 'And those that remember how Sepoys were treated after Cawnpore will find the execution at least intelligible.' Davis, pp. 124–25.

[2] In an American magazine for October, 1927, there appeared an article by an English nobleman defending the atrocity of Amritsar and holding the slaughter to have been necessary. Every word he says in its defense might be urged in behalf of the course of Charlemagne at Verden.

Widukind. He came bringing with him a horde of savage Northmen, Frisians, and Slavs. Together they went forth to burn, slay, and lay waste in the name of Odin.

Charles had spent the winter at Thionville. On April 30 of the next year, 783, he suffered a heavy personal loss in the death of his wife Hildegarde, the beautiful Alemannian for whom he had sent away Desiderata. She had been more than wife to him; she had been faithful counselor, wise confidant, sympathetic friend. He had scant time to pay above her tomb the tribute of his sorrow when he must mount his horse and speed away to the war in Saxony. His army had hardly gathered itself before he traversed the Rhine and entered the enemy country at the head of his advance guard. And there in the middle of July the heavy news reached him of the death of his mother, the Dowager Queen Bertrade, his other wise friend and adviser.

At the first encounter, Widukind showed again that he had learned something in the art of war. He had dug himself in upon the heights of Osneggebirge, near the present city of Detmold. Charles attacked them in person, without waiting for his reënforcements. The Saxons fought stubbornly. It was at a heavy loss that Charles drove them from their entrenchments. When they went they withdrew in good order to re-form in another strong position on the river Hase. Charles held them there until his additional troops arrived. Then he attacked the Saxons in their new position, drove them headlong from it, and won a complete victory,[1] taking thousands of prisoners, all of whom he treated mercifully. The rest of that season, there being no enemy in sight, his army was employed in laying waste the country. But not a Saxon came in to beg for peace.

The winter of 783–784 was spent at Heristal. Charles had already married again and his bride was this Fastrada, daughter of a German count. We have encountered her be-

---

[1] Hodgkin, p. 116; Vétault, pp. 286–87; von den Steinen, p. 21; Einhard, *Life*, p. 16; Einhard, *Annals*, p. 71; Halphen, pp. 167–69.

fore and unpleasantly. We shall meet her again. So long as she lived she was the evil star of his career as Hildegarde had been the good.

With the coming of spring he returned to his heavy task at the North. The Saxons retired before him and left their country to its fate. From one end of it to the other he marched without a sign of opposition. When the campaign ended with autumn, he returned to Worms, the army laden with booty, but without having fought a battle.

The eldest son of Charles, who bore his father's name, was now twelve years old. He had accompanied the King on this campaign and was left on the banks of the Lippe with a small force of occupation. As soon as Charles had turned his back, the Saxons returned as usual and with other activities attacked the force nominally commanded by this boy. The Franks, ably marshaled this time, beat off the assailants, and when the young Charles reached Worms he was hailed as a conqueror — to gratify other minds as young as his, no doubt. But the incident stirred the King to an unprecedented strategy. In that climate with its heavy snows and biting frosts military operations were deemed impossible in winter. Yet in the dead of that savage season he led his troops forth. Fiercely and sullenly they went on together. They saw the final Saxon stronghold destroyed, the final Saxon force scattered, Widukind a fugitive among the wild tribes to the North. Then they rested. They had made a wilderness: they were entitled to call it peace.

Charles established himself in Saxony and directed in person the work of reconstruction.[1] The missionaries were brought back, the churches rebuilt, the government was firmly constituted. Then he sent messengers to treat with Widukind.

The beaten leader was wandering with a few followers along the south bank of the Elbe. His spirit was broken at

[1] Vétault, pp. 288–89; von den Steinen (a clear succinct account), pp. 21–22; Hodgkin, p. 118; Einhard, *Annals*, pp. 73–77.

last, not so much by his defeats, perhaps, as by the demonstration that the god in whom he had trusted was powerless to help him. He was invited to surrender. For his safety he demanded hostages. Charles sent them, assuring the fugitive he had nothing to fear. He entered the Frankish camp, was received with honor and kindness, and Charles in a personal conversation did not attempt to conceal his admiration for a bold and skillful adversary. He invited his guest to consider the advantages of the Christian religion. According to the legend, a miraculous apparition assisted at the conversion and Widukind announced his readiness to be baptized. Charles himself acted as godfather, having invoked the blessing of the Pope and the assistance of Offa, King of Mercia, a converted Saxon ruler of England. Hadrian I ordered special ceremonies and prayers of thanksgiving in the churches. Widukind was loaded with gifts and assigned a comfortable residence in Westphalia. There he passed his days in dignified retirement. It is an odd footnote to the history of all these things that long afterward a descendant of Widukind and a descendant of Charles were married and from their union sprang a new line of European rulers.

In Saxony the end seemed to have come at last, after so many years of struggle. Charles thought so, and turned him to other matters. Saxony was Frank; Saxony was Christian.[1]

He was not yet through with these pugnacious people. In the spring of 793, when he was about to set forth on an expedition against the Avars, a post-haste messenger brought him at Regensburg the worst of news. The North Saxons had broken into rebellion, had ambushed and destroyed a Frank detachment under Count Theodoric, the savior of the remnants of the army after the disaster of Süntel, and had slain the Count himself.[2] The Avar affair must wait and Charles must turn north with his forces again to combat his old-time foes.

It was a conflict quickly concluded. He led one army from

[1] Halphen, pp. 173-77; Hodgkin, p. 113.   [2] Mombert, p. 129.

the southeast, his son, the Crown Prince, led another from the west. The insurgent Saxons were gathered at Sindfeld, south of Paderborn. The two Frankish forces caught them in a trap and they surrendered without striking a blow.[1]

The next year, part of them revolted again, killed Witzin, Duke of the Abodrites, the close allies of the Franks, and once more threatened the kingdom. Charles marched again through their country and again brought back peace with the sword. In 797, convinced that the iron code of Draco was no model for lawmakers in that region, he canceled the severe Capitulary of 782 and issued another that substituted conciliation for suppression and good will for terror.[2] After that he had little trouble. The main body of Saxons was steadily being absorbed into the Frankish Empire. For six years there were sporadic upheavals from the Nordalbingians, or Saxons north of the Elbe, but by 808 the last of these had been subdued, and a war that lasted more than thirty years was done with.

One of the last movements in its checkered story had for succeeding generations an interest that Charlemagne could never have dreamed of. Wearied of the incessant revolt and incurable bad faith of the Nordalbingians, he deported a body of them, men, women, and children, said to have numbered ten thousand, settled them in Holland, and gave their lands to his allies, the Abodrites. In Holland, the infrangible Saxon spirit, mingled with that of the ancient and worthy Batavians, mollified by Christianity, enlightened at last with ideals, flowered to the world in the siege of Leyden and still later had a curious effect upon the American revolt and American Declaration of Independence.[3]

[1] Einhard, *Annals*, pp. 92–93; Einhard, *Life*, p. 21; Halphen, pp. 189–90; Vétault, pp. 351–52.

[2] Mombert, p. 133. The new laws are supposed, on insufficient grounds, to reflect the spirits of Alcuin and Queen Luitgarde.

[3] Douglas Campbell, *The Puritan in Holland, England and America*, vol. II, pp. 420–22.

CHAPTER IX

ROLAND AND THE HEAVY DAY OF RONCESVALLES

A MYSTERY overhangs the historic relations of France and Spain.

By a strange fatality, to mix in Spanish affairs has always been to France a forerunner of disaster. Stupid interference with one Spanish succession resulted in Sedan and utter ruin for Louis Napoleon; with another signaled the overthrow of Louis Philippe; with another plunged France into a disastrous war and extended the hateful tribe of Bourbon. It was his intriguing and campaigning in Spain that began the downfall of Napoleon the Great, and it was an ill-advised expedition to Spain that drew upon Charles of the Franks an underscored disaster to his arms and seemed to inaugurate a series of misfortunes checkering to the end of his life what was otherwise a career of almost unexampled splendor.

We go back now to those peculiar and fascinating people, the Saracens. After their defeats by The Hammer and other Christian leaders had swept them out of France, the Moslem hosts remained for centuries in possession of Spain except for the northern regions and a little Christian kingdom called the Asturias. Wise as they were, the Saracens were not wise enough to avoid the human pitfalls of dissensions, bickerings, and jarring ambitions. A quarrel grew up about the succession to the Caliphate of Cordova. The all-powerful Franks were near neighbors; the temptation to win their help for one side or the other was too strong. As early as 760, Soliman-Ibn-el-Arabi, Governor of Barcelona, had sought the support of King Pepin and became in some vague way a vassal of the Frankish State. Thus was presented the odd spectacle of Saracens appealing to the son of the man that had ruined their hopes at Tours, and faithful scions of the Prophet going hob-and-nob with those they usually called dogs of unbelievers.

In 777, while Charles was at Paderborn intent upon the problem of the Saxons,[1] this same Soliman, or another that bore the same name and was now Governor of Saragossa, came at the head of an embassy of Saracen[2] chiefs with an offer of all northern Spain in return for help against the government of Cordova.

As a matter of fact, Charles had no good reason to take up this quarrel. It is true that a part of the Christian population of Spain complained of the tyranny of Abd-el-Raman-ben-Mousala, calling him 'the cruelest Mussulman that had ever governed Spain,'[3] and equally true that Charles was the titular defender of the faith and foremost Christian ruler. But in general the Saracens had shown a disposition to be tolerant[4] toward the Christians in their territories and the aggressions of Abd-el-Raman might have been assuaged with an embassy and a few words of caution. The share Charles took in the story seems on the whole gratuitous and suggests that judgment went dumb before a prospect of new peoples to be governed.

However that may be, and nobody knows, a treaty was concluded on the banks of the Lippe by which Spain as far as the river Ebro was ceded to the Frankish King in return for an army of invasion that he was to lead to the liberation of the people oppressed by the insensate emirs. The winter had already set in when this compact was signed. Charles paid a short visit to his farms in Austrasia and then gave himself to the organizing of his forces. How large an army he gathered is not set forth, but the chroniclers seem to have been impressed with its unusual size. From the Danube to

[1] Einhard, *Life*, p. 17.
[2] Einhard, *Annals*, pp. 64–65.
[3] Vétault, p. 248; von den Steinen, p. 17.
[4] Gibbon, chap. LI, p. 106.

Italy and the sea, he called out his reserves and drew them to a place of rendezvous in Aquitania.[1]

Easter found him at Chasseneuil with his family, and there Queen Hildegarde bore him twins, of whom one, Lothar, died in his cradle, and the other came to have a place in history as Louis the Pious.

For the war, Charles followed his usual plan of dividing his forces, giving the command of one army to that same uncle, the stout Duke Bernard, who had been his chief lieutenant in the Italian campaign, and leading the other division himself. They crossed the Pyrenees by different routes and came together in Spain.[2]

No enemy opposed the advance of the great host. Charles appeared before Pampelona. At the mere sight of his banners it was surrendered by the Governor, Abou-Thor, who was one of Soliman's confederates. Other places followed this example. The Governors of Barcelona and Gironne opened their strongholds and gave hostages for their good conduct. Saragossa was menaced but not taken, and then Charles gave himself chiefly to the work of organizing the new territory as part of the Frankish State.

This seems to have been more than either Saracens or Christians had counted on. They wished the Frank to help them in their quarrels, but expected to return to power themselves as soon as he should have soundly beaten their enemies for them — a delightful illustration of the naïve immaturity of the governing mind. When he should have won their battles, Charles was to go back to his own country and presently thank God that he had been of assistance to deserving persons. The practical Charles had a different notion about this. When the resident Christians found that in the captured cities the native governors were being dismissed and Frankish counts were supplying their places, the murmurs arose to heaven. The Christians in Spain were Ostrogoths. Against the Franks they had an ancient grudge,

[1] Vétault, p. 249.   [2] Hodgkin, p. 146.

grown from many defeats. They now assumed an air of grievance, declaring they had rather be ruled by heathen Saracens than by the ever-detestable Franks. The Christian Kings of Navarre and the Asturias said so without reservation. Forthwith they sought an alliance with the Mohammedan Caliph of Cordova rather than open their strongholds to their old-time enemies, even though these were of their own faith.[1]

In other words, kaleidoscope. One month they appealed to Charles to beat the Mussulman and the next they appealed to the Mussulman to beat Charles.

No chapter of mediæval history is vaguer than the rest of this story. It appears that Charles intended to capture Saragossa and then gave up that purpose. It appears also that he may have been disgusted with the nature of his reception. The old chronicler of Metz, whose fragmentary narrative is most often followed, says that Charles received word of a serious outbreak of the Saxons and so left Spain for the North. Others have suggested that he found it too difficult to provision so large an army in so hostile a country. All we know for certain is that he determined to return without capturing Saragossa; that he deemed northern Spain to have been added to his dominions; that he left a force to keep it in order; and that he seemed incensed as well as disappointed. He seized the unfortunate Soliman that had negotiated the treaty and carried him home in chains,[2] a fact perhaps more significant than any of the others. About the most that could be said otherwise for the invasion was that it had given him new territory, extended his influence into a new region, and laid a foundation for later conquests.[3] This is not much. In fact, the whole story would not now be worth an extended telling if it had not included one incident hardly to be equaled for dramatic intensity and since then more celebrated and more besung than any other in mediæval history.

On its way home, the army of the Franks had left the

[1] Vétault, pp. 250-57.   [2] Hodgkin, p. 147.   [3] Vétault, pp. 251-52.

Saracens far behind. On August 18, 778, the troopers reached the summit of the Pyrenees. No enemy was in sight; the march was peaceful and care-free. The first division had crossed the divide and was swinging down the descent toward the north. The rear guard with the baggage was threading the crest of the pass, which led thence through a gloomy and narrow defile, once the bed of a little lake. No suspicion of danger entered any soldier's mind.

Of a sudden from concealed places in the hill slopes, there swept down upon the troops a wild and furious horde of shrieking savages that began a desperate assault. The Franks, taken by surprise and encumbered with heavy armor and the baggage, were thrown into confusion. Stretched out in a long thin line where the defile made maneuvers and military formations impossible, they were at the mercy of their assailants. The battalions from the forward files that hastened back with assistance only added to the fatal disorder of their comrades, hemmed in a road so narrow that at no place could three men walk abreast in it. Hour after hour went on the hopeless strife, Frank locked in deadly encounter with his inevitable fate. The assailants, often shielded by cliffs and boulders, often hardly visible, poured down upon the struggling legions a torrent of rocks and arrows. Then as the confusion grew they flung themselves bodily upon the bewildered soldiers and with swords butchered them like cattle or hurled them down the steeps of the pass.[1]

The rear guard was virtually annihilated. The slaughter was grievous. No reënforcements could avail to stem the disaster. Night alone put an end to the butchery. As soon as darkness fell the assailants disappeared — with the baggage.

Charles at the head of his troops had issued from the bottom of the pass upon the plain when he heard of what had happened to his rear guard. He re-formed his broken columns and started the next day in pursuit of his foe. There was

[1] Vétault, pp. 254-55. He is following Einhard; *vide Annals*, pp. 65-66, and *Life*, pp. 17-18. The details are scanty. Mombert, p. 159; Capéfigue, p. 233.

none in sight nor could the scouts discover traces of the warriors that had attacked so ferociously. They had come and gone like a flash, and Charles was obliged to return empty-handed. Under the severest humiliation he ever encountered he moved northward to his winter quarters.

This was that battle of Roncesvalles that for so many years charmed the imaginations of poets, troubadours, romancers, and historians. The deeds of valor done that day in fact and in fiction came to have a deathless renown and a singular impression upon both letters and art. Among the Frankish nobles that fell in the pass were Eggihard, the King's high steward; Anselm, the seneschal; and above all 'Hruoland,[1] warden of the Breton March,' who became the immortal Roland of songs, sonnets, ballads and ballades, rondeaus, triolets, stories, legends, innumerable. 'Hruoland, warden of the Breton March' — that is all we positively know about him, and out of that single half-line has sprung an interminable literature. From so trifling a source flowed never so vast a river.[2] It is the most astonishing thing in literary history and beyond explanation except the unsatisfied thirst of a world wandering in a fictionless desert and suddenly charmed by the mellifluous clang of a name. Hruoland became Orlando in Italian, Roldan in Spanish, Roland in French, the language of the troubadours. Of Anselm and Eggihard, who also perished that day in the pass, we know as much as we know of 'Hruoland, warden of the Breton March,' but nobody has ever celebrated them in ballade or distich. Reasonably, perhaps. Eggihard — it will hardly scan, and surely would sound but ill on lips of troubadour or minstrel.

The wealth of the detail with which the mediæval imagination, long pent up, now running a romantic riot, adorned this bare pole of fact must astonish every investigator. 'The Warden of the Breton March' was the greatest knight that ever lived, the bravest, boldest, wisest, most adorable. The

[1] Einhard, *Life*, p. 18.　　　[2] Capefigue, p. 234; also pp. 238-50.

deeds performed by him that day surpassed all others known to man; by him with his good sword and by Oliver his comrade in arms. Where Oliver came from we know not, but he must be ever by Roland's side and ever bright and fair. When all possible changes had been rung on Roland's prowess at Roncesvalles, he was taken to every part of Europe and even to Iceland, performing everywhere dazzling feats of bravery. Songs about him and his companions in arms became the favorite literature of every land. One of them [1] was heard at the battle of Hastings. Next he was involved in the copious legendary accretions of the Rhine, and a ruin and a town there still bear his name. The local legend of Rolandseck, totally ignoring Einhard, says that he died in this castle — heart-broken when he discovered that in his absence, Hildegunde, his lady love, had taken the veil and entered a convent. Finally the figures of the mighty paladins, Roland and Oliver, came to be embalmed for us in painting and sculpture. In many an old church we may still see their warlike effigies.

All this from the battle of Roncesvalles, insignificant in object and results. The assailants possessed themselves of much baggage and other spoils, but except in one immaterial respect they effected nothing else. The one exception was the mark they left upon the military reputation of Charles. Critics have pointed out with justice that to thread that pass without protecting his flanks with scouts and guards was an extraordinary carelessness. But probably there is a fracture of this kind in the record of every famous military commander if the everlasting tribe of Einhards would let us find it out.

It remains to be noticed that in the popular and long-accepted accounts of this battle was firmly embedded a singular historical error.

[1] Sung by Knight Taillefer as he led a Norman charge. But the most famous 'Song of Roland' is of a later period, its author unknown. The preferred date of its composition is about 1100. The most perfect extant copy is in the Bodleian Library, Oxford, England. *Vide* Appendix.

For centuries the idea seemed fixed in the human mind that the blow had been struck at the Franks by the Saracens,[1] who thus achieved upon the grandson of The Hammer their measure of revenge. This reminds one forcibly of Napoleon's celebrated remark about the fabulous nature of history. Roncesvalles did not have even so much dignity as Saracenic vengeance might have given to it. As nearly as can now be determined no Saracens had part in it. Who, then, were these savage people that, planning so adroit an ambuscade, struck so resoundingly upon the foremost soldier of Christendom and one of the outstanding military geniuses of the world?

They were the Basques, the inhabitants of the Pyrenees, the survivors of an almost lost and unusual people that had once inhabited much of Europe. Basques — and they had no impulse to so fierce an attack except plunder and animal delight in killing.[2] The great host of Charles winding southward through their mountains they had watched and made no sign. Suddenly, upon the return march, they leaped as if from the earth upon the weary Franks and with insatiable fury cut them to pieces.

No stranger eruption of an apparently irresponsible force is of record among men, and the weirdness it of might have held the wondering attention of mankind even if there had been no romance of Roland. It was as if there had suddenly been created a new power of destruction that sprang once into a devastating flame and then disappeared.

The leader of the Basques was one Lupus. Part of the fiction about Roncesvalles, long received as truth, represented Charles as overtaking, capturing, and hanging this Lupus. It remained for a modern Frenchman [3] to dig up the fact that Lupus lived long and in great prosperity.

[1] Walter Scott repeats this common error in the stanza referring to the horn that told 'imperial Charlemagne' how 'Paynim sons of swarthy Spain had wrought his champion's fall.'

[2] Vétault, p. 255.

[3] Lucien Double, *L'Empereur Charlemagne*, p. 272. Another error made by some

CHARLEMAGNE, FIRST OF THE MODERNS

Heavy of heart, since he had lost so many brave men and good friends, Charles returned to his winter palace to learn more of the gravity of the uprising in the North. For the first time in his life he tasted the bitterness of adversity. All reports told of trouble.

historians is to the effect that Lupus was the chief that had betrayed Waifar to Pepin the Short. M. Double has set this also straight.

CHAPTER X

THE STORY OF THE UNLUCKY LIUTBERGA

FROM its beginning the career of Charles of the Franks pivoted at every crisis upon the influence of women or a woman. It was his mother that inspired some of the best measures of his early rule. His separation from Desiderata helped to precipitate the Lombard war. Gentle counsels of Queen Hildegarde often guided him aright in the troublous days of the Saxon insurrections. The headstrong Fastrada, who seemed to her contemporaries to have the soul of a wolf, plunged him into other difficulties than the massacre on the Weser. Another woman now interfered in his destiny with results important for him and most evil for her.

This was Liutberga, Duchess of Bavaria, daughter of Desiderius, the King of the Lombards, whom Charles had deposed and sent to a monastery. She was therefore a sister to Desiderata, whom Charles had divorced. For more than one reason she hated him. Another sister of hers had been married to Arichis, Duke of Benevento in Italy. Benevento was nominally a vassal state of the Frankish King. It had never really accepted its place in the imperial congeries, chiefly because its rulers were too stiff of neck and too confident of their own power as undefeated Lombards to acknowledge obedience to anybody. Probably, the wife of Arichis found something congenial to her soul in fostering this spirit.

Hadrian I, the wise and enlightened Pope that we saw so intelligently active at a former crux in Italian affairs, had much occasion to complain of Duke Arichis. In imitation of his royal father-in-law and apparently uninstructed by his father-in-law's fate, he amused himself by seizing and annexing such cities belonging to the Papal States as lay nearest

159

to his own dominions. In 786, without reference to his suzerain, he began a war of aggression upon the people of Amalfi, which was a province belonging to the Duke of Naples.[1]

Hadrian informed Charles of these developments, and Charles, perceiving clearly that trouble was at hand in Italy, crossed the Alps late in the autumn, passed Christmas at Florence, paid his third visit to Rome, and there consulted long with Hadrian. In the middle of the winter of 787, he led an army toward Benevento.

Arichis sent his eldest son, Romuald, with presents, kind words, and a petition that the army of Charles should not enter Beneventan territory.[2] What he expected to gain by this is beyond guessing, unless he had a notion that because Charles was placable he was foolish. On this point there was soon no chance for illusion.

'Your messages of good will are pleasant enough,' said Charles, 'but what does your father purpose to do?'

The young man seems to have made some vague and scattering response, whereupon Charles put him under arrest. Then he dispatched a messenger to Arichis demanding in explicit terms that the Duke should without further delay restore to the Holy See the possessions he had seized from it, should acknowledge his obligations to the Kingdom of the Franks, and should furnish satisfactory guarantees of his good conduct thereafter. It was an ultimatum, straight, simple, direct. Do these things at once or Benevento will be treated as a conquered province and its Duke as a vassal in rebellion.

When he heard of the arrest of his son, Arichis, who was, maybe, only another sufferer from neurosis, fled from his capital and took refuge at Salerno, which, being a seaport, offered him some chance to escape out of the country. He was looking about for means to reach Constantinople and join there in congenial exile his brother-in-law Adelghis when

[1] Vétault, pp. 295–96.   [2] Einhard, *Life*, p. 18; Hodgkin, p. 133.

he received the ultimatum of the King.[1] He seems to have been rejoiced that the terms were so easy; what he had expected them to be can only be surmised — execution by wild horses, may be. The haste he made to comply with every demand seems almost comical. He sent his second son, Grimoald, with the Bishops of Salerno and Benevento, to kneel before the King with the most humble promises of obedience and on the spot to restore to the Pope the six cities he had taken from the Papal States. He signed an agreement to pay an annual tribute equal to about $120,000 and sent along twelve hostages as a pledge that he would keep faith. One of them was this young Grimoald, who was also the treaty-maker on this occasion. Thereupon Charles released Romuald and led his army back to Rome, where he celebrated Easter.[2]

Without shedding a drop of blood he had reduced the duchy of the stiff-necked to subjection and extended the actual front of his kingdom almost to the southern point of Italy. But before he had fairly entered Rome from these easy triumphs, he had word of the machinations of Liutberga and the ugly situation opening in Bavaria.

Nominally, Bavaria was a subject province of the Frankish Kingdom, but Tassilo, urged by his wife, was at pains to make the connection as slight as possible. Charles was no great stickler for the forms of vassalage, but in time the hostile attitude of the Bavarian court became too marked to be overlooked. Tassilo desired that Bavaria should be independent in name as well as in fact. As far back as the war with Aquitania he had refused to furnish his contingent of soldiers, declaring that he would never again enter the presence of the King of the Franks. No Bavarians were supplied to Charles for the Italian and Saxon campaigns, and Tassilo coolly ignored all attempts to remind him of his pledges and his duty.

[1] Einhard, *Annals*, pp. 77–78.
[2] Einhard, *Life*, p. 18; Hodgkin, pp. 133–34.

In 787, Charles, who had not disregarded any of these conditions, was at Rome on a visit to the Pope. As we have noted, part of his usual policy was to avoid war whenever he could.[1] At Rome he related to Hadrian the ill behavior of Tassilo and suggested that the Pope should send an embassy to the Duke and remind him of his obligations. The Pope was only too glad to comply. The ambassadors must have been of a convincing eloquence, for they succeeded in inspiring Tassilo with a wholesome fear. On condition that hostages should guarantee his safety, the Duke agreed to visit the King that winter. When he fulfilled that pledge, Tassilo renewed his oath of allegiance and promised to furnish the share of the military establishment to which he was bound.

The most interesting question that these annals continually provoke is whether the typical ruler of that age was more child, more constitutional liar, or more congenital imbecile. No sooner was Tassilo back in his own territories than he disregarded everything he had promised at Worms and resumed his former course of contemptuous indifference to the overlord.

Still Charles was slow to wrath. While he was at Rome after the subduing of Benevento two Bavarian envoys appeared before the Pope ostensibly to beg his intercession between their master and the King. The Pope gave them open hearing at which Charles was present. The envoys stated their case, declaring the willingness of Tassilo to fulfill all his obligations and promises.

'But what guarantee does your master offer,' thundered Charles, 'that he will this time keep the faith he has so often broken?'

The envoys said they had no authority to do more than to present their message and bear back the Pope's answer.

'Then this is my answer,' said the Pope. 'Tell your master that he and you are alike liars and falsifiers and that on pain

[1] Hodgkin, p. 130. He 'first tried spiritual means.'

of the utmost penalty of the Church he shall keep to the letter the promises he has made.'[1]

To this the envoys made no response, but set out at once for Bavaria, while Charles returned to Worms.

It was now woman against woman. Charles took counsel of the energetic Fastrada, who urged him to immediate war. Tassilo was guided by Liutberga, who had added another to the deep-seated grievances she felt against the masterful Frank. He had obliterated the Lombard country of Benevento; he had humiliated the Lombard Prince Arichis, her brother-in-law; he was now triumphing over her husband. It is an illumination of character that Charles made one more effort to adjust the difference without an open rupture. He summoned a council of his nobles and laid the case before them. On their advice he sent one more embassy to Tassilo to urge a pacific understanding. It failed and the Franks declared war.[2]

It was all over before it had more than begun. The master strategist of the times must have long before matured his plans for this contingency. He made up three armies. The first moving from Italy was commanded by the brother of the Crown Prince, now called Pepin, though he had not been so named at his birth.[3] Charles himself led the second, which moved from the west. A third composed of Saxons and Thuringians descended from the north by way of Ingolstadt. The three had Tassilo in a trap. It was one of those swift and grandiose moves of Charles by which he often conquered an enemy without striking a blow.

The Duke perceived that his situation was hopeless and surrendered at discretion. He went in person before Charles, performed all the ceremonies of vassalage, and gave his son as hostage for the faithful performance of his obligations.

No sooner was this arrangement ratified than it was shattered. Tassilo returned to his own country. There

---

[1] Hodgkin, p. 135; Einhard, *Life*, p. 17; Einhard, *Annals*, pp. 78–82.
[2] Hodgkin, p. 135; *Annals* of Lorsch, p. 82.   [3] Hodgkin, p. 130.

Liutberga goaded him into fresh offenses. By her counsel he opened negotiations with the Avars,[1] the fierce Mongols on the Danube, seeking an alliance in a final movement against the Franks. He went even farther than that, for there is fairly good evidence that he plotted the assassination of the King that his wife hated with so fierce a hatred.

Some one reminded him of the peril to which he was exposing his son, left a hostage in the hands of Charles.

'If I had ten sons,' said the Duke, 'I would lose them all in this cause. It is better for me to die than to live a vassal on such terms as I have sworn to.'

The inscrutable patience of the King was exhausted. He had Tassilo arrested and brought a prisoner to Ingelheim. There before an assembly of nobles that represented every part of the kingdom, including Bavaria itself, he was put on trial. The evidence was all of a kind. Tassilo attempted no defense. He even avowed what was urged against him. Unanimously he was found guilty and sentenced to death.

Charles was unwilling to carry out this sentence. He asked of the assembly that it might be commuted. When the nobles had agreed, Charles asked Tassilo what he wished to do. Tassilo is said to have responded that he wished to enter a monastery, 'there to do penance for his many sins that he might save his soul.' Seclusion in a monastery was so often the fate forced upon defeated monarchs in those days that one reads this with amused skepticism. But whether voluntarily or otherwise in this case, Tassilo was shut up, first in the monastery of Saint Goar on the Rhine and then at another place in what is now Normandy. In one respect he fared better than that Childeric III with whom these chronicles begin. He asked as a favor that his long hair, the symbol of his rank and nation, should not be cut off, lest he be too much humiliated in the eyes of his people. The request was granted; he suffered only the tonsure.[2]

[1] Einhard, *Life*, p. 17; Einhard, *Annals*, p. 82.
[2] *Annals* of Lorsch, pp. 84–85.

The entire family shared his fate or salvation, whichever it was. Liutberga, the haughty, the maladroit, the revengeful, who had been responsible for all the upheaval, became a nun.[1] The two sons, Theodon and Theodebert, and two daughters of whom the names have not been preserved, were forced to take holy orders. 'The repose of the world demanded that this family should be extinguished in obscurity,' remarks Vétault.[2] Probably he makes a correct diagnosis of the case.

Two other entries concerning the restless Tassilo are to be found in the records. The annalist Angilbert[3] says that the fallen Duke lived in the cloister with sincere heart as piously as he had entered it. In 794 he was brought before the assembly at Frankfort, where he formally renounced all claim to the throne of Bavaria, a mysterious formality the purpose of which has been lost, since he was now but a private person.

With the fall of the last member of the old Bavarian house, Charles became Duke of Bavaria, and the boundaries of his actual as well as of his nominal sovereignty were extended eastward to the frontiers of the Avars.[4]

[1] So-called Nazarian *Annals*, p. 85.   [2] Page 304.
[3] If he wrote the things sometimes ascribed to him.
[4] Einhard, *Life*, p. 19.

CHAPTER XI

THE PEOPLE THAT DWELT IN THE NINE RINGS

Of the strange barbarians that in the morning of the Christian era threatened Europe and civilization, the strangest were these Avars.

About the end of the sixth century they suddenly came swarming in from Central Asia and for the next two hundred years were the terror of Constantinople and its degenerate emperors. Scarcely another people in any stage of the world's story has swept so quickly to a place commanding and then faded so quickly from view. Once they were powerful enough to levy upon the senile Empire a tribute for those times as enormous as it was disgraceful. The Emperor Maurice revolted at the shameful burden. Then the Avars showed to him and to all the world how perilous they were in battle. With a skill that now causes us to wonder, they succeeded in maneuvering him and his forces into an impossible position. To avoid destruction he allowed them to levy a new and greater tribute and to impose such humiliating terms as shamed anew the name of Roman.[1]

After some wanderings and adventures, these flat-faced intruders from the plains of Tartary seized upon a commodious region that the Latinized Franks knew as Pannonia. It stretched from almost the Dalmatian coast of the Adriatic north and east to the corner of the Danube and was rich and fertile. There they made a country and a government of a nature Europe had not seen before and is not likely to see again. It was purely Asiatic, despotic, and so nearly as we can now make out, marvelously efficient for the ideals of Avar life. For generations they shook the rest of Central

[1] Davis, p. 141; Gibbon, chap. XLII, pp. 454–58; chap. XLV, pp. 96, 99, *et seq.*

AN AVAR RAID
By Ulpiano Checa

Europe with incessant alarms while they lived in a way different from that of any other people of whom we have knowledge. They seem to have been originally by profession active and competent brigands, but at the time when they came to rest around the Danube such a means of livelihood naturally conferred much less distinction than the unusual means they took to safeguard their booty when once they had gained it.

With what must have been prodigious labor they surrounded themselves with a series of gigantic fortifications or circular earthworks, being rings within rings that protected perhaps a hundred square miles of enclosed territory and created by their strangeness and mystery even more than by their formidable strength an impression of almost superstitious terror upon all their neighbors. 'The people of the rings' became the great bogymen of the Middle Ages and left a certain mark on common speech that survives to this day.

Of the general outlines of this story, fantastic as it may appear, we have enough warrant in the records, and confirmation has been had in excavations that revealed traces of the long-vanished ramparts. But for the details, curiously enough, we are indebted chiefly to the memory of one boy.

Once more the witness is the singular person known in history and literature as the Monk of Saint Gall.[1] He has recorded that when he was a lad he was wont to listen (sometimes unwillingly) to the tales of old Adalbert, a veteran warrior that had fought against the Avars. The chapter the old man liked best was a description of the marvelous Avar fortifications. When the boy had grown up he wrote [2] this account of one of the conversations between him and the grizzled soldier.

---

[1] Professor Halphen has virtually succeeded in identifying him as one Notker, an industrious scribe of the end of the ninth century. *Études Critiques sur l'Histoire de Charlemagne*, pp. 138–39.

[2] Monk of Saint Gall, pp. 46–48.

'The country of the Huns,'[1] began the veteran, 'was surrounded with nine rings ——'

'Rings?' asked the boy.

'It was protected with nine walls or palisades. The diameter of the first ring was equal to the distance from Zurich to Constance' — about thirty-five miles.[2] The old man went on to explain that each ring had walls of logs filled in between with stones and lime and covered with sod. Each wall was twenty feet high and twenty feet thick. On the top trees and shrubs were thickly planted and so trimmed that they should offer every obstacle to the invader. The ninth or final ring enclosed the citadel of the nation, the residence of the Chagan or Chief, and the treasure, which was the accumulation of generations of plunder. It was not until after the Avars had ceased to be a factor in continental affairs that men learned, with a kind of awe, about the excellence of the riches concealed within that ninth ring.

Between the rings were the farms and villages, so spaced that a trumpet blown in one could be heard in the next, and thus the inhabitants might be easily alarmed and summoned. Aliens dwelling in a hostile land, the Avars evidently purposed to take no chances with their neighbors. The rings were constantly patrolled; the whole country was kept easily under guard. At intervals strongly protected doors allowed communications through the rings and a path by which marauding parties could issue upon their raids and return with their booty.

When the Avars tore their way westward into Europe they were like so many other Tartar tribes, nomads and shepherds as well as bandits. From dwelling so long in the fixed boundaries of their rings they had developed something of the arts and habits of settled agriculturists. For a long time

[1] The Huns and Avars, though quite distinct, were commonly confused by writers in that period and long afterward.

[2] Either the worthy Adalbert was experimenting in fictionalized biography or the excellent Monk's memory went askew. The Avar rings were veritable, but could hardly have been of the size here reported.

peace did not tame their arrogant spirit nor impair their physical vigor. They came of tribes that for its own sake loved fighting; they never allowed the pleasures of husbandry to interfere with the serious business of loot. Squat, broad-shouldered, supple, and strong, they seem to have been alert in the field, marvelous bowmen, marvelous horsemen. Pure Mongols, their yellow skin, slanted eyes, long braided hair, fierce aspect, strange weapons, and the exceeding swiftness of their maneuvers revived the terrors of Attila's hordes. No doubt their numbers were exaggerated, so that the timid believed the Avars a great and invincible nation and the most terrible foe that had threatened Christendom. Yet with all allowance for the additions of fancy, it is manifest that such works as their fortifications could not have been reared by a negligible population. We need not wonder that for generations the mysterious rings along the Danube were to the generality objects of superstitious surmise and to the statesmen of grave concern.

Come from the same great human cradle of Asia out of which had poured the Huns,[1] the Avars seem to have been in every way as capable a race as their cousins and still fiercer. Unluckily, the world has lost all definite knowledge of their culture, but they must have had some of the arts well developed, for they made effective weapons [2] and armor and they could negotiate and trade as well as fight. The title of their chief, the Chagan or Khakan, reveals their Tartar origin. His rule from the citadel in the ninth ring went not always undisputed; more than once Avarland was distracted with civil war. And with these meager facts about one of the most interesting peoples in history, inquiry stops short.

As the tribe increased, many of its members began to live on lands outside of the rings, where they came into contact with Christians, and cemented an understanding with the

[1] Gibbon, chap. XXVI.
[2] *Vide* letter of Charles to Offa, King of Mercia, written in 796.

remains of Attila's invading Huns. As to the Christians, the
difference in racial traits and interests, and the belief that the
aliens were perilous heathen, speedily bred trouble and would
have led eventually to Frankish intervention even if there
had been no other irritant. Disputes were continually arising
about the borderlands that the Avars occupied; the Avars
were accused on plausible grounds of annoying and persecut-
ing their Christian neighbors. But beyond all these the
kingdom had its own grievance. The Avars had supported
Tassilo of Bavaria in one of his revolts. They had marched
out of their ramparts and made war on the Franks. With
difficulty they had been repulsed. So far as could be learned,
they had now returned to the rings only to prepare through
the winter another expedition. The Christians looked to
Charles.

They could hardly have sought him at a worse time. The
difficulties into which he had been plunged by the unlucky
Spanish expedition were a needless addition to a plenitude
of other distractions. His kingdom lived surrounded by
enemies; as the old writer says of another man so beset, he
walked amid fires. Among them was one of a new origin.
On the northwest frontier of his dominions was a savage
tribe of Slavs that were known as the Wiltzes. They had long
been an ugly cloud on the borderland, into which they often
raided, and just at this inopportune moment they broke
through with an organized invasion and Charles must lead
an army against them.[1]

'The Saxons served in this campaign,' says old Einhard,
'as auxiliaries among the tribes that followed the King's
standard at his summons, but their obedience lacked sincerity and devotion. War was declared because the Slavs
kept harassing the Abodrites, old allies of the Franks, with
continuous incursions, despite all commands to the contrary.
A gulf of unknown length [the Baltic] but nowhere more than
a hundred miles wide, and in many parts narrower, stretches

[1] Einhard, *Life*, p. 19; Einhard, *Annals*, p. 88.

170

off toward the east from the Western Ocean. Many tribes have settlements on its shores; the Danes and Swedes whom we call Northmen, on the northern shore and all the adjacent islands; but the southern shore is inhabited by the Slavs and Aisti. The Walatabians [Wiltzes] against whom the King now made war were the chief of these. But in a single campaign, which he conducted in person, he so crushed and subdued them that they did not think it advisable thereafter to refuse obedience to his commands.'

He had left his new capital of Aachen in May, crossed the Rhine near Cologne, marched through Saxony (as it then was), recruiting his forces with Frisians, Abodrites, and Serbs. At the Elbe he threw across the river two bridges on which his troops advanced and were in the country of the Wiltzes.

'Warlike as they were,' says Einhard, 'they could not withstand the impetuous assaults of the King's army. When they saw him approaching their capital, the old chief, Dragowit, who, because of illustrious descent and great age had preference over all the other chiefs of the tribe, gave himself up with all his possessions, delivered the required hostages, and with all the other princes of the Slavs swore fidelity to the King of the Franks.'

When he had brought the campaign to this happy ending, Charles turned south to take up the case of the Avars.[1] So great was their prestige and so profound the mystery and awe brooding over their unknown dwelling-places that he believed he was facing one of the crises of his career and was about to begin a holy war to rescue Christendom from such a foe as at Tours had fronted his grandfather.

In 789, the Avars had sent an embassy to him at Worms, asking him to adjust amicably a dispute they were having with their Christian neighbors concerning land boundaries.[2] The only result of the meeting had been to show him that the ideas of the two peoples were irreconcilable and that either

[1] Einhard, *Life*, p. 20. [2] Vétault, p. 321–22.

Christianity or heathendom must go down. In the early spring of 791 he began to move toward the Avar frontier. As usual, he divided his army,[1] and the campaign has additional interest from the fact that one of the divisions was led by his second legitimate son, now Pepin, but first known as Carloman, whose military novitiate we have previously reported. Pepin's army came northward from Italy. The main division, commanded by Charles, marched eastward from Regensburg. One may sense something of the unifying energy that the Frankish system had developed when one reads that in this army went Bavarians whom Charles had conquered, Saxons whom he had chased and harried, Serbs, Frisians, Abodriti, and even Czechs. For the peculiar people that had come from the east to settle in Bohemia were in the ranks fighting for the first time under a Christian banner and for a Christian cause — heathen fighting against other heathen, for the sake of Christianity.

The whole enterprise was over in eight weeks, but not too prosperously. The armies were united at the appointed place. They marched down both banks of the Danube, while the immense commissariat for so large a host was floated along in boats. They drove Avars and Huns from the forts about the river; they met with no reverse. The three days of prayer for victory with which they began their advance seemed crowned with an abundant blessing. And yet it is clear now that the adventure was largely futile and they were like a man striking at nothing or seeking an invisible foe. The Avars abandoned to the invader all their country outside of the rings that they might concentrate the greater part of their forces within those mystical fortifications.[2]

Meanwhile Pepin with his division reached the first or outer ring, and broke through it against what seems a feeble resistance. For one night the soldiers pillaged the villages within that circle. This only achievement of the campaign quickly proved fruitless. The next day they were unable to

[1] Einhard, *Annals*, p. 88.   [2] Vétault, pp. 323–24.

172

penetrate the second ring and the rapid approach of Avar reënforcements drove them away.[1]

Thereupon what was then deemed a mysterious malady,[2] and probably produced by the incantations of the heathen, broke out among the horses of Charles's command. It had then no name; to-day we should know it to be epizoötic. It proved strangely fatal; the entire cavalry was speedily and of necessity transformed into foot soldiery pitted against the expert horsemen of the Avars.[3] The summer was over. The royal army without material signs of triumph returned to Bavaria. There was no annexation of enemy territory, no submission of armed hosts, no baptism at the point of the sword. For once the hosannahs of the annalists go lamely. The regions the Avars had abandoned and the Franks had overrun would be difficult to hold and not worth the holding. For the present the effort to remove the Avar menace came to an end. The next year, according to the King's plans, it was to be renewed.

Four years passed before another Frankish army saw Avar territory, and as for Charles, he was destined never to return to it. Before the spring for which he had planned so much came again there befell a strange combination of events that drove from his mind then and for a long time afterward the Avars and all their affairs.

Within the compass of a few weeks the structure of government and system of civilization that with such toil and pains he had been rearing was struck on all sides. Every enemy he had in the world and had left outside of a monastery seemed to spring at once into activity against him. New complications multiplied, some of them most perplexing and painful; conspiracies against his life no less than against his government; plots at home and stalemates abroad.

Saxony centered one of these upheavals. The faithless and indomitable people there suddenly arose, abandoned their

[1] Vétault, p. 324.   [2] Einhard, *Annals*, p. 89.
[3] Einhard, *Annals*, p. 89.

173

new religion, returned to Odin, and struck two heavy blows against their conquerors. In July, 792, they fell upon a detachment of Franks stationed at the mouth of the Elbe and cut it to pieces.[1] The next year came the disaster in which Count Theodoric lost his life and his army was scattered at the river Weser.

In the Church of which Charles was in a theological as well as a material way the protector, a new schism broke forth and for a time threatened a ruinous division. In the fever of unrest and disruption that had come upon mankind, scarcely anything gained for order in so many years of effort seemed to be secure.

This was the severest test to which he was put and ought to show whether he was really of the band of the great. One fact stands out. In the midst of so many, so diverse, and so crucial besettings he seems not to have lost his head nor known the sinking of the heart that assails the contemplative. It is enough of a standard of character that a man shall keep steadfastly his faith in the work he has undertaken and not withhold his hand from the best of his effort. He had begun to restore civilization in Europe. A smaller man would have been crushed now with the reflection that evidently Europe did not wish to be civilized. It does not appear that this suggestion ever occurred to Charles of the Franks. In the midst of a gloomy circuit of reverses he was able to fix his eyes and his faith on the Europe that was to be and not the Europe that immediately faced him.

The story of these troubles we shall have to deal with at length hereafter. For the present we should go on with the Avars.

In 795, Charles found himself again in a position to take up the Holy War.

As so often happened in his career, opportunity seemed to ripen to his wish. The people of the rings fell into fresh disputings among themselves.[2] In an uprising of their poorer

[1] Einhard, *Annals*, p. 90.   [2] Hodgkin, p. 161.

orders, their two chiefs, the Chagan and the Ouighor, were assassinated. At the same time, certain Slav tribes to the south of the rings, people that had been conquered by the Avars, broke into revolt. A lieutenant of Pepin's, the Duke Herric of Frioul, just beginning his advance upon the Mongols, was able to give the insurrection his helping hand, although he lost his life in the first battle. It was an assault upon a place called Tarsacoz, and we are left to guess at the fate of his army.[1]

But young Pepin, meanwhile, with the bulk of the forces from Italy and Bavaria, entered the Avars' territory from the west and went to a speedy and final success. He overwhelmed the Mongolians in battle, he swept them back into their rings. Then he penetrated one ring after another with unresting perseverance until he stood at last in the ninth and before the Avar citadel that had been to so many generations the center of surmise and romance. It fell, the Chagan surrendered,[2] and the power of the Avars was broken forever. Europe was at last relieved from a singular and degrading terror.

And now a strange thing happened with results more remarkable upon Europe's economics and more enlightening to us than the political consequences of the victory. The whole rich treasure of the Avars, accumulated in two hundred years of banditry and tribute-laying, fell into the hands of the young conqueror. For once popular rumors about such things proved not to have been exaggerated, a fact in itself enough to mark the event for our astonishment. Heaped up in the citadel was a store of merchantable wealth that surpassed anything of the kind the most avaricious had ever dreamed of.[3] Pepin laid hands upon it all. According to the chroniclers, fifteen great wagons each drawn by four oxen carried the spoils away. We might be inclined to scoff but for collateral testimony that leaves no doubt. The Frankish nation,

[1] Vétault, p. 363.
[2] Einhard, *Life*, pp. 20–21; Einhard, *Annals*, p. 93.
[3] 'In no war, so far as human knowledge goes, was the booty so great.'

175

says Vétault,[1] had never been in possession of so many pieces of money of such value. 'Poor men became suddenly rich,' says Einhard.[2] In the autumn the procession of carts made its entry into Aachen, as a replica of an ancient triumph. Charles for the first time was able to make to his soldiers a distribution of substantial rewards. A large part of the treasure he devoted to the Church,[3] making a present of it through Pope Leo III, who used it in the restoring of the Basilica of the Lateran at Rome. Most of the rest was shared by the army and its officers.

The sudden accession of such large amounts of current money brought down an economic revolution. The purchasing power of gold was diminished by a third. Taking the livre as a standard of value, it appears that before the victory over the Avars it was worth in our money something like $42. After the distribution of the Avar treasure had been completed the livre was worth only $28.[4]

It was in recognition of the gifts to the Church that the Pope caused to be made the oldest representation of Charles that is now extant. It is a mosaic picturing the King as receiving from the hand of Saint Peter the sacred banner of Rome.

Pepin made a thorough job of his victory. He leveled all the rings and left the crestfallen Avars without defense. Once the most arrogant of invaders, dictating terms to Roman emperors and having their will upon all, they now became humble suitors for clemency. Michelet [5] says that they seemed to have lost their spirit with their gold. Thudun, the Chagan, and a crowd of his chieftains were brought along in Pepin's triumphal train. They professed a desire to embrace Christianity and were baptized at Aachen, doubtless to the inexpressible joy of the King, ardent propagandist of the Christian faith.

[1] Page 363.   [2] *Life*, p. 21.
[3] Conf. Monk of Saint Gall, p. 44.
[4] Vétault, p. 363.   [5] *Histoire de France*, vol. I, p. 328.

As with the Saxons, the conversion seems to have been no more than an expedient.[1] In 799, Thudun, thinking he saw in the troubled state of the kingdom an opportunity for revenge, recanted from the Christian religion, returned to his idols, and proclaimed the rising of his people to throw off the Frankish yoke. An army of Bavarians was sent against them and made short work of their insurrection. After a few encounters Thudun was crushed.

Then the country that the Avars had occupied was turned into a desert, and nothing ominous was left of a once terrible people. Einhard wrote that even in his time it was a land empty of inhabitants. The spot upon which the citadel had stood was a wilderness where one could discover not a trace of a human dwelling. The surviving Mongolians asked and were allowed to migrate into Bavaria, where they settled and were absorbed into the population.[2] 'To disappear like the Avars' was a common saying in Europe long after the generality of men had forgotten what Avars meant.

But few historical facts are more suggestive than that there should have been poured into the Teuton veins so large a mixture of Mongolian blood of which there is left no trace. Evidently the supposed difference between race and race is no better than a clumsy fiction.

[1] Einhard, *Annals*, p. 94; *Annals* of Metz, p. 103.   [2] Hodgkin, p. 163.

CHAPTER XII

A TIGRESS RIDES IN STATE

How happens it that the woman of the Dark and Middle Ages has not had an analytical study? For any one that cares to consider justly all sides of the human evolution she would seem to abound in a priceless instruction. We commonly think, for instance, of woman as having been mostly suppressed and inarticulate until modern enlightenment came to set her free and give her a place by the side of man. Whatever may have been the state of the mass of women in early Europe,[1] nothing inarticulate or suppressed can be discovered about a long line of eminent or notorious queens and princesses that diversified the career of the Franks. The terrible story of Fredegonde and Brunhilda seems more a type than an exception. There were Fredegondes and Brunhildas in every generation, and one of the worst of them about this time broke into the current drama with a passage amazing for boldness and cruelty.

It was woman, again overshadowing the life of Charles of the Franks. The haughty and savage Fastrada [2] was now supplying his days with a liberal assortment of troubles, but presently arose a greater than Fastrada, and for a time it must have seemed uncertain which of the two forces of evil was to be the more fruitful in mischief.

We go back to the fragment still visible, as the eighth Christian century came to an end, of the old Roman Empire. After the Northern barbarians had seized all of western Europe and trodden out the last embers of the old imperial power at Rome, the Eastern division of the realm as Theo-

[1] Conf. Theodore Krabbes, *Die Frau im altfranz. Karls Epos.*
[2] Einhard, *Life*, p. 31.

178

dosius had separated it continued to exist, by name at least, at Constantinople. There the emperors that ruled, sometimes in rapid succession (when the assassin was unusually busy) called themselves the legitimate successors of the Cæsars and kept up the fiction of the old Roman system. Besides the territories in Asia and eastern Europe that these monarchs dominated, they laid claim to Sicily and to certain lands in Italy, by which they were frequently involved in disputes with the Papal States.

In a long line of worthless creatures, elevated by murder or intrigue to the throne at Constantinople, came, about this time, one Constantine V, known familiarly as Copronymus, who amid many defects of character seems still to have been a man and not a manikin.[1] The world will never be able to determine definitely about him, because he was involved in a furious religious controversy in which one side showed him to be a hideous devil, and the other a wise, pure, and unselfish servant of good, both lying magnificently. About all that is clear now is that he tried to set straight the intorted affairs of the Empire, and had some purpose to improve the eastern branch of the Church, which had fallen under Asiatic influences not good for it. Men have even supposed, though upon slight and improbable grounds, that he had at times some thought upon the millions that sweated and toiled and bled and bore a boundless misery for the sake of his ease and the ease of his kind. However this may be, he must have had some independence of will, for he astonished and appalled the conventional by going out into the wilderness and choosing a bride from a tribe of wild Tartars dwelling near the Caucasus. She bore him a son and successor named Leo IV, and it was Irene, the wife of Leo IV, that now strode upon the stage of Frankish affairs.

Few careers have been more romantic. For a time it looked like a realization of King Cophetua and the Beggar Maid. She was born in Athens, and flattering souls have

[1] Gibbon, chap. XLVIII, vol. v, pp. 301–03.

tried hard to glorify the conditions of her life there by asserting a noble birth. It appears, nevertheless, that when Leo met her she was penniless,[1] an orphan, and friendless. He was then Crown Prince. At one glimpse of her face he fell desperately in love with her, and rested not until he had made her his bride, she being then seventeen years old.

They went to Constantinople to live, where Constantine Copronymus still reigned in portly state. Of a sudden he sickened and died. What he died of the physicians did not know; it was a disease wholly new to them.[2]

Leo now ascended the throne with Irene as the real directing power. He reigned long enough to show that he was weak, vain, and foolish. At nightfall he also was smitten with the same mysterious disease that had ended his father's days, a disease that baffled the physicians even to give it a name.[3] To a throne already stained black with murder, and now of aspect more than ever sinister, came his son and Irene's, known as Constantine VI.[4] He was a mere boy; his mother had purposely kept him in ignorance and encouraged his vices, and she now seized the reins of absolute power.

In history she has borne an almost equal reputation for beauty and savagery, and deserved still another for an unresting addiction to intrigue. To her it was the breath of life, and, unless the records do her wrong, her fancy was for the boldest varieties. It was devotion to this pleasure that brought her into the life of Charles of the Franks.

He had a daughter named Hrotrud. Irene knew well enough that her empire sailed amid a thousand shoals, the local rebellions against her rule and incessant attacks from the wild tribes on the frontiers being not the least of her troubles. She conceived the idea of securing the powerful

[1] Gibbon, chap. XLVIII, vol. v, p. 304.

[2] Gaillard, *Histoire de Charlemagne*, p. 294.

[3] Gibbon, chap. XLVIII, p. 304. It was given out that he died from wearing a certain crown of jewels, which alone would justify suspicion.

[4] Gibbon, chap. XLVIII, p. 305.

180

support of the military genius and disciplined forces of the King of the Franks by marrying Hrotrud to Constantine.[1] In 781, while Charles was in Rome, she sent to him an embassy with a formal proposal of this marriage. The prospect of a united empire of such great dimensions must have dazzled the mind of Charles. He gave his approval to the match, the boy Emperor and the girl Princess were betrothed, and a learned man came from the Constantinople court to Aachen to teach Greek to the bartered bride to be.[2]

But there was one factor in the arrangement that Irene, Charles, and Constantine seem to have overlooked, although it was most important of all. Hrotrud's mother, the wise and gentle Hildegarde, was dead, and Fastrada ruled the household hearth. This matchmaking was not to her purposes. She probably hated Irene as she hated most other persons, and she had another reason to interfere. Among the unattractive traits for which she shone conspicuous, jealousy had its due place. If Hrotrud were to marry Constantine, Hrotrud would be an empress, Fastrada would be but a queen. Her stepdaughter, for whom it is to be surmised she entertained no liking, would outrank her.

With this knowledge of Fastrada's endowment and of her fondness for interfering, which amounted to a passion, we have a credible clue to a mystery that is otherwise without explanation. The engagement lasted six years. Then it was abruptly broken off from the Frankish end. The chroniclers give us the fact and are reticent about the reasons. Discerning commentators have concluded that Fastrada rested not until she had outwitted and defeated Irene and prevented a marriage utterly hateful to her and humiliating to her prestige.[3]

But it happened that the heart of the boy Emperor was

[1] Einhard, *Life*, p. 29; Einhard, *Annals*, p. 96.

[2] The project of uniting these dominions by a marriage was not new. Before Leo had seen Irene, his father, Copronymus, had designed to marry him to the Princess Gisela, sister of Charles. Gaillard, p. 293.

[3] Hodgkin, p. 173; Vétault, p. 309.

set upon it. We have no record that he had ever seen Hrotrud, though she may have been sent to Constantinople on a visit to the court. Whether it was mere wounded vanity or frustrated desire or imagined slight, we shall not know. But by a phenomenon sometimes observable in persons of his nature, there awoke in him a will nobody had suspected him to possess. The pliable suddenly became rigid, the soft and yielding became headstrong. Hrotrud he would have, no matter who should gainsay him, and when he found he had been thwarted he resorted to a revenge that made history.

Irene had mind upon a revenge of a different kind. She had been deeply affronted by the abrupt breaking of the engagement, for which she blamed Charles. She was then maintaining at her court as a refugee the almost forgotten Adelghis, son of Desiderius, King of the Lombards, whom Charles had defeated and deposed. No doubt he was only too ready to strike a blow at his ancient enemy; possibly he suggested it in the ready ear of the Dowager Empress. At least she entered into a conspiracy with him and with Arichis, the beaten Duke of Benevento, for the final undoing of Charles.[1] They were first to invade Italy, expel the Frankish forces, seize the Papal cities, restore the Lombard Kingdom, and then enter Frankland from the south and conquer it.

Irene for this purpose organized a mighty expedition. As it was about to set forth, Arichis, the ablest and most dangerous member of the alliance, suddenly sickened and died. The others landed a great army in Calabria and started forward to effect first the conquest of Rome.

Charles must have been well informed of these events. He did not himself move to meet the invaders, but sent an army commanded by Winighis, one of his wisest generals, who had with him the Lombard Duke of Spoleto and the new Lombard Duke of Benevento. The inclusion of Benevento seems surprising in view of the fact that the old Duke had been Arichis, one of the conspirators. But Charles had now in

[1] Hodgkin, p. 174.

the young Duke a seemingly loyal subject, and had won this unexpected support by an act of generosity of which he could hardly have foreseen the results. All this time he had been holding as a hostage Grimoald, Arichis's son. As soon as he had word of the father's treachery he would have been justified by the savage code of the times in putting the son to death. Arichis died; Grimoald became the normal successor to the dukedom. Charles was seriously advised not to allow him to mount the throne. Instead, he sent him home with honors and acknowledged his succession, with the result that Grimoald became his vassal and his troops fought against the conspirators.[1]

The war in Italy was quickly over. All the fortune of Irene's enterprise was set upon one battle. The trained Frankish warriors, graduates of a school of instruction that had made them the best soldiers in the world, outfought and crushed the Greeks, and the whole project of conspiracy fell to pieces. By some slip of fate Adelghis escaped and made his way back to Constantinople. It was his last appearance on the stage of action and the last visible reminiscence of the Kingdom of the Lombards.

As a penalty for this assault upon him, Charles seized the province of Istria, which had belonged to Irene, and added it bodily and unceremoniously to his dominions.[2]

But it was in Constantinople that the sequel was to be tragic and terrible. In the boy Emperor that had been so docile under his mother's iron rule awoke, at the touch of his passion for Hrotrud, a will untamed as that of his Tartar ancestors. His mother provided for him in the place of the Frankish Princess he had lost a beautiful maiden of Armenia. He turned in wrath from a loveless union. All his deference for his mother was gone. To revenge himself for his lost love he formed with some of his nobles a plot to seize Irene and banish her to Sicily.

Constantinople was probably the worst place in the world

[1] Hodgkin, p. 174; Vétault, p. 315.   [2] Hodgkin, p. 175; Vétault, p. 316.

for the ingenuous and the inexperienced to venture upon plot-making. The imperial palace was a nest of spies and a citadel of treachery. The throne was surrounded with eunuchs, crooked counselors, eavesdroppers, and hired thugs. Just as Constantine's plans were about to take shape in action, they were told by spies to Irene.

The vengeance that fell upon the conspirators was characteristic of the place. The leaders were tortured to death; the rest banished. As for Constantine VI, Emperor of the East, Most Noble Augustus, successor to the Cæsars, and the rest, his mother attended in person to his punishment. With her own hand and, we may believe, a thorough enjoyment, she whipped him like a slave or hound.[1] Then she had him shut up in a dungeon.

It was Constantinople, eighth century, and accustomed to deeds of violence and disorder. But Irene this time went too far. Her own overweening and haughty temperament had made her many enemies. The army rose in revolt against the imprisonment of its sovereign. His troops broke into his prison, set him free, and proclaimed him sole Emperor. Irene's creatures were scourged from the palace. Irene herself was thrust into the same dungeon cell where lately she had imprisoned her son.

The spirit he had shown must have been but a passing fire; all his experience in Constantinople must have taught him nothing. After a time he released his fond parent and attempted to live with her upon terms of amity. She pretended to reciprocate his affection while she contrived new plots against him.[2]

It may be well to show what life really was then in the Eastern Empire. Constantine had five uncles, half brothers of his father. With all the most sacred and solemn engagements and oaths that a Christian can take, they had sworn to uphold and support him, to defend him against all enemies, to

[1] Gibbon, chap. XLVIII, p. 305; Hodgkin, p. 176.
[2] Hodgkin, p. 175; Vétault, p. 316.

184

befriend him in every necessity. They violated these promises by engaging in plot after plot against him. He was at
the time but the shadow of a ruler; Irene was the real power;
and it is possible, of course, that the efforts of the uncles were
directed against her. If so, she responded in the true spirit of
her times and training. One of her conspiring brothers-in-law
she blinded; from the mouths of the other four she had the
tongues torn.[1] For years they lay in a dungeon. One day
they managed to escape and showed themselves at the
Church of Saint Sophia, now a Mohammedan mosque. The
blind man, who alone could speak, told the passers-by their
terrible story. A tumult arose; the populace, inured to horrors, could not endure the dreadful spectacle. Then Irene
laid all the blame for the mutilation upon her son,[2] while a
wily agent of hers led with soothing words and many promises
the wretched men from the public's sight. They were carried
away to Greece, where eventually they were put to death.[3]

But the plotting against Constantine went on and in the
next recurrent wave of it he was seized and hurried away to
prison. His captors hesitated to use violence upon him,
anointed sovereign of the Eastern World. The furious Irene
told them that unless they fulfilled her commands she would
lay bare all the conspiracies in which they had been engaged.

Thereupon, with savage thrusts of a dagger, they put out
Constantine's eyes, and Irene reigned alone.[4]

Her luxury, her lavish display, and her passions made her
conspicuous even before a world not nice about depravity.
Through the streets of Constantinople she rode in a chariot
of pure gold, drawn by milk-white horses, the reins of each
being held by a noble going afoot. She oppressed the people
and burdened them with taxes. She met plot with counter-
plot, crime with crime, lie with lie. The Eastern Church was
riven at the time by the controversy about the worship of
images. Constantine V had been opposed to this worship;

[1] Gaillard, p. 296. [2] *Ibid.*
[3] Gibbon, chap. XLVIII, p. 306. [4] Gibbon, v, p. 306.

Irene was in favor of it; and in the eyes of the image-worshipers, this fact atoned for her deeds. But forever and ever when religious controversy comes in at the door, common sense flies out at the window.

The chief minister of her violences, perfidies, and vices was one Storacius. Although he had received great favors from her hands, he now headed a conspiracy against her. She discovered it in time and rushed to the Senate, for Constantinople still had a Senate, to denounce him. That night Storacius was seized with the same mysterious disease that had carried off Constantine V and Leo IV and perished almost as suddenly.[1]

For five years Irene maintained herself at the head of the Eastern Empire, sole ruler and authority. While thus she stood red with crimes and a sign of enduring horror to all mankind,[2] Charles of the Franks, according to one eminent authority,[3] thought seriously of marrying her. Fastrada was dead; for the moment there was in sight no other candidate for the royal consortship so many had occupied, and the allure of the reuniting of the Roman Empire must have been tremendous. The political consequences are beyond surmise; the personal consequences were fraught with chances fitted to appall the stoutest heart, including poison, blindness, and dungeons. In any event, Charles with his downright ways thrust into the atmosphere of cogging and fraud inseparable from the Eastern establishment would have been as good as wrecked from the beginning.

From such a fate he was providentially saved. Yet Irene and her cruelty and crimes exercised upon him and his affairs a profound influence and became in the end the most powerful cause of a great historic scene in which he was chief actor, and whereof the results before the world lasted for a thousand years; lasted, indeed, until they were obliterated by the im-

[1] Gibbon, v, p. 396; Hodgkin, pp. 178–79.
[2] Gaillard, p. 297.
[3] Theophanes, *Chronographia*, cited by Vétault at page 449.

186

patient foot of Napoleon.[1] For Irene, the cruel and rapacious, became indirectly and involuntarily the founder of the Holy Roman Empire, and made of the grandson of Charles Martel the successor of the Cæsars.

When the rule of Irene in Constantinople came to an end, it was Charles himself, if we may believe the Eastern chroniclers, that precipitated her ruin with his ill-considered notion of marrying her. If it seems strange that he should have been willing to wed with one that had but a few years before led a coalition against him, we are to remember that this consideration weighed little with him against the prospect of a colossal and universal empire. One might think that, on the other hand, Irene would be no particularly loving wife in view of the disaster Charles had brought upon her army, and his seizure of Istria. But the wound of this defeat must have been a long time healed, and she was one without sentiment except about her own selfish pleasures.

Charles is said to have sent his ambassadors to Constantinople to negotiate for her hand, and Irene to have received the proposal with favor. The news enraged the parasites and courtiers, for they saw in the proposed union the certain end to their own power and profits. One of the parasites, the patrician Aëtius, had long meditated a conspiracy. He now used the unpopularity of Charles as a useful weapon and loosed his plot. It succeeded. Irene was dethroned and exiled and Nicephorus, the brother of Aëtius, was crowned as Emperor.[2]

The end of her story was a singular tragedy, almost Æscylean in its proportions of retribution. When the successful revolt burst upon her, and she saw her house of life falling, she sought the infamous Nicephorus, and exercised her wiles upon him to secure her own safety. He had been her co-conspirator, she had protected and rescued him, but he

[1] Bryce, *The Holy Roman Empire*, pp. 356–59.

[2] Gibbon, vol. v, pp. 306–07; Vétault, p. 449. Vétault rejects the story of the proposed marriage, holding that it was concocted and circulated at Constantinople for the purpose of undermining and ruining Irene.

187

would do nothing for her except to banish her. She was borne first to an island in the Sea of Marmora, and then to the Island of Lesbos, where she was left to shift for herself. The beggar maid was again a beggar; King Cophetua had gone with King Pandion, and the Athenian maiden that with her bright eyes and classic features had bewitched Leo IV, Emperor of the East, must earn her daily bread with her distaff.[1]

[1] Gibbon, chap. XLVIII, p. 307.

CHAPTER XIII

THE FAMOUS ACADEMY OF AACHEN

MODERN interests as far apart as certain operas of Richard Wagner and the making of Rhine wine are among the connections that bind us to Charles of the Franks, this unusual person, for both we owe to his restless activities.

As to the operas, that happy bond came about through those employments of his as diligent collector [1] and preserver of classical texts and the old heldenlieder and legends of his country and countrymen. By reason of this service we are blessed with ancient native works as well as older classics that otherwise would have slipped away, even from the vague grasp of tradition.

Among these hero tales of his rescuing were the great Dietrich and Siegfried sagas.

The first celebrates the deeds of Theodoric, King of the Ostrogoths, and was written by Dietrich von Bern. The second tells the struggle between Fredegonde and Brunhilda, of which we should have known from other sources, but it also contains a large part of the Nibelungenlied [2] as Wagner used it and the beautiful Hildebrand saga.

The Rhine wine laurel wreath he added by virtue of two sharp eyes, a habit of observation, and an inquiring mind. One of his palaces stood at Ingelheim, about eleven miles below Mainz. From his windows there he noticed that in the spring the snow melted first on the tops of the hills along the river. This led him to believe that as the climate was plainly milder on the hillsides than elsewhere, grapes might be grown upon them. He sent to Tirol for the vines, had them planted,

[1] Mombert, p. 267.

[2] Dieffenbach and Vogt, p. 351. 'Our lordly Nibelungen lieder,' these authors call the legends.

and launched an industry that for all these centuries has clothed with vineyards that long succession of sunny slopes whereon the traveler looks with wonder and pleasure.

Far greater is the world's obligation in respect to its articulations of learning. Of that vast and complicated machinery for public education that now moves forward in every country he made the first working model, he designed it, put it together, and gave to it the impetus of motion.

This is a subject that, important in itself, bears with it so close and intimate a view of the man's daily life, we ought to look at it again and more heedfully.

When we have made all possible allowance for friendly exaggeration, emotional zeal, and the magnifying influences of time, there is left about the court at Aachen in this reign a residuum of fact likely to cause wholesome astonishment. By the side of empire as it was administered in any former span of European history after the Northern invasions, it is a startling innovation. Compared with the dens of wild beasts offered to our gaze in the time of Chlothar II, for instance, it is an inspiration. The days of government by the dagger and the poison cup are gone, and with them a host of other conditions that made nothing for our joy in the human race, but much for the red pages of chroniclers.

Of the intellectual state of any period, popular amusements may be taken as a fair test — amusements, and the trend of social manners. The recorded diversions of the fortunate before and long after Charlemagne's day cause us to gasp when we turn to what went on at the oasis he maintained in this desert. We have seen his school at work for youth of all classes. To further its benign influence he drew together such a body of learned men as was not to be found in one place elsewhere in all Europe, then or for centuries afterward. They lived at his palace and his expense, pursued their studies under his protection, taught in his school, provided him with retreat and relief from the troubled affairs of his state, and managed so to entrench learning that it with-

OCTAGON OF THE CATHEDRAL AT AACHEN WITH THE BRONZE
CHANDELIER PRESENTED BY FREDERICK BARBAROSSA
The Octagon is virtually as Charlemagne built it

stood new assaults from the barbarians after he had passed.

The first of these teachers and scholars was of course the celebrated Alcuin, a native of Northumberland in England, and one of the leaders of the group of good men and good minds that made the monastery at York a repository of learning and a kind of dynamic center whence learning radiated into a pitch-dark world. He was born about 735, and came of a family that had already furnished to the calendar Saint Willibrod, missionary to the Frisians.[1] His education began at a school maintained at the cathedral of York. There he distinguished himself as an apt pupil, eventually becoming the institution's head. His first meeting with Charles was probably as far back as 768, while Carloman still lived and the Frankish realm was still divided.[2] Alcuin had been to Rome on a mission. In returning he passed through Frankland and visited its court. Charles kept him well in mind. When next they met, at Parma in 781, the King drew from the scholar a promise to come to Aachen and make his home there. He came in 782, and thereafter for fourteen years was foremost teacher, counselor, sworn brother of Charlemagne, and first national educator.[3] The world owes to him an immeasurable debt. To perfect that court school of which we have spoken, to use it as a model upon which the other schools throughout the kingdom were to be established and fostered, was his first employment. In all those institutions, the enduring homes and nurseries of a diligent tuition, that came to be founded in so many cities in the reign of Charles of the Franks, virtually all of the teaching talent came from Aachen and all had been trained by Alcuin. It seems much to say of any man, but is here the attested fact.

Although the brightest of the company that gathered at the new capital, Alcuin was not the first to walk in that

[1] Davis, p. 166.   [2] Davis, p. 166.

[3] In 786 he returned to York for a brief visit and repeated it in 793. Three years later he insisted upon retiring to the monastery of Saint Martin at Tours, where he spent the rest of his life in seclusion and meditation, but maintaining a correspondence with his 'dearest David.' He died in 804. Conf. Davis, p. 167.

academic grove. Peter of Pisa, the grammarian, had been
there for years, since in fact the days of Pepin, who had
brought him from Italy to teach the royal children. Paulus
Diaconus, historian and poet, Charles had brought from
Lombardy. Paulus of Aquileia, Arno of Salzburg, and
Amalar of Trèves were others distinguished in that group.

With the coming of Alcuin the Aachen school reached its
best development. It was no longer a filling station for the
youths in and around the court, but expanded into a national establishment of scope and efficiency. King and monk,
working together, made it model [1] and example. From this
partnership and these discreet labors are to be dated some
of the most famous seats of learning in Europe. The University of Liège, which a few years ago all the world thought
of with a tender solicitude, is one of them. Charles established there a school; the zeal for learning thus implanted
grew first into a Jesuit college, and then, long afterward, expanded into the university. Utrecht's university, founded in
1636, is another. In France, if it is not true, as once asserted,
that he directly originated the Sorbonne, that great institution was a fruit of his innovations. Such celebrated schools as
those of Fontanelle, Saint Denis, Saint Germain, Aniane, Cor-
bie, Saint Bénoit,[2] are indubitable monuments to his efforts
and Alcuin's under him. In Belgium, in Germany, in Switzerland, are schools developed from his foundations, and it was
in these that through the dusk centuries following his death
the light of learning survived and was not again extinguished.[3]

So great and genuine a service would outweigh a multitude
of errors. Upon civilization the effect went beyond esti-
mate. The immaterial spirit of man had been carried away
in a black flood, and these two, a peasant king and a cowled
monk, grasped it drowning by the hair and drew it back to
life.

The democracy of the thing must have been an immeasurable forcing-house of good. As we have noted before, no dis-

[1] Hallam, chap. ix, p. 602.   [2] Vétault, p. 426.   [3] *Ibid.*

tinction of rank or caste bothered that place. According to tradition the King himself, a pupil in his own school, sat by the side of the son of his cellarer. Even if that delightful incident should some day prove to be but the embroidery of mediæval and febrile imagination, the record is fairly sure that among the pupils were two sons of the town miller and that two of the King's sons were fellows with them.[1] Homespun and velvet went together in this curious little temple of applied democracy — went together to attack the problems set by the fathers of the Church and pick up what little was known of the world in which they must live. It is an odd glimpse of knowledge the leveler, at its inevitable work so early to knock down the barriers of caste and rank, bringing men together and shrinking the dimensions of the world.[2] So eleven hundred years later it was clearly thus busied in India, almost the last citadel of caste, but not even in India was its vivifying influence more needed than in the intellectual doldrums into which Charles and his monk friend had precipitated themselves.[3]

His colleagues in the business of ruling were not of his mind about such things. No other kings then had much higher intellectual tastes than were manifested in a fondness for roast hare and the exploits of a juggler that could balance three swords on end. Fat feasts, fat women, and much drink were the fashionable refinements of court life — great courts and small. The merest baron that kept his robbers' roost by the Rhine or the Adige must lord it in what state he could, having his little imitation court and his little imitation joys in fat things. The best of them, small or great, lived in a way cruder, fouler, and more bestial than now the poorest peasant

---

[1] Vétault, p. 428; Monk of Saint Gall, p. 12.

[2] 'The World was made small so that all men might be friends,' says Henry Mouquin, a nineteenth-century philosopher.

[3] Dieffenbach and Vogt, p. 348; J. Bass Mullinger, *The Schools of Charlemagne*, p. 65. 'He himself was wont, along with the more intelligent of his courtiers, to take his seat in the midst of the learners, stimulating their ardor by his example and gratifying his own thirst for knowledge by discussion and inquiry.'

knows — in most countries. And now even the Indian ryot in his mud hut may begin to glimpse hope, while to the peasant of the Dark Ages hope must have been as much of a stranger as books. Dirt was everywhere. Even in the palaces, the conveniences of life were still those of the jungle. With their fingers or their daggers, diners fished their food from a common dish, ate it from their unwashed hands, threw the bones or other remnants upon the floor. Smoke from the kitchen fire half choked the dining-room. Soap, cleanliness, gentle ways, the courtesy that is respect for the feeling of others, were as unknown as the electric telegraph. While the great man of the manor sat and gorged and gnawed bones and grunted and filled himself from huge tankards of ale or wine, the acrobats stood upon their heads or the poor paid jesters made coarse jokes until my lord slept from weariness or the labors of the trencher or became so drunk he saw double.

Children they were, the adults of that day, primitive, unreasoning, impulsive, sensual, stuffing themselves on a narrow choice of coarse dietary, satisfying appetite at whatsoever cost, dying young, usually incapable of moral reflection or of introspection, playing like uninformed children at such costly games as war and banditry, living for the hour, careless about to-morrow in this world, occasionally trying to propitiate it in another, uninformed, superstitious, fond of unprofitable amusements, coming back from them to run amok, sometimes as half-mad berserkers, sometimes revenging with senseless cruelties the emptiness of life.[1] The best of them were more or less like this. Even the shrewdest leaders were ignorant enough to act on childish resentments or to rush headlong upon the spears of foolish acts.

We do not have to credit all or any large part of the offerings of the panegyrists to see that Aachen must have presented a startling contrast to all this. The King of the Franks comes to his dinner simply clad and surrounded, not by jug-

[1] Hallam, chap. IX, pp. 487–92; especially his account of the strange superstitions that even the most enlightened persons cherished.

glers and jesters, but by his Academy, by the men of learning he has drawn to him from every corner of Europe; Alcuin
from England, Paulus Diaconus, Theodulf, learned monks
from Ireland. The amusement of that company is to have
one read from a classic, Plutarch or Livy[1] preferred, or Saint
Augustine, who is the King's favorite author. Then they discuss the thing that has been read. What Einhard tells us
about the abstemiousness of the King may be mere fiction. It
may not be true that he restricts himself at table to two or
three simple dishes, never drinks more than three glasses of
wine, and sternly denounces indulgences and drunkenness in
others. But we can be fairly sure that the account of the
favorite pursuits of the company at his board is substantially
correct because Alcuin and other witnesses better than Einhard have testified to it.

That company constituted the Academy of Aachen, distinct from the school, and the first thing of the kind recorded
since the deluge from the woods. It must have been a gathering of easy and informal manners. They lay aside their titles
and call one another by familiar names. Charles is David,
Alcuin is Albinus, Angilbert, a young man said to have been
an able poet, is Homer, Pepin, the King's son, is Julius,
the Princess Gisela is Delia, Fredegis is Nathaniel, Queen
Liutgarde is Ava.[2]

Angilbert is said to have been greatly admired, a brilliant
scholar, handsome and daring, with as much reputation for
courage in the field as for learning at home. For years, according to report, he was at work on a Latin epic from which
he was accustomed to read extracts at the dinner table. To
our loss, may be, no other trace of it has come down to us.
Tradition has made him the hero of a love story with the
Princess Bertha. Some aver he married her. In the early
books of romance such stories are as plentiful as blackberries.
There is no better basis for this than for the others. It was
the open season for that kind of hawk-flying.

[1] Einhard, *Life*, p. 33.   [2] Mullinger, p. 74.

Another poet in the group was this Theodulf, the gray-haired Abbot of Fleury, afterward Bishop of Orleans.[1] He, we are told, had a ready wit and a bitter tongue that made him feared in court circles. At the table sometimes he used to read satirical poems of his making and be criticized by the Irish monks and defended by others. It is related that on one such occasion he turned his caustic muse upon the soldiers of his time, whom he ridiculed as fat of paunch and slender of wit. A warrior that was present began slowly to perceive that his order was under fire. He sprang to his feet in a rage to meet the power of satire with the power of blows. Then, according to the story, which is not too authentic, the King looked at him and he slunk out of the chamber.

Sometimes, we are told, Alcuin reads at the table a passage from Vergil, expounds it, considers it from different points of view as a poet, as a rhetorician, and as a grammarian. Grammar is the part of it that more interests the King. He is himself a grammarian and has composed a grammar of German. The monks compare Vergil with Horace and Ovid.

This is the delectable picture as sketched by Einhard, by the Monk of Saint Gall, and by Alcuin, and then embellished by other and abler hands. We can believe what we please of it. Probably it is much overwrought. Yet for evidence of this King's novel interest in learning and books we have no need to depend upon the fancies of the laudators. His letters and the record of his reign offer so many and such genuine proofs that the natural sarcasm of the incredulous is stilled in its own despite.

The school is different. There the pupils recite to Master Alcuin and others. They produce at each session the compositions on which they have been busy since the last assembly. We are told that their employments include much verse-making. Unluckily, those other barbarian ancestors of ours, the Norsemen, rubbed out these achievements, too, with others. Many of the pupils write prose instead of verse.

[1] Mullinger, p. 97.

Among them is this Einhard, a youth destined to be one of the most famous and most discussed writers of antiquity. He came from the valley of the Main, where he was born about 775. The beginning of his education he gathered at the monastery of Fulda, to which he had been admitted through the efforts of the good Abbot Baugulf. He was about sixteen when he came to the court at Aachen as one of the youths that because of superior industry at their studies were invited from all parts of the kingdom to be inmates of the royal palace and live as the King's guests while they pursued their studies.

He was small of stature and therefore nicknamed Nardulus, but he soon became distinguished as a scholar. In the Academy they called him Bélzeléel. He is supposed to have been, in the latter years of the reign, secretary to the King. The *Vita Caroli Magni* that for eleven hundred years has been a chief source of supposed information about Charlemagne came from his pen.[1]

Young Einhard's specialty at the school was the production of prose essays on specific subjects. One of his fellow pupils was the King's steward, Lentulus. Because of his slow speech and deliberate motions he was at first a butt of ridicule to the younger students. He turned this upside down by proving to be one of the smartest pupils in the school. It was he, we are told, that produced the best and ablest criticisms on Einhard's essays.

Poetry must have been a great thing at this hall of learning. The King himself wrote it. The well-known classical hymn that to this day the priests sing on occasions of special solemnity, the 'Veni, Creator Spiritus,' is ascribed to him.

> Veni, Creator Spiritus
> Mentes, tuorum visita;
> Imple superna gratia
> Quae tu creasti pectora.

---

[1] It is supposed to have been written between 830 and 836. In 828 he retired to the monastery of Seligenstadt, where he lived until his death March 14, 840.

CHARLEMAGNE, FIRST OF THE MODERNS

The origin of the air to which it is sung is uncertain, but without question it is of great antiquity and may have been composed in Charlemagne's own time. As we shall see, he was as meddlesome about music as about learning.

Music and poetry. Under Clovis it was lying and the battle-axe; under Theodoric II, murder and mead. In two hundred years we seem to have advanced a thousand. Poor Einhard lost his balance at so great a revolution and that seems nothing wonderful.

The cheerful account of halcyon days at Aachen goes on. Women have a place in the proceedings. The Princess Bertha with whom, according to the romance, Homer Angilbert has the unsuccessful love affair, writes verses, and examines and criticizes the verses of others. She has a specialty; it is antiquities. Among the other ladies of the court is one Gunrada, who is called by the poets the most beautiful woman in Europe, a distinction that the world has always regarded with tolerance if not with conviction; it has been conferred so often. We are told that her educational attainments became as celebrated as her good looks, at which the eyebrow will probably be lifted. Gisela, the King's sister, who so narrowly escaped marriage with the worthless Prince Adelghis, comes from her nunnery to help at the school and put to use the studies she has been making since her retirement.

The curriculum followed a plan devised by Alcuin. Judging from its remains there was nothing dilettante or perfunctory about instruction at the royal court of the Franks. Students must have gone there to work, not to frivol. The range of the subjects pursued was in two main classes, the *trivium* and the *quadrivium*. The first included all that was then known of the sciences, what were then called 'the seven liberal arts,' and what was called 'philosophia.' This brought in what was called grammar, which embraced much more than we now denote by that word, being also rhetoric and dialectics. Under *quadrivium* were included arithmetic, music,

198

THE PONT-TOR, ONE OF THE ANCIENT GATES TO THE CITY OF AACHEN

THE CATHEDRAL OF AACHEN

The central part was built by Charlemagne and consecrated by
Pope Leo III in 805

geometry, and astronomy. Religious instruction dominated all the studies.

As a public school pupil Charlemagne seems to have been much of a success, but allowance must be made for the extravagance of the reporters. He was nearing middle age when he learned at his own institution the elements of arithmetic, a fact that tells us compendiously the state of civilization, since he was accounted a cultured person and had the rare distinction of having been tutored in his youth. With energy he pursued dialectics, astronomy, philosophy, and rhetoric. According to eulogy he was a gifted orator. When he started to speak the words flowed from his mouth without pause or slip, well-chosen words, eloquent words. Thus Einhard, strewing the imperial way. There is nothing to gainsay him. From Charlemagne's letters, the true source of information about him, it appears that he believed all persons should learn to speak well and that no one could, with a decent reverence, read the Scriptures that did not know the full meaning of the words he was reading.

To his other accomplishments he tried to add the skill of the expert penman. His failure to achieve this, as recorded in Einhard, is the sole foundation for the assertion, repeated by hundreds of authors through eleven centuries, that Charles the Great was unable to write. But as Vétault points out,[1] what Einhard meant was that he essayed in his old age to acquire the art of the calligraph which he so diligently fostered at his capital. It was this art that his fingers stiffened in sword play could not compass. Otherwise he could write well enough and often.

But he must have been at times a somewhat troublesome pupil. 'The monarch himself,' says Dr. Mullinger, 'in an ardor of a long unsatisfied curiosity, propounded queries on all imaginable topics — suggesting, distinguishing, disputing, objecting — a colossal figure, gazing fixedly with bright blue eyes upon his admired guest.'[2]

[1] Page 400.   [2] *The Schools of Charlemagne*, p. 71.

The 'admired guest' was Alcuin, whose method of teaching was the catechetical. We have left to us some curious examples of the questions. Alcuin wrote an imaginary conversation between a Saxon boy and a Frankish boy, interspersed with comments of the instructor. It probably gives a fair notion of his idea of effective teaching. It is all swift question and answer. In another similar paper he gives an alleged report of an examination conducted by himself of one of his students, Pepin, the second son of Charles. The amount of scientific knowledge then possessed by even the most learned may be gauged from a few extracts.[1] The pupil propounds the questions, the teacher answers:

Pepin — What is light?
Ans. — The torch of all things.
Pepin — What is day?
Ans. — An incitement to work.
Pepin — What is the sun?
Ans. — The splendor of the universe, the beauty of the sky, the glory of day, the distributor of the hours.
Pepin — What are the stars?
Ans. — The pictures on the roofs of the heavens, the guides of sailors, the ornament of night.

It appears that instruction in arithmetic was somewhat more exact.

When Alcuin retired to the monastery of Tours, he was succeeded at Aachen by his young countryman, Fredegis, who doubtless pursued the Alcuinistic methods.

This was the school which went on at all times no matter where its founder might be. As for the Academy, when he traveled he took with him as much of that as was mobile. From beating Avars by day to studying Augustine at night — one would like to know more about the mind that could compass that leap. When he was not leading troops to battle somewhere, he had mind upon the task of snaring all visitors, travelers, or others that might contribute to school or Academy. Meginfrid, the chamberlain of the palace, had for one

[1] Cited by Wells at much greater length, pp. 328–32.

of his duties the search for such men and their entertainment while guests. The irksome number of them seems to have made at times serious inroads upon Meginfrid's allowance and even affected the royal revenues. Therefore, we may think it the more wonderful that in the face of this condition a statesman so careful as Charlemagne should have continued expenditures that were without precedent in his times, without warrant in any known policy, and no doubt the subject of the worthy chamberlain's protesting groans.

The men he entertained were specialists in some line of learning — grammarians, rhetoricians, prosodists, mathematicians, theologians. It must have been the theologians that most delighted the King's heart. He was himself a theologian and had all the tireless ardors of the guild. It appears that he put away in his memory what the learned visitor had to say and then was accustomed to beat it to pieces when alone with Alcuin.

The practical value of the Academy was that it started or nourished a passion for learning among minds that could carry it elsewhere when there was no printed word and when the means of communication were only the flimsiest. 'With equal truth it may be said,' observes Dr. Mullinger, 'that the history of the schools of Charles the Great has modified the whole subsequent history of European culture.' [1] Compared with that fact whether the material empire he founded endured or crumbled was not of the slightest importance to any human interest.

[1] Mullinger, pp. 50–51.

CHAPTER XIV

GRAFT IN THE DARK AGES

THIS man had inherited from his father the largest realm in Europe. He had now more than doubled his inheritance.[1] One of the greatest empires that ever acknowledged a single ruler was his dominion. From the Adriatic, southern Italy, the Mediterranean, and the river Ebro in Spain, it stretched northward to the North Sea and the edge of the Baltic. East and west, everything from the Bay of Biscay and the English Channel to the city of Vienna was Frankish territory.

To us in this day the most perplexing question that arises as we look upon this huge structure is not so much how one man had compacted it as how he managed to govern it and cause it to hold together overnight. There never was a greater *mélange* of antagonistic races, peoples, languages, and interests, and no empire ever contained more intractable and irreducible elements.[2] According to the views of a later generation, to do no more than to cause the Neustrians and Austrasians, French and Germans, to keep from one another's throats was task enough for any man. Yet here they dwelt not alone in peace, but in amity and seeming forgetfulness of ancient feud. But besides Neustrians and Austrasians were all these other variants from the human garden, ever-plotting Beneventans on the south to wild-eyed Abodrites on the north, so many that enumeration wearies, most of them about two degrees from the jungle, all jealous, irascible, reckless, and all devoted disciples of the gospel of swords and quick blows. Most of them would as lief fight as eat. Yet throughout the greater part of Charles's reign he kept the most of them not only from their chosen trade of throat-cutting, but

---

[1] Einhard, *Life*, p. 22.　　　[2] Vétault, p. 403.

202

THE MOSAIC MADE BY ORDER OF POPE LEO III AND NOW IN THE
CHURCH OF SAINT JOHN LATERAN, ROME

The right-hand figure is of Charlemagne, made in his lifetime. At the left is Pope
Leo. The inscription, in Mediæval Latin, reads, 'Blessed Peter, grant long life to
Pope Leo and victory to King Charles.'

GRAFT IN THE DARK AGES

pulling with him more or less toward his purposes,[1] all of which in their eyes were alien and absurd. There may have been greater administrative achievements, but one might find it hard to recall them offhand.

We are to remember, also, that there was scarcely anything in the way of a workable precedent by which an administrator could be guided. The old tribal system that the barbarians had brought with them from the woods broke down whenever it was applied to more than a handful of men. The system of old imperial Rome, in its main particulars, had long faded from the human memory, and in the existing conditions, probably would not have worked at all.

There was one other notion more or less common that viewed the King or ruler as the sole and absolute dictator about everything and admitted no laws but his wild, untrammeled will. Upon some such basis all the small kingdoms about Europe, the Kingdoms of the Lombards, the Aquitanians, the Duchy of Bavaria, and the rest had risen and fallen. There must have been something in this man that revolted instinctively at such a dispensation. Possibly it was the peasant in him; possibly he was one of those that have an undefined but inevitable sense of the future. Even if he had been enough of a despot or enough of a megalomaniac to try for the old style of autocratic enginery, it probably would not have motioned far or lasted long in a society so large, complex, warlike, and insubmissive. The system that Charles of the Franks used seems to indicate that he was as much of an executive as a military genius.[2] So far as one can see now, it was the only process that could have held together this vast agglomerate, and certainly it is, after the decline of Rome,

---

[1] In a letter written by Nithard (d. 844), son of Poet Angilbert, occurs a remarkable statement of this fact. Von den Steinen, p. 118.

[2] 'To myself, the theory that Charlemagne was a man of the broadest statesmanship seems to explain the facts much more perfectly than any other, though one must certainly hesitate to affirm that he was conscious to the full of all the bearings of his policy that we may seem to detect.' George Burton Adams, *Civilization During the Middle Ages*, p. 155.

the first showing of a governmental machinery that had a competent model.

Not all the credit for it belongs to Charlemagne. His father, the capable Pepin, had instituted a part of it, but with features and ideas exemplified in the fate of Waifar, for instance. Assassination was not included in the system of Pepin's son, and neither, strange to say, was any discernible kind of political weather-gauge work.

First, he gave to each nation comprised in his federation a governor or count whose functions were to supervise the administration of justice, to hear complaints, to weed out abuses, to keep order and security. To him, in the first instance, came the petitioners, who thus had a magistrate of their own race, speaking their own tongue, and were not obliged to travel long distances and make their appeal to an alien. The law department was controlled by a chancellor at the central capital; the affairs of the Church by an arch-chaplain. But above all other authorities in civil, military, and ecclesiastical matters was Charles himself. The operation of his great machine he directed, inspired, and chastened indefatigably and conscientiously. Subordinates might steer the course, but he laid it, and usually brought up with a round turn any one that went astray from it.

The legislative department of his system comprised two annual assemblies of delegates from all parts of the nation,[1] one in the autumn to propose measures of national importance, one in the spring to adopt or discard them. If these bodies had been elected by the people they would have meant an innovation a thousand years in advance of the rest of the social organization, but even the measure of representation that they included signified something. The assemblies in the Kingdom of the Franks were made up of the dignitaries of the Church and State, the dukes, counts, and other nobles, and then of persons appointed by the King. They had no power to adopt any measure over the King's veto, nor to re-

[1] Vétault, p. 404, following Adalhard.

ject a measure that he favored,[1] but equally with him they
had the power of initiative. So far the measure of democracy is small; the wonder is that there is any. The assemblies did not represent the common people; on the contrary,
the noble legislators, after the manner of their kind, hated
the common people with great heartiness, so that often the
democratic King was obliged to interfere to protect the common people against his delegates. It was not a good system;
for later times in the tangled story of mankind, it would have
been an exceedingly bad system. But it was better than any
system that had preceded it since the skin-clad folk had come
out of the woods. The assemblies were not really legislative
nor exactly deliberative. Yet they had in them the germ of
the true legislative assembly, the germ of the thing that was
in the slow course of time to remake life in France as in the
rest of the world.

But the real democracy in the government of Charles of
the Franks was not manifested so much in these assemblies of
nobles and dignitaries, whom he often disregarded and often
must have despised, as in his system of *Missi Regii*, his personal messengers or traveling inspectors. These he kept
moving constantly about the kingdom, observing the work
of the courts, watching the local administrations, listening
to complaints, reporting upon all conditions, even the condition of the pawns or human Things at the bottom. As a
rule, and unavoidably, the dukes and counts and the like,
to whom the local governments were entrusted, were half
savages, of the business brotherhood of fighting and plundering, to whom the pawn order was contemptible. They had
never been taught any other view of life; they had to the full
the prejudices of the aristocracy; they rejoiced in a consciousness of class. The gravest task of the democratic King
was to restrain the cruel impulses of these tyrants and to
compel them to be decent. The dogged resolution that was
one of his conspicuous traits was not put to a harder test.

[1] Hallam, chap. xi, Part. ii, p. 213.

The story of these struggles is to be drawn from the Capitularies, the official letters that, upon the receipt of the reports of his inspectors, he was accustomed to send to his counts and governors. There are some in which he complains bitterly of the oppression of the toiling masses, and commands, reiterates, and insists that there may be an easing of these burdens. He wishes all taxes to be levied justly, all extortion to be abolished. He orders that the vassals of the counts shall cease to rob travelers; that the tillers of the soil shall be left in peace; agriculture and industry shall be safeguarded and encouraged; life and property shall be protected; the Church shall be extended; the clergy shall diligently perform its functions. A great part of the documentation is taken up with these deliverances. Of course, if there had been no Charles of the Franks, no Capitularies, and no coördinating mind in control at this juncture, there would still have come in the course of time deliverance from the anarchies and tyrannies that beset the midnight of Europe. If any credit pertains to the first understanding of the situation, it seems to belong to him. He planted or replanted (as you will) the hope and dream of equality and justice, and after his day no tyrant, although there came many, was ever able to trample that growth to death.

How did the system he inaugurated work in practice? I cite the case of the Istrians as an example.

Istria, a province of Italy, had been conquered and annexed in 789.[1] As usual a duke was sent there to take charge of the government and represent the King.

After a time the *Missus* or inspector that was observing things in Istria made ill reports about the doings of this duke. It appears in fact that the Duke had run a long distance ahead of his times and at the end of the eighth century had instituted some business methods of the twentieth. The modern press would have called him a grafter. Having a chance to fill his pockets at the public expense, he diligently filled them all.

[1] Vétault, pp. 316–17.

206

This was the report. The King sent his inspector back to make a complete investigation. On his findings a court was summoned, a jury impaneled, and the astonished Duke dragged summarily before it.

The event was new in the history of the European nobility, and perhaps for that reason the testimony, or much of it, has been preserved. It showed that the Duke regarded even the free people as his slaves. As slaves he bestowed them in squads upon his sons, his daughters, and his favorites. As slaves, their owners drove them to service.

With such enforced labor the Duke had built palaces and constructed pleasure grounds. From the slave population he was accustomed to annex anything of theirs that pleased his ducal fancy; cattle, horses, tithes, wives, daughters, pots, pans, anything. He was fond of dispossessing small land-owners of any piece of property that seemed good in his eyes; a stretch of fertile meadow, or maybe a good site for a new castle. The meadow land he had rented at good rates to people he had imported from the Slav country, and the castle sites he used handily in his everyday interests, which seem to have combined highway robbery with ardent pursuit of pleasure.

With difficulty these facts were brought out.

'If we say anything,' complained the witnesses, 'he swears he will kill us.' Nevertheless, the story comes forth piecemeal. The Duke had ships, and drove the people aboard them to work as galley slaves. He maintained an army, and on pain of death drove other people into it to fight his battles. His was a thrifty soul; he despised not the day of small things. It appears that when nothing else was toward in his line he stole clothes from the backs of his unfortunate victims, and fish from their nets.

More pertains to this story than is visible on the surface. It is, in fact, a good cross-section of the society of the day. It lights up the difficulties confronting a ruler bent upon introducing the primitives of justice, and, in the end, it compels some tribute to a ruler that in the face of such odds would persist in such intentions. For note well what happened.

The jury found the Duke guilty of the offenses charged against him. Then the King compelled the grafting nobleman to make restitution. He must restore his thievings, compensate every poor man he had wronged, give back lands, cattle, horses, or the value thereof to the last penny. He must release his galley slaves; he must discharge his other slaves in the army. He must acknowledge publicly that he had erred, and give securities that thereafter he and his households and his dependents and retainers and gad-flies and the rest would transgress no more, but deal justly with the people of the country.

That was all. Charles did not hang the Duke, nor displace him. It would be pleasant to think that enlightened in other ways he was on principle opposed to hanging folks; but he had other reasons. The noble orders against which he contended were too powerful and too closely united. He must govern as he could and not as he would. The raising of a hand in punishment of the Duke of Istria might be the signal for civil war. If the predatory nobles were to be restrained, they must be restrained by policy rather than by force. It was better to let one nobleman like the Duke of Istria go unhanged than to put fifty noblemen like the Duke of Istria in a position where they could rob, murder, and oppress at will. Powerful as Charlemagne was, he was not powerful enough to withstand that threat. It seems to have been the course of a practical man bent first on results, and not on a nominal triumph. In all probability he had no thought of being poignarded for the sake of an ideal that his death would in no wise further, and the Duke of Istria was restored to his post. The lesson he had been taught must have been salutary. There is no further record of complaint.

Like Napoleon and like Augustus, Charles visualized great public improvements, but his best designs were spoiled by the incapacity of his engineers and artisans. He planned a great canal to join the river Danube to the Main, and so to the Rhine, a work that would have been of inestimable value to mediæval commerce. When the construction had proceeded some miles, it encountered swampy ground, and the engineers could devise no means by which the banks could be retained.[1] Centuries afterward, that same canal was constructed by King Louis of Bavaria, and in 1929 it became the axis of a gigantic plan made public at the waterways convention to unite the Rhone, the North and Black Seas in one network of streams.

Charlemagne designed and built at Mainz a bridge across the Rhine that was for the time being one of the wonders of the world.[2] 'All mankind,' says one enthusiastic chronicler, 'was engaged in the building of it.' A burning ship drifted against it, set it on fire, and the whole structure was consumed.[3] He did much to improve harbors, notably at Boulogne and elsewhere along the north coast, and he developed his fleets against the Norseman pirates that more and more threatened his seaports. Yet even these matters he was never able to order to his desire, and for a most significant reason. He had no money to pay workmen, and he could not conscript labor. In the case of the Mainz bridge, indeed, the nobles furnished the labor by bringing up vassals of theirs that by an old custom were obligated to work upon bridges and roads, as well as to do military service. But there was no such obligation about dredging harbors, no coin in the treasury to pay for the labor, and most of the improvements must be postponed to a later age.

[1] Mombert, p. 277; Vétault, p. 332.   [2] Einhard, *Annals*, p. 90.
[3] Einhard, *Annals*, p. 124. The fire happened in 813. The bridge was of wood. Charlemagne had planned to replace it with a structure of stone.

CHAPTER XV

THE MIDNIGHT PLOTTERS IN THE CHURCH

IT was in 793 that the Danube-Main Canal project failed, but shortly before there had come about so many other disasters and misadventures the bad work of the canal engineers was in the mass hardly noticeable.

That strange, infectious restlessness we have previously noted as one of the mysteries of the Middle Ages now seemed to seize the spirits of men. Plottings and contrivings appeared in unexpected places.[1] Beyond the eastern frontier trouble with the Avars was growing. In Italy the Duchy of Benevento cast loose its allegiance. To the north what was left of the Saxons staged one of their periodic outbreaks. On the south the Saracens, after so many years of quietude, began a significant movement northward. At home there was trouble in the Church. If we can believe the testimony of Einhard, the cruelty and violence of Queen Fastrada often clouded the household horizon, and in his own palace had swirled around the King a fresh conspiracy against his life.

The other troubles were accidental; the conspiracy was in a way the result of the laxity of his own private morals. A little more and we should have had the materials for a Lear-like tragedy of fate and the retribution that falls upon our pleasant vices. Before his marriage with Desiderata, his mistress Himiltrude had borne him a son named Pepin. It would have been easy in those times to legitimatize this youth, and make him the royal heir; for it is not to be forgotten that Charles Martel was born of a similarly irregular union, and Charles himself, by some reports, came of a nuptial as yet unauthorized. But the King would not legitimatize Pepin and

[1] Vétault, p. 328.

210

for a reason that multiplied the young man's sense of wrong.

The reason was that he was a hunchback. Yet he was a singularly handsome youth,[1] able, and, despite his physical misfortune, of a pleasing address. Otherwise we know little about him, but may surmise from certain events that he would have been a more promising heir to the throne than he into whose possession it finally passed.

But according to the prejudices of the times, the deformity of poor Pepin was an insuperable barrier. He could not whirl a sword, he could not brain a foeman; on horseback he could make no figure to awe the groundlings. Against these defects what availed mind, even the most brilliant?

He dwelt about the court in comfort and honor, recognized as one of the blood royal, not recognized in that sonship he felt rightfully to belong to him. He was not Crown Prince and first heir to his father's throne. As he grew older, the sense of injustice weighed the more heavily upon him as he brooded over one intolerable affront of his youth.[2] In his family the name Pepin was of peculiar luster and esteem. Pepin of Landon, Pepin of Heristal, Pepin the Short, had borne it with honor. He had been proud to have it for his own. But then it had been taken away from him and bestowed upon legitimacy, his half-brother, born Carloman. Evidently, therefore, he had been permanently relegated to strut in silks and chew his finger-ends in a corner. His half-brother Louis had been made King of Italy; his half-brother Carloman, filcher of his own name, was the King of Aquitania. Of their claims he lacked only this word legitimacy and a straight back. Yet he was nothing and it was evident that nothing he would continue to be, an idle and illegitimate hunchback dawdling around an empty court.

The wrath that burned in him might have smouldered indefinitely if the unlucky Fastrada had not interfered to make it flame. The eternal feminine was at work again, Charles's

[1] Einhard, *Life*, p. 30; Einhard, *Annals*, p. 89.
[2] Vétault, p. 326; Hodgkin, p. 130.

feminine, the sinister woman that comes at the instant of fate to do her item of decisive ill. Charles had deliberately chosen this one to be his consort; Charles, who seldom made errors in choosing. The wisest of men have blundered thus about their love affairs. But the wife of Charles of the Franks was much more than the mother of his children. In the scheme of government he had erected she had important parts to play. Whenever the King might be from his capital she was the ruler, clothed with his power.[1] At all times and wherever the King might be, the Queen was in charge of certain departments of the government. The treasurer, the constable, and the marshal received their instructions from her and looked upon her as their executive officer. She had her own palace, a mile from that of the King; you can still see the site at Aachen and some outline of its proportions. At all times, too, it is to be gathered, this King was subject to the influence of his Queen. He was accustomed to consult her about many affairs of state, and, as he had a respect for the intuitive wisdom of women, he seems sometimes to have followed a woman's advice when it conflicted with his own judgment.

He was often absent for months at a time from Aachen; absent about his wars with the Saxons, the Avars, or what not. At such times Fastrada steered the ship alone and according to her natural propensities. The incomplete and maybe misdrawn picture we have of her heightens her overbearing ways and insolent demeanor.[2] As in the case of Brunhilda, the nobles resented the government of a woman; government by this type of woman they seem to have regarded as intolerable.

This is what Einhard would have us believe. It seems an inadequate reason for a revolution that was to begin with murder, but most ventures then were made on inadequate reasons or none. Vétault [3] suspects that the nobles had an-

[1] Davis, pp. 146–47.   [2] Vétault, pp. 346–47.
[3] Page 325.

212

other incentive in their disappointment over the results of the first campaign against the Avars, which had just been concluded. Whereas much booty had been expected, little was had. This again falls short of enough to justify so perilous a movement against so alert a chieftain. But there was another and much more plausible source of unrest among these nobles. The unconventional ways and democratic innovations of the King must have disturbed and disgusted them. His strong hand was heavy upon them; above all he had interfered with their business, in all ages the intolerable outrage. From murmuring about the unreasonable humor of Fastrada they came to conspire for the King's overthrow and took Pepin the hunchback as their ostensible head and handy claimant to the throne.[1]

The most formidable part of this combination was in Bavaria, where the nobles, Bavarian and Frankish, most had reason to resent the King's attempts to abolish robbery and oppression. In Germany more than in any other country at that time [2] robbery had been commercialized and standardized. It had, in fact, grown there to be a vested right. The policy of the King, all hostile to it, met with the reception that in all ages has attended every attempt to interfere with such a right. Furiously the nobles resisted the invasion and resolved to defend even with assassination their ancient privileges. It is now an old story in the history of human affairs; it was then comparatively new.

The war had made its usual demands.[3] Certain noblemen of Bavaria had managed in one way or another to avoid leading their troops into the struggle. They were now footloose for dark-lantern purposes.

[1] Einhard, *Life*, p. 30.

[2] Hallam, chap. IX, p. 506. 'Germany appears to have been, upon the whole, the country where downright robbery was most unscrupulously practiced by the great. Their castles, erected upon almost inaccessible heights among the woods, became the secure receptacles of predatory bands.... Robbery, indeed, is the constant theme both of the Capitularies [Charlemagne's] and of the Anglo-Saxon laws.'

[3] Einhard, *Life*, p. 30.

The center of the conspiracy was at Regensburg. At night when the town was asleep and the great Church of Saint Peter was deserted, it was their practice to steal into its recesses and debate their plans. Attached to the church was a poor deacon, a Lombard named Fardulf.[1] One night when he was later than usual in his duties he sat down and fell asleep. About midnight he was awakened by voices and looking up saw by the light of torches a body of armed men stealing through the church. He divined from their attitude and the words he heard them drop that they were not worshipers. They gathered at one side of a monument. Fardulf crept to the other side and wormed his way until he was close enough to hear what they said. There he listened while they discussed the final details of the murder of the King and the seizure of the government.

When the plans of the conspirators [2] had been fully arranged, their meeting was ended and they started for the door. Fardulf crept into a corner until they could be gone. On the way a sudden suspicion seemed to seize one of them. He said that in the darkness some one might have overheard them and that before they went the church should be searched. With torches and their drawn swords they poked hither and thither and dragged out the trembling Fardulf.

They set him in the midst of them with daggers at his throat. He admitted that he had heard all. Then most of the knights were for killing him on the spot. But others argued that to shed blood in the holy church would surely ruin their enterprise. No good could befall it after such a beginning; they would not take upon their souls so black a crime. But to carry away their shivering captive and murder him in another place would be no better. Still they would be violating sanctuary and laying hands of violence upon a man of God. Let him live, therefore, said these, if he will swear by all the

[1] Vétault, pp. 325-28; Einhard, *Annals*, pp. 89-90.
[2] Monk of Saint Gall, pp. 65-69.

saints and otherwise that he will keep in eternal silence what
he has heard.[1]

Forthwith, upon the relics of the saints, and by the bones
of the martyrs, and by his faith, and with the most sacred ad-
jurations a Christian could lay upon his soul, they swore him
that never, no matter what might befall, would he make
known to any human being a word of what he had heard that
night. And so sworn many times and ingeniously, they left
him and went their ways.

After midnight a shaken and half-clothed figure knocked
at the palace gate and asked admission on the ground that he
had to make a communication of the first importance. There
were seven wards that he must pass; it must have been by his
extraordinary earnestness that he convinced the guards at
each portal he was on an errand of honesty. At last he stood
before the royal apartment and knocked violently.

The attendants coming to the door saw before them a man
haggard and distraught that begged admittance to the King.
They took him for a lunatic and with laughter closed the door
in his face. But the noise they made awakened the King, who
demanded to know the cause of so much clamor and mirth in
the middle of the night. They said:

'It is a miserable beggar without a beard, or probably some
crazy merchant that pretends that he must speak to you at
once.'

'Let him in,' said the King, struck with the strangeness of
this appeal at such an hour, and Fardulf the Lombard, the
hereditary enemy, threw himself on his knees and told all
he had heard.

That morning all the conspirators were arrested. A court
was summoned for their trial. It heard the testimony of Fardulf, found unanimously a verdict of guilty, and sentenced
the band to death. Einhard is fond of dwelling upon the
mercy and tolerance of the King. He did not in this instance

[1] Einhard, *Life*, p. 30; Vétault, p. 327, who follows the Monk of Saint Gall, pp.
65–66.

intervene on the side of mercy except in behalf of his son. All the rest were hanged, beheaded, or exiled.[1] Pepin the hunchback was shut into a monastery, where he lived twenty years.

Fardulf the Lombard, who at such a risk had saved the life of the destroyer of the Lombard monarchy, was well rewarded. He had acted on the principle that a promise extorted is not a promise binding.

In this instance mankind accepted enough of that doctrine to absolve him from any blame for the breaking of his oath.

Queen Fastrada, alleged by Einhard to have been one cause of this tragedy, was to play but little longer on the stage she had darkened with her lowering presence. She died two years afterward and the realm seems to have been the lighter of heart for her passing.

[1] Vétault, p. 327; Hodgkin, pp. 139–40; Davis, pp. 146–48.

CHAPTER XVI

KING AND CÆSAR

OF this career of vicissitude and achievement, unequaled for its span of years, range of endeavor, and average of success, the summit came in an extraordinary scene that on almost the last day of the last year of the eighth century dazzled the world.

It was a thing unexpected by the generality of mankind and maybe as little desired, it was over in a space of minutes, and yet it became the most enduring and, in a spectacular way, the most important political event of the reign. Historically, it involved the greatest honor the age could confer. The man that received it seemed to look upon it without enthusiasm. Yet in the years to come, for the sake of the emblem shown glittering that day in Rome, Europe was to be shaken with wars, men were to spend their lives in restless scheming and heart-breaking struggle, thousands of the pawns from the bottom of the human pyramid were to be marshaled and hurtled in ranks to beat one another to death. From one viewpoint it looked that day like nothing but play-acting, not particularly well done. For a thousand years afterward, the scene was still set and actors were still rehearsing it. Yet of those that played first the leading rôles, one seemed to be actuated chiefly by a sudden and childish impulse, and the other to be seized at once by regret.

So slight are the threads that pull men's affairs this way and that. In this case, the principal thread went back to one woman, and was determined by her character. If Irene of Constantinople had been a good wife and tolerable mother, Charles of the Franks might have ended his days much as he began them. It was the spectacle of this depraved and reck-

217

less woman reigning from the throne of the Cæsars and threatening the peace and stability of civilization that drove a few thoughtful men to look level-eyed upon actual conditions, and move illegally toward the only hope. Here was the once great, once splendid, Empire of Rome, mistress of the world, titular head of the Christian religion, titular leader of civilization; these were the creatures at Constantinople that swayed and governed what was left of this former supremacy, these wretched degenerates that reigned, plotted, assassinated, wantoned, and wallowed. What chance had Christianity with such champions to lead it?

In the whole orbit of the Empire there had been for years mostly a surfeit of vice at home and a flabby invertebrate of weakness abroad. Long the astute observers of men and measures had known this, but, as so often happens, evil was not acute nor at its worst until all men knew that it was known to all men. What brought it to the universal knowledge was the extravagance and crimes of Irene. Then all wise men agreed that the condition was intolerable.

Exactly why Western and Central Europe should have been so much concerned that things should go well at Constantinople may not be clear now, unless we remember the infancy of the human mind. One of the childish tricks of the times was to turn confidingly and instinctively to the tattered remnants of the old Roman power, and to the person that bore the old Roman title. The mere name of Emperor, Imperator, Augustus, Cæsar, was adored as the greatest potentiality in Europe. Kings were well enough, the thousand princes and princelets that buzzed about and battened upon the toil of the common herd were well enough. But the Emperor was traditionally the overlord of the Christian society, the successor of the mighty Constantine, the shield against the barbarians that encompassed and tried to throttle it. As a matter of fact, the Emperor at Constantinople had not for many years protected anything except his life (when he could), and the vicious pleasures of the stews in which he

218

lived. As another matter of fact, the worth of his bulwark against the barbarians might have been judged from this that annually he paid them money to let him alone. And yet the superstitious belief in his strength survived, although he might not be able to muster more than a guard of eunuchs, and in his divine wisdom, although he might be a chattering idiot. In the popular mind he was still Theodosius, Constantine, Emperor, Cæsar, sword, and buckler of the Church.

With reason, therefore, Europe was shocked and alarmed when it mastered the fact that this abandoned woman had seized the old place of power, soaring upon the two wings of murder and criminal intrigue. Even the most credulous and childlike in a credulous and childlike age could see that a throne so possessed could have no moral influence and no leadership. A sexual distinction is always to be observed in the depravities of history. Constantine V might have been as wicked as Irene without upsetting the machinery of the world. With a woman, all was different. For one thing, the old fiction of physical force in the Empire could no longer be maintained. That alone was enough.

In those days news traveled slowly; men's minds were untrained to seize upon the meaning of great events. Two years passed before the Christian world grasped what had happened at Constantinople. Then it began to see the meaning of these conditions and their deadly menace to the faith with which civilization had come to be interwoven.

All along the frontiers of that religion the outlook was bad and growing worse. Fresh barbarian hordes were pressing down from the north and northeast.[1] The Mohammedans were returning to the attack on the south and southeast. If aught was to be done to resist these attacks, it must be done quickly.

One place in the Western world was the natural rallying point for such resistance, and at this most inopportune crisis Rome was torn with civil war. We need from time to time

[1] Hodgkin, p. 194.

concrete events and outstanding facts to bring us back to the truth that essentially the world still was close to the primeval wilderness. One of them is that in those days ambitious men did not scruple to lay hands upon the venerable head of the Christian religion. The civil war in Rome centered about the Pope.

Hadrian I, the wise, the virtuous, the friend of Charlemagne, the friend of civilization, died in 795. His successor was a Roman prelate that took the name of Leo III. Hadrian's rule had been unusually long, unusually beneficent. Men accustomed to his ways were doubtful of his successor. On other grounds the new Pope was unpopular in Rome. A faction grew up against him, headed by hot-headed youths, nephews of Hadrian, but not like him. The mainspring of their conspiring was that they had been members of his household and now saw themselves ousted from fat and desirable drippings of their uncle's table. They and their associates planned to depose Leo with force, and to choose a pope after their own will. Doubtless other motives contributed; conspiracies are seldom woven around one strand. But throughout, the chief impulses were envy and greed.[1]

One Pascal, a monk who had been a prior, and one Campolus, who had been a treasury officer under Hadrian, were members of this band. They now concocted and formulated charges against the personal character of the Pope, charges of gross crimes and immoralities of a nature not to be ignored.

These they presented to Charles with the notion that he would attend to the deposing part of the programme. Charles refused to accept offhand these extraordinary creations, but asked his old friend Alcuin to undertake an inquiry. Alcuin sent to Rome an inspector to make the investigation. In the main, his report was favorable to the Pope, but did not clear him from all imputations of misconduct. The prejudices of Charles were all with the clergy. He construed

[1] Vétault, p. 368.

the inspector's report as sufficiently establishing the Pope's innocence and erased the matter from his concerns.

But the conspirators at Rome were grimly set upon their object. The Pope refused to abdicate. The conspirators resorted to other means of ousting him.

One day Pope Leo, mounted on a horse, was leading through the streets of Rome a solemn religious procession. From a concealed hiding-place a band of ruffians suddenly leaped upon him, drove off the processionists and guard, and, with clubs and stones, beat the aged Pontiff to the ground.[1]

Then they started to put out his eyes and cut out his tongue, that he might be incapable of performing the duties of his office.

Even among these outcasts must have persisted some remnants of conscience. Their villainy failed them before this hideous mutilation. The eyes of the Pope were injured, but not destroyed.[2] As he lay on the ground, he was beaten insensible, and then was dragged off to be imprisoned in a monastery.[3]

So far as Rome knew, he had vanished, for the place of his imprisonment was kept a secret. The conspirators seized the city and set in motion their machinery to elect a pope of their own.

Leo had strong friends and faithful followers. These were not convinced that he had perished, but sought for him zealously in out-of-the-way places. Among the searchers was the chamberlain of his household, stout and trusty. He went from prison to prison, from monastery to monastery, until by judicious inquiry he discovered the building where his master was confined.

It stood upon a hillside so steep that some of the windows in the part occupied by the Pope opened upon almost a sheer declivity. As these windows were deemed unreachable, they were not watched.

[1] Capefigue, p. 348.   [2] Von den Steinen, p. 41; Hodgkin, p. 285.
[3] Einhard, *Annals*, p. 97; Fletcher, p. 256.

221

By night, and after toil and dangers, the chamberlain succeeded in scaling the cliff and reaching a spot whence he could have speech with his master. He returned to the ground, obtained the necessary tackle, reascended the cliff. Then he performed the all but impossible task of getting the august prisoner out of the window, and down the side of the rock to his waiting friends below. These carried him without discovery to Saint Peter's Church, where he had sanctuary.[1]

News of the revolt in Rome had reached the Duke of Spoleto, whom Charles had appointed to be lieutenant or governor of that province. He had out his army, and marched to the city to restore order. The conspirators slammed the gates in his face and defied him from the walls. If he had come with a notion that this was an ordinary riot, he was quickly aware of his error. He found it impossible to force the walls, and ingloriously gave up the attempt. But he did one good thing. The Church of Saint Peter's was outside the city. He stopped there, took the Pope under his protection, and escorted him to a place of safety in Spoleto.[2]

All this was reported to Charles while he was at the head of his troops leading a final campaign against troublesome remnants of the North Saxons. The iron in his blood was aroused, but not even for such disquieting news would he leave the work in hand. He ordered the Pope to be brought before him at Paderborn, far in the heart of the conquered country.[3]

At once all the eulogies of the adoring Einhard fade before the light this imperious gesture throws upon the age, its manners, and the incomparable power of Charles. He ordered a pope to be brought before him for trial. In a few more years, and for centuries thereafter, an offending or accused monarch might come before a pope for judgment or vindication. Mankind was not to see again such a spectacle of temporal power as was afforded when a pope threaded the

---

[1] Vétault, p. 369. The story is in Anastasius.
[2] Von den Steinen, p. 41.   [3] Vétault, pp. 364–70.

rough passes of the Alps and journeyed almost a thousand miles to make his defense before a monarch in a rude camp of soldiers.[1]

Arrived at Paderborn, Leo appeared before a select council of the most eminent men in the King's service. That is to say, and not to put too fine a point upon it, the Pope was on trial, the council was the jury, Charles was the inquisitor — a soldier cross-examining the successor of Saint Peter. It was a time when men were not supersensitive, and when the King's prestige was great. Yet even then murmurs arose against the apparent disrespect toward the head of the Church,[2] and in after times it was viewed as still worse. The trial at Paderborn came to be regarded as illegal and impertinent. In some men's minds the fame of Charlemagne was impaired by it.

Yet it is easy to see that he had no thought of arrogance or disrespect. His plain, practical mind looked upon the performance as unavoidable. A vital issue had arisen in the Christian world. He was the only power that could settle it. Because of serious business in hand, he could not go to the Pope. Let the Pope come to him; the result would be the same.

He was right about the serious nature of the business he had in hand. At all times there was at the North the growing menace of the Norsemen. Now the Northern Saxons had made an alliance with these sea-raiders, and, unless the junction of Norse and Saxon forces could be prevented, there promised to be shortly the torch in a hundred churches and the land again laid waste. Nothing could prevent such a junction but one of those swift and daring movements that he alone knew how to make. Therefore, he could not leave his troops.

But meanwhile the Church was virtually without a head. Civil war was raging in Italy. Rome had been seized by banditti. The Pope was in exile. Until his place should be

[1] Einhard, *Annals*, p. 97.   [2] Vétault, pp. 374-75.

filled, Christendom would rock with unrest, and until the charges against him had been proved or disproved, no man could say whether he should be restored or the Church proceed to the election of another. There might have been some subtler way out of this emergency, but it was one that such a mind would never discover. All he knew was to go straight to the end, just as a peasant would plod across a field by the shortest route and taking big, straight steps ahead.

Yet for all his care, the verdict seems to have been of the order of Scotch. Leo was not found guilty, but, as before, he was not wholly cleared. Charles held that the result was decisive enough for practical purposes and the time being. He sent Leo with an escort back to Rome,[1] that he might be restored there to his palace and his office until another investigation should determine all the counts in the indictment.

The ease with which all this was carried out is the convincing proof of the extraordinary nature of the man's prestige. When his emissaries and forces reached Rome, the conspiracy collapsed. Peace was restored to the city. Pascal and Campolus were surrendered and bundled off to Charles as his prisoners. The Pope resumed his functions, and men stood patiently to see what next would be done by the one strong man whose handbeck thus dominated the world.

He pressed on with his campaigning, overawed the turbulent Saxons, and came back to Aachen, where he passed the winter of 799–800. In the spring he moved from his capital, but not at first toward Italy. He went about the kingdom attending to many matters while he waited to see if time would not show the best way out of the perplexing situation. He was well used to difficult problems; none in his experience had possessed so many ugly aspects as this. If, at the coming inquiry, the Pope should be found guilty and yet (as was most likely) should refuse to abdicate, there was no precedent for his removal. He must needs be cast out

[1] Vétault, p. 371.

by force to the imminent peril of the Church. On the other hand, if he should continue in office after his guilt had been shown, or even when there was a general doubt of his innocence, the whole Christian organization would be torn apart or wrecked.

It was the 24th of November, 800, when Charles reached Rome. Under an outward calm and armed truce, feverish agitation shook Church and State. The Church, so far as it was represented by Leo, was threatened with a deadly loss of prestige. The State, so far as the foolish and decadent Empire at Constantinople represented to men's minds the idea of a state, promised soon to be contemptible and impotent. Civilization was fighting for its life against the barbarian siege. On all sides the heathen hordes were pressing in, and its two natural bulwarks were breaking down. Men demanded a new protection against impending chaos. The wise saw one that promised to work. It was to establish the strongest possible power in the West, and let the old Empire of the East wallow on its downward way, wherever that might lead.

After the requisite days of celebration that followed his arrival, and after the ceremonies for which he had so little taste, Charles assembled his council for the final trial of the charges against Leo. Before a tribunal composed of distinguished clergy from all parts of the kingdom, he produced Pascal and Campolus, whom, still in chains, he had brought back with him from the North like so much baggage.

There ensued a singular scene. It was demanded of these men, once and for all, that they substantiate the charges with which they had so long shaken Christendom. Then appeared in stark daylight upon what flimsy basis rested all this turmoil. They had no proof, they had no considerable witnesses, they had nothing but idle imaginations and winehouse babblings. The farther they floundered in their examination, the more clearly men saw that this was so. When they had made an end of their lamentable performance,

225

the innocence of the Pope was triumphantly acclaimed, and with full honors and powers, amid the general rejoicing, he was restored to his throne. For once the adage was footless; smoke there had been and of an ill odor, but no fire.[1]

And then Leo III showed that he was worthy to take the seals that had fallen from the hand of the great Hadrian. The court that vindicated him condemned to death the conspirators that had disrupted the Christian State. With the tongue they had tried to tear from his mouth he pleaded in behalf of the men that had so cruelly tortured him, and succeeded in winning for them that they should be banished, and not slain.

His exculpation was complete on December 23, year 800. Two days later, in old Saint Peter's, with unusual pomp and fervor, as by men released from a great fear, the festival of Christmas was celebrated. The church was gorgeously decorated and filled with communicants exalted into a new hope, both by this happy deliverance and by the presence of the greatest Christian warrior. Rumors were abroad that the day would see on that hallowed spot a most important and memorable event that all good citizens would wish to witness.

Charles was there with two of his sons. The Pope himself said mass. Charles descended into the enclosure before the shrine of the Apostle, and knelt to make his devotions. Profound silence reigned in the church. His prayers ended, Charles arose and started to reascend the few steps to the level of the choir.

Then the Pope snatched from the altar a crown of gold and placed it upon the King's head. At the signal, the great throng burst into loud cries of congratulation, and men shouted the words that in so many generations had not been heard in Rome, the acclamation that hailed a new imperator:

'To Charles the Augustus, crowned of God, the great and pacific Emperor, long life and victory!'[2]

[1] Vétault, p. 375, following Anastasius.
[2] Einhard, *Life*, p. 46; Einhard, *Annals*, p. 101; Monk of Saint Gall, p. 34. He

THE CORONATION OF CHARLEMAGNE
From the painting by Raphael in the Vatican

The Western Empire had come again after three hundred and twenty-four years. Charles had been placed upon its throne. Henceforth he was not merely King, but Cæsar and Emperor.

Yet for an event of such magnitude, what happened that Christmas morning was and is covered with a curious mystery. For eleven hundred years, historians have debated about it, striving to knit together its apparently irreconcilable features. Was the coronation with the foreknowledge and approval of Charles? Did he plan for it and desire it? Was he sincere about it, or only mumming? These questions have been batted to and fro by innumerable commentators, and are as far from answer now as when the debate began.

To be Emperor of the West, lord paramount of the civilized world, and successor to Theodosius, would seem a natural ambition for any man to cherish if he could. In the existing conditions of chaos, it would have been in Charles not merely understandable, but praiseworthy. What then is the difficulty? A few lines in the book of this same Einhard, supposed secretary and assuredly biographer to the King. According to his account, Charles not only did not desire the coronation, and was unprepared for it, but when done he resented it.

'He was in the beginning so hostile to the title of Cæsar and Augustus that he declared that although the day was a high church festival, if he had known the Pope's intention he would not have entered the church.' [1]

Thus his Boswell. The problem is to reconcile this remark with the facts of the coronation. It is unthinkable that the Pope should dare to thrust upon so great a prince so notable a ceremony without full knowledge on all sides. To suppose

says that Pope Leo summoned Charles to Rome for this purpose, which is clearly absurd.

[1] Einhard, *Life*, p. 36. Charles may have disliked the title of Augustus at the beginning, but he quickly adjusted himself to it, and used it in all his correspondence.

that the nobles were gathered there and instructed as to the acclaim they should raise, and Charles know nothing about it, is preposterous. It appears from certain documents that Alcuin was well advised, some weeks before, that the coronation was to take place. That he in Tours should know of it, and Charles in Rome know it not, is again beyond belief.

The act was in itself wholly illegal.[1] No precedent existed and no authority for the crowning of an emperor by a pope. No one can well believe that the Pope would have ventured upon so violent an innovation without consulting the man that was not only most concerned in it, but was also ruler of the Western world, spiritual and temporal. Finally, it appears that the coronation had been considered and decided upon some days in advance by a council that Leo had called, and we know too much about the careful supervision Charles had over all matters connected with the Church to suppose that any important council could be held anywhere without his knowledge.

It was not a humorous age. Men were not usually cynical or sophisticated. A time of simple intensities and primitive emotions is not one oversuspicious. Yet it is to be noted about this event that in some quarters scoffing and scurrilous comment followed. Before that first inquiry at Paderborn, Charles and the Pope had conferred long and secretly.[2] Afterward, Charles had performed for the Pope a great and signal service, vindicating him to the world, setting him again upon his throne. When as the next scene in the drama the Pope puts the imperial crown upon his benefactor's head, behold winks and nods and tongues in cheeks — covertly. Here must have been bargaining, said the cavilers; for so much vindication, so much crown.

The only part of the ceremony that day for which warrant existed was the outcry of the throng. This partook of the nature of accredited elections in the old days; for whatever might have been the pretensions of the Senate in the long de-

---

[1] Bryce, *The Holy Roman Empire*, pp. 59–60.   [2] Hodgkin, p. 188.

cline of Rome, it was by the acclamation of the army that the Emperor was chosen. There was one spirit in that age bold enough to devise and to carry out a notably radical step, a long departure like this from established usage and the law of custom. That was Charles himself.

All this seemed to make a sure case for foreknowledge and design.[1] And yet there is Einhard's report. 'Would that I had not entered Saint Peter's on Christmas Day!' was the burden of the Emperor's lament, according to the scribe that knew him best. In scouting for a way around this discrepancy, some have supposed that Charles regarded with concern the assumption by the Pope of a power that did not belong to the Papacy, which is most unlikely. Some have through thick and thin held to the notion that Charles was really taken by surprise, and the Pope alone knew what was to be done.[2] Bryce makes a plausible deduction that Charles knew the coronation was planned, and hoped for it, but was unprepared for it at the time it happened and regretted it because it interfered with his own plans.[3] He also cites the differing opinion of Dr. von Dollinger that Charles wanted to be Emperor, but was disconcerted by the action of the Pope when he thought of the perilous complications that would ensue with Constantinople.

One other explanation is more likely to occur to a modern than to a Victorian investigator. It is that Einhard was a foolish person, and his report after all need not be taken as embodying gospel. His business was to represent his hero always as reflecting what seemed to him the grandest virtues and most resplendent self-abnegations. Nothing would appeal more to the Einhard order of mind than to picture Charlemagne as without personal ambition and actuated by only the highest motives. To parade him as never having thought of so great an honor as this until the Pope suddenly

[1] Vétault, pages 379–80, does not think so.
[2] Vétault, for one, pp. 379–80; Fletcher, p. 258.
[3] Page 57. Conf. Monk of Saint Gall, p. 35.

229

thrust it upon him might have been an irresistible temptation, and the probability is that Charles never made the remark upon which debate has pivoted for a thousand years. Or, if he made it, meant by it nothing seismic.

We might be slower to discount the famous biographer's words on this occasion, if he had not in so many others shown himself to be a most indifferent reporter. Why should we imagine that modern times have had a monopoly of propaganda and amiable distortion? For much of this appearing in Einhard allowance can be made. He was Charlemagne's secretary, let us say; he was awed by the greatness of his subject; he desired the world to be impressed with a notable example of piety. He wrote his book fourteen years after Charlemagne's death, and perhaps did not clearly remember some things that he asserts with confidence. All this is well and charitable. But when it comes to taking passages from Suetonius and applying them unchanged to Charlemagne,[1] the modern reader, though patient and good-natured, will think the limits of propaganda have been passed.

But, however this may be, Charles, King of the Franks, was Emperor of the West. Emperor he remained, and at the moment when first he felt on his brows the imperial crown was founded the Holy Roman Empire that endured henceforth until Napoleon dashed it to pieces.[2] Two great men stand forth between Julius Cæsar and our own day, both rulers of France. It is remarkable that one of them began this institution of power and moment, and the other destroyed it.

If Charles had really been disturbed by the thought of possible opposition from Constantinople, the next two or three years showed how footless was any such fear. At the moment of the coronation Irene was reigning in the full tide of her arrogance and success. Two years later the revolt of Aëtius drove her from the throne. The end of the tigress

[1] *Études Critiques*, etc., pp. 91–92.
[2] Bryce, pp. 359–60.

Charles had once thought of marrying was not long delayed. The health of the Eastern Empire was not replenished when she was reduced to plying the distaff at Lesbos, but the menace to Christian civilization she had once represented had been banished with her.

CHAPTER XVII

THE MAN, SELF-DRAWN

EVERY day we are in intimate contact with something in civilization that resulted from or has been affected by the deed or dream of this strangely throned Cæsar. Yet to most of us he remains a figure as fabulous as Jack of the Beanstalk or Guy of Warwick Who Slew the Great Dun Cow. For this strabismus we owe the eulogists of his own time or a little later. If we can see the man at all, it is no more than a dim, elusive shadow glimpsed through their clouds of incense. With whatsoever gravity they may repeat their assertions, the normal mind intuitively balks at them. Without stopping to debate much of the matter, the average reader finds no conviction in his Einhard and Monk of Saint Gall, because there never was a merely mortal being so good, so wise, so gentle, and so infallible as the man they pretend to describe. Men are not so constituted, we say; and an atmosphere of unreality having been thus created in one respect, the whole narrative takes a like tinge and goes presently with other fairy tales to be forgotten.

Because Einhard was so near to his idol, assumably knew him so well, and wrote with so much authority, he has, nevertheless, been tolerated as the best available source of information, although long ago men pointed out in him apparent and grievous errors, improbabilities, or slips. He says that Pope Stephen II deposed Childeric III,[1] the last of the *fainéants*, and came to France that with his own hand he might crown Pepin. The records easily prove that the Pope to whom Pepin appealed was Zacharias and the crown-

---

[1] Page 28. So many historians, biographers, writers, and philosophers have been deceived by this error that it amounts to a historical and literary curiosity. Among those misled by it was the great Napoleon himself. *Vide* Bryce, p. 354.

232

CHARLEMAGNE
From the painting by Albert Dürer in
the Germanic Museum, Nuremberg

ing was by Saint Boniface. He says that so great was the
love of Charles for his children [1] that he carried them with
him on all his campaigns, for he could not endure to be separated from them. It is obvious that the statement is impossible. He says [2] that King Pepin divided his kingdom on
the lines that had been followed by Charles Martel. It is
evident that the division was wholly different. He cites as
portent of Charlemagne's death the mysterious fall of the
portico of the royal palace. Charlemagne died in 814. The
portico fell in 817. He tells us there were other portents,
such as terrible eclipses and earthquakes.[3] Our natural
skepticism is easily verified by reference to historical fact.
The earthquakes and eclipses took place at different times,
but long before the passing of his idol.[4]

Yet these too friendly narrators have a certain distinct
value to us, though not in the way they intended. If the
incidents they record are worthless as history, they are
nevertheless a roundabout index of character. Stories about
a man of whom everybody knows must be in line with the
general knowledge of that man if they are to be circulated
and accepted. The incidents recorded by Einhard and the
Monk of Saint Gall may not have happened, but might
have happened. If the residual of these labored writings and
of others of the period is the parade before us of a figure
almost impossibly good, they prove that underneath their
stuffy tributes must have been something fairly genuine and
respectable. He must have been a man of worth or all these
stories in his favor would not have been invented.

But in trying to learn what kind of man it really was that
remade Europe, salvaged civilization, restored learning, and
still reaches out to us across eleven centuries, we are not
bound in by speculations founded upon amiable fiction.
Many things in Einhard, the Monk of Saint Gall, and the
others are verifiable facts; many cohere with credible records

[1] Page 28.   [2] *Annals*, p. 55.
[3] *Annals*, pp. 101–03, 109.   [4] Halphen, pp. 93–94.

like those of the pontificate; many are on their face probable. From these we can gather much. But far beyond and above all of them is the marvelous source of knowledge that exists in the Charlemagne Capitularies or circular letters. In these he has drawn himself; unconsciously, therefore indubitably. As von den Steinen justly remarks,[1] we can cast aside Einhard, the Monk, and all the other writers of the time. In these incomparable letters we find the real image of the man, the full revelation of his peculiar ideas about government and life; we can discern the causes of his success, the secrets of his great and abiding influences, and even some of the idiosyncrasies of his character.

The letters cover the greater part of his reign and almost every subject vital to the man and his work. Most of them were sent out to bishops, counts, governors, other persons in authority, giving them explicit instructions as to the conduct of various offices and the work of public administration. They constituted, in chief, the legislation of the kingdom as well as its executive impulse. Men were told what to do about everything and how to do it; told sometimes in an astonishing detail. No one can read these letters now without perceiving a contact with an untrammeled and dynamic mind; after all these centuries and the total extinction of the occasion, few persons can read them without a stirring of the mental pulses. These straight, stern, bullet-like sentences, written in a spirit so uncompromising and still often in a spirit so lofty — for all our modern superiority, they still lay hold and stir.[2]

There are extant seventy-five of these Capitularies, embracing all told 1151 capitula, or articles. A great French historian and philosopher [3] has assorted them according to the main topic dealt with. Eighty-seven are devoted to moral legislation, matters of conscience, the intellectual responsibility of men; eighty-five to religious legislation con-

[1] Page 61.   [2] Conf. Wells, *The Age of Charlemagne*, p. 244.
[3] Guizot, *History of Civilization*, Lesson XXI.

234

cerning ecclesiastical affairs and the relations of the clergy with the people; three hundred and five to topics related to discipline and faith; two hundred and eighty-three to political subjects, embracing all the branches of the public administration, one hundred and thirty to matters pertaining to the administration of the criminal law; one hundred and ten to the administration of the civil law; eighty-three to subjects of domestic concern; and the remainder to subjects connected with special occasions.

As to the man that writes them, the first and most vivid of the impressions one gets is of his singular attitude toward religion. He has accepted it, not as a necessary seventh-day ceremony, nor as a convenience, nor as a handy sop for occasional application to a loaded conscience, nor yet, like Napoleon and other rulers, as a kind of valet or handmaid to his politic aims; but with fervency, persistence, the plainest honesty. He takes it with him, even into affairs where it has seldom entered. 'By the Grace of God, King,' and so forth is in his documents no formula. He believes it, he repeats it with an astonishing gusto; he puts it into his private correspondence, dwells upon it, evidently construes it to have a peculiar and potent meaning. Not fanatically; that is the strangest part of it. There is nothing of the fanatic in this man's make-up. He never appears to have thought of himself as 'the Scourge of God,' or invented a divine commission to cover brigandage. That we could understand, having had so many modern examples of it, first and last. But this is all different; this is the case of a man that looks upon religion as a practical, everyday, natural, feasible asset of life that he utilizes himself and wants others to make the most of.[1]

He is always at it. He seldom writes a letter on any subject or to any person that he does not bring in this before he is through. About all of it he is as honest as the skin between your brows. There is not a hook in any of his letters on which one can hang one charge of insincerity — about this, anyway.

[1] Almost any of the Capitularies can be cited in evidence of this.

235

It is among the most remarkable facts in the whole remarkable story. Alone it is enough to make him a historical figure of overpowering interest.

When he writes to a brother king, whether on state or personal topics, he reminds him in burning phrases of his duty toward God and religion.[1] When he unceremoniously rebukes the nobles for laxity about the administration of justice, he thunders at them like an audacious preacher. He wants everybody to be good — but not on philosophical grounds, as being productive of happiness. Not at all; they must watch their steps because it is so commanded in the Scriptures. In proof, he can cite you offhand to chapter and verse; can, and does so. And these things that in any other ruler or executive or commander would be taken as trick-playing and camouflage or worse — here they come upon you with an irresistible conviction. No chance is left to scoff or even to doubt. He means all he says; he feels it to his fingertips.

His mental processes revolve upon this one axis, but that always sufficient. He believes that when he wins a victory, it is because God overwhelms his enemies for him, never stopping to think that possibly his enemies have besought God with the same fervor. If he writes to a friend about indifferent matters, he is certain to land somewhere with an exhortation. Writing to Fastrada in the autumn of 791, he begins his letter in exactly the same way as when he writes to kings, counts, or bishops:

'Charles, by the grace of God, King of the Franks and Lombards, Protector of the Romans, to his beloved and very courageous wife, Queen Fastrada.' He gives her a 'friendly greeting' and sends the same to his daughters and the household servants, a somewhat unusual salutation in persons of his line of activity. He then tells her the news. A messenger

---

[1] *Vide* his two letters to Offa, King of Mercia, numbered 9 and 10 in von den Steinen's collection, and his letters to the Emperors Nicephorus and Michael I, numbered 23 and 24.

has lately arrived from his dear son Pepin (the legitimate Pepin) telling him that the health of the Pope is good and that the Italian territory has been freed from his enemies, which gives him great satisfaction. And next there is news that his troops, advancing out of Italy and invading the country of the heathen Avars, on August 23 met them in a pitched battle. 'And Almighty God in his mercy gave to our troops the victory and they have killed many of the Avars. It is said that not in a long time has such slaughter been seen among them'; which again forcibly reminds one of the human spiral and the telegram that Kaiser William the First sent to his wife at the close of the battle of Sedan. After slaughter, booty. 'Our troops plundered the stronghold [of the Avars] and camped there that night and the following day until the third hour, when with their booty they returned home in peace.'

They brought away one hundred and fifty Avar prisoners that they are holding for the King's pleasure. He does not say what he intends to do with them.

Throughout this letter, as all the others, there recurs, despite unpleasant and gruesome passages like the foregoing, the same spirit of religious exaltation that so evidently mastered him. A man may and probably will pretend many things to the wife of his bosom. He will not pretend to her a piety that both know to be fraudulent. In this letter he goes on to tell of a three days' service he has ordered in the church. To celebrate this triumph? Not at all; 'to seek God's mercy that he will assure us peace and health, victory and favorable results, and that he may be to us in his mercy and goodness a helper, counselor, and defender in all our necessities.' Also, he has ordered the priests to proclaim a three days' abstinence from meat and wine, a general fast to be observed by all — with penalties for disobedience. Whosoever in these three days shall eat flesh or drink wine shall pay for the benefit of the poor a shilling; if unable to pay a shilling, at least a penny. Further, he orders special masses and processions and

237

gives special directions about the singing of the Psalms. He desires Fastrada to see that all these commands are carefully carried out in her part of the realm, he being thus absent from Aachen. Finally, he reverts humanly to his part of husband and wonders why she does not write to him. She has sent him no word in many days and he wishes she would write oftener and tell him about her health and the like.[1]

A royal and indefatigable evangelist for whom I am unable to think of a prototype. Thus in one of his encyclicals to the clergy he writes:

We wish to ask the ecclesiastics themselves, and those that have not only to learn but to teach out of the Holy Scriptures, who are they to whom the Apostle says, 'Be ye imitators of me'; or whom that is about when the same Apostle says, 'No man that warreth entangleth himself with the business of the world'? In other words, how is the Apostle to be imitated, how the priest is to war for God?

Further, we must beg of them that they will truly show us what is this 'renouncing of the world' that is spoken of by them; or how we can distinguish those that renounce the world from those that still follow it? Whether it consists in anything more than this, that they do not bear arms and are not publicly married?

We must also inquire if that man has relinquished the world who is daily laboring to increase in every manner and by every artifice his possessions, by sweet persuasions about the blessedness of heaven and by terrible threats about the punishments of hell; who uses the name of God or of some saint to despoil simpler and less learned folk, whether rich or poor, of their property; to deprive the lawful heirs of their inheritance and thus to drive many through sheer destitution to a life of robbery and crime that they would otherwise never have embraced?[2]

This last question, put so keenly to the conscience, sounds like a reforming voice of our own day. More than a thousand years were to elapse before it should be again prominent in men's thinkings.

In a letter [3] furthering education, addressed primarily to Baugulf, Abbot of Fulda, but to be circulated among all

[1] No. 7 in von den Steinen's collection.
[2] Cited by Hodgkin, p. 234.   [3] No. 4 in von den Steinen.

238

bishops and abbots, he commands all to betake themselves diligently to the study of letters to the end that 'those that wish to please God by living properly shall not neglect to please him also by speaking properly.' It was a characteristic thought. And he reminds them that 'it is written, "Thou shalt be justified or condemned by thy words."' Although, he continues, it may be better to act well than to have knowledge, they should never forget that it is necessary first to know how to act well. If all men owe a duty to avoid error, how much greater is that duty upon those whose calling in life is the service of the truth? He says in plain terms that he has had too much reason to complain of slack and slovenly modes of expression among the priesthood. 'What a sincere devotion faithfully dictates in the thought is lamely expressed in language because the speakers have brought to their studies neglect and indifference.'

There has been so much of this he has begun to fear that, the reports to him from the clergy being often so badly expressed, there must be a defective intelligence in the interpretation of the Holy Scriptures. 'If errors in words are dangerous, we all know that errors in meanings may be far more dangerous still.' Therefore he exhorts them, not merely against neglect of the study of letters, but that they should prosecute that study with the utmost zeal and diligence under the blessing of God. There are in the Scriptures many figures, tropes, and other similar adornments, and it is obvious that the meaning of these can be grasped quickly and surely only by one that had been equipped thereto by study and research. The letter ends with this blunt adjuration:

Do not on any account neglect to send copies of this letter to all the bishops, your suffragans, and to all the monasteries if you wish to have our good will.

It seems the strangest of all business for a conquering soldier and successful empire-builder to be engaged in, but such minute directions and explicit commands to the clergy form a large part of the Capitularies. Queen Mother Bertrade must have been a prime instructress to have drilled into his youthful mind a conviction that neither years nor wars nor success nor ambition could displace.

Even in confidential letters to his closest friends he was the same. In 796 he wrote one [1] to his intimate, Angilbert the poet, who in the circle at Aachen was known as 'Homer.' 'Charles, by the grace of God, King and Protector of the Holy Church, greets Homer the Aurikolar,' is the beginning of this letter, which is one of instructions, Angilbert having been sent as a special envoy to Pope Leo when Leo was crowned as successor to Hadrian. He did not hesitate to remind even popes of their duty.

When the divine goodness shall have led you safe and sound to the apostolic head, our father, then admonish him to a zealous propriety in all his life and especially to the observance of the holy statutes and to the pious leading of the Holy Church of God, so far as your talk with him permits of this and his mind is in accordance with it. Remind him how brief is the honor that he enjoys at present, how everlasting is the reward that waits on one that in his position discharges its duties well. Counsel him most urgently to abolish heretical venality that in many places disgraces the body of the Church, which, as you know, we have frequently complained against. Do not forget to remind him of the negotiations I have had with his predecessor, the blessed Pope Hadrian, concerning the building of a monastery to Saint Paul, and when by God's will you return to me bring me a definite answer.

The Lord lead you in all health, there and back. The Lord govern and lead him that he may zealously do that which will serve the Holy Church, that he may be for us the pious father and powerful intercessor.... Depart in health, advance in the Truth, and come again in peace, my Homeric child.

To Amalar, Bishop of Trèves, he writes [2] about things that in a military genius and world-ruler are enough to make one marvel. He wants to know how he and his suffragans interpret to their flocks the sacrament of baptism, how they seek to make religious converts of the children, what a religious convert is, about the *Scrutinium* and what the *Scrutinium* is,

[1] No. 12 in von den Steinen.   [2] No. 21.

240

the Creed and how the Latin fathers have interpreted it. Then about the renunciation of the devil and all his works and insolence, and what are these works, with many other points besides. The Bishop evidently made a satisfactory reply, for there follows another letter to him from Charles thanking him, but not foregoing the joys of exhortation. Although he knows that the excellent Bishop is diligent in spiritual and Christian learning, nevertheless he urges him to more and more thorough endeavor, more tireless instruction and holy preaching for all that are under his guidance and the fountain of his influence.

If we found one such letter from a worldly ruler, we should surely suspect it; ten would constitute a portent. Charlemagne seems to have written many of this purport and with the same extraordinary fervency of spirit.

He had next a concern, wholly abnormal for one of his times and occupation, in the condition of the poor of his realm. He is continually and almost frantically commanding the counts and governors to see that the poor have justice, that no man shall be oppressed, that for every complaint there shall be a ready and impartial hearing. He threatens with his direst wrath any noble that shall attempt to prevent the poor from access to him.

One of these Capitularies [1] is put forth in the name of the *missi* or inspectors that are about to go upon their tours through the country. It is addressed to the counts, and says:

Take care that neither you nor any of your officers are so evil-disposed as to say 'Hush! hush! say nothing about that matter till those *missi* have passed by, and afterward we will settle it quietly among ourselves.' Do not so deny or even postpone the administration of justice; but rather give diligent heed that justice may be done in the case before we arrive. [2]

If in such documents we came upon one or two references to the poor and the unfortunate, we might ascribe them to formula or policy or a passing fancy. They recur here so

[1] No. 22.   [2] Cited by Hodgkin, p. 244.

often and so forcibly that we are driven to conclude the concern must have been genuine and instinctive. In a Capitulary of 802 he writes:

> And let no one by his cleverness and astuteness, according to the customs of many, dare to interfere with the written law, or to disturb the course of justice, or to set himself up against the churches of God or against poor persons or widows or children.

And instructing his envoys or *missi*, he urges them diligently to 'make inquiry whenever any one complains that wrong has been done him by another, as they desire to keep the favor of God for themselves and to preserve with fidelity what has been entrusted to them, so that in all places everywhere in regard to the holy churches of God, and in the case of poor people, children, and widows, they may administer the law fully and with justice for all.'[1]

It is easy to see that when Einhard[2] says he spent great sums in charity and sent money to the distressed even as far away as Syria and Africa, the adulating secretary may have been for once fairly accurate.

Two refugees from Britain, banished from their native land, sought an asylum with him. According to an undated letter of his, written about 793[3] to Archbishop Athilhard and Bishop Ceolvulf of Britain, he harbored these exiles for a time and then sent them to the Archbishop and Bishop asking them to intercede with King Offa in their behalf, that they might be allowed to live in their own country. Because, says he, with a lack of sophistication that seems odd in a king, he has examined them and they promise to amend their ways and purge themselves of every fault. But if his royal brother is obdurate and refuses to allow them in his kingdom, then Athilhard and Ceolvulf are to send them back to Frankland, where Charles will care for them.

'For,' he observes, 'it is better to be an outcast than to die,

---

[1] Printed by Wells at pages 246–47.
[2] *Life*, p. 26.
[3] No. 11 in von den Steinen's collection.

242

it is better to find labor in a strange land than death in one's own.'

But he believes his royal brother will be merciful and reminds him of the example of Christ. Unluckily there is no letter that gives the rest of this story, but as the two exiles are not mentioned again in the annals or elsewhere, it seems likely that Charles's appeal carried home. Most of his messages to his fellow sovereigns had that effect — after the strength of his legions had been proved.

He makes heroic efforts to stop or mitigate the banditry that goes on along the highways, the vested right of robbery to which we have before referred. Many of the Capitularies are devoted to this subject.[1] It appears that even he with all his powers was unable to extirpate this form of profitable enterprise. The most he could do was to restrict it. He established the principle that travelers need not go out of their way to be robbed, which, improbable as it may now seem, amounted to a notable concession.[2] Previously a baron with a good castle and an active band of miscreants in his employ used to insist that whosoever came within sight of his hold must journey up to it and pay tribute. The general practice of thievery on the highway continued for centuries after his time — if, indeed, it has ever been abolished. Perhaps the nobles he rebuked made response to him that they were not in business for reasons of hygiene. If so the parallel with certain modern conditions was fairly complete.

He had gifts as an organizer; that is evident from the efficiency to which he brought the Frankish legion and the care with which it was equipped and managed through the vast territories that his operations covered. One of his letters to Abbot Fulrad [3] reveals the minute attention he gave to details and so probably supplies us with the reason for his success. It was written about 804, early in the spring, and was doubtless but one copy of a circular sent to all his provincial governors. He was at that time engaged in his final

[1] Hallam, chap. IX, p. 506.   [2] *Ibid.*   [3] No. 15.

operations in Saxony and orders his troops to be ready and perfectly outfitted. It is interesting to note that in those days prelates were also sometimes military commanders.[1]

'Know ye,' begins the Capitulary to the Abbot,[2] 'that we have called our national assembly this year to meet in East Saxony at the place called Stassfurt. Therefore we command you that with your full contingent of men, all well-weaponed and with full armor, shall come on June 17 to the place I have named.' And then, his religious habit being indomitable even about such stern business as army equipment, he reminds the Abbot that the seventeenth of June is seven days before the festival of Saint John the Baptist. The soldiers are to come not only fully armed, but with all the necessary tools for warfare, all clothing, food, and all other things needful. Every man must have shield, lance, sword, dagger, bow, and a quiver full of arrows. On the wagons are to be loaded the tools, namely, hatchets, crowbars, drills, axes, mattocks, iron spades, and what else is required for field operations against the enemy. The wagons are also to carry provisions for the troops for three months, and arms and clothing for half a year. Particularly he cautions his subordinate, whatever way he and his troops may take to the assembly, that they should proceed peacefully and be careful not to disturb or displace anything as they go, except, of course, 'grass, wood, and water.' And let every leader stay close by his people lest the absence of the commander from his troops should give an opportunity for encroachments upon the residents.

A careful and thrifty soul, he overlooks nothing. 'But the present that you intend to bring us at the Assembly, send it to us by the middle of May.' In case the marching of the Abbot and his troops should fall in with that of the commander-in-chief, the commander-in-chief will be well pleased.

[1] In the Song of Roland one of the great heroes of the battle of Roncesvalles is a supposititious Archbishop Turpin of Reims, pictured as a great warrior.

[2] No. 16 in von den Steinen.

He appears next as a strangely artless and unsuspicious soul to be at the head of a great nation and contesting with minds supple in statecraft. He seems to have wanted to believe that men told him the truth and clung as long as he could to that naïve belief. To the last it was manifestly hard for him to adjust himself to the fact that men lie. He did not lie himself and probably could see no reason why any one else should lie. It was simple of him, for example, to believe the Saxons; yet again and again he took their fallacious promises for truth. It was simple of him to believe Hunold, believe Tassilo, believe Arichis, believe Irene, believe anybody that could gain an end by lying! He believed them all. They all lied to him. He believed the next no less readily. Perhaps the most singular fact about his correspondence and all the great mass of stories and legends concerning him is the absence of guile. He had a sufficiency of other weaknesses and faults, but he seems to have been without duplicity.[1] This in a man that for forty-three years [2] had the unshared control of a great empire and steered it through negotiations as well as wars seems incredible but is still true. He was perfectly willing, at one time, for the advancement of his empire, to give his daughter in marriage to the foolish Constantine and willing at another time to marry the fiend Irene. But he did not lie about things.

What seems more, he did not resort to the futilities and puerilities of the international chess board that even in his time had begun to be played in the fashion with which we are but too familiar. 'If I move here, he will move there, and then I will move there and have him mated' — he seemed to have no facility in such gaming. Whether he disdained its fripperies, as he is said to have scorned ornamental clothing, or whether his mind was not able to grasp its subtleties, no

[1] In the main, English writers have always been unfair to him. Gibbon accuses him of promising to bestow upon the Pope that tract of land in northern Italy that was never delivered, but no one ever discovered a document to this effect and later historians have conceded that the alleged gift never was made.

[2] For two years he shared the rule with his brother.

one can tell. But either way in his dealings with other nations he seemed more an antique Roman than a Dane.

We have found him in his Academy pursuing poetry and making it. Music he knew and may even have made that also — in the intervals of smiting paynim Avars. In his efforts to improve the singing in the churches, he labored like a man on the wheel. It is more than once the subject of his Capitularies and in other ways he demanded attention to his pet reform; sometimes with unexpected results.

In the Supplement to the ancient 'Annals' of Lorsch [1] appears one of these adventures. Charles when in Rome asked Pope Hadrian to help him in his laudable campaigning for better music. The Pope sent to him two of the most celebrated singers of the Roman Church, Theodor and Benedict, who had been taught after the Gregorian School. He also gave to Charles the Antiphonies that Saint Gregory had set forth in the Roman manner. One of these masters Charles sent to Metz and the other to Soissons to start schools of singing there. All the schoolmasters of all the cities of Frankland were commanded to study the Antiphonies and from them to learn how to sing.

The innovation wrought a kind of revolution in the Frankish Church. But we are told the Franks could not master the tremulous and tender tones the Romans used and their naturally rougher voices seemed to break in their throats. The teacher that went to Metz had the better success; the Metz School of Music became the foremost in the kingdom. By so much as the Roman School surpassed Metz, so much Metz surpassed all others in Frankland.

Similarly, the Roman masters instructed the Franks in the art of playing the organ.

With the musicians came the teachers of grammar and mathematics. Thus, remarks the chronicle, knowledge, science, and art were scattered broadcast over the country,

[1] In the Monk of Saint Gall, p. 13.

whereas before the time of King Charles no man had given the least heed to such things.[1]

In the same 'Annals' it is related that on one occasion when Charles was in Rome, celebrating Easter, a strife arose between singers he had brought with him in his *entourage* and singers of Saint Peter's Church as to which sang the better. The Franks maintained that their singing was the more tuneful and beautiful. The Romans declared that the Franks made a loud noise and spoiled the flow of the melody, whereas they themselves sang correctly as taught Saint Gregory. The Franks said they sang with the more feeling. The Romans said the singing of the Franks was stupid, rural, and uneducated; like the braying of beasts, said they cheerfully. The controversy waxing warm and coming to the ears of Charles, he sent for his singers and said:

'Speak frankly now and tell me, which is the better water, that in the living fountain or that in the brook that flows away from it?'

They all replied with one accord:

'The fountain, because the brook becomes contaminated and the farther it flows from the fountain the muddier it grows.'

'Then go back to the fountain of the holy Gregory,' said the King, 'since it is obvious that you have muddied the stream of the church service.'

In a Capitulary dated March 23, 789, he commanded the Roman method to be learned and sung in all the churches of the kingdom.

That dear old dreamer of dreams and anthologist of pleasing romances, the Monk of Saint Gall, tells us that the King had not proceeded far with his musical reforms when he encountered the Musicians' Union of that day. Things had gone so well with the two masters he had imported that he asked the Pope to send him more. Accordingly twelve instructors were chosen from the staff in Rome and sent over

[1] Supplement to the *Annals* of Lorsch, p. 80–81.

the Alps. But on the way they fell into talk among themselves and decided that it was not to the advantage of their
craft that its secrets should be thus scattered among barbarians.

When they arrived in Frankland, Charles received them
with honor and distributed them among the places not already supplied with masters. One of his customs was to go
about the land, particularly at times of religious festival, and
observe the state of the services, being a kind of self-appointed ecclesiastical inspector. At Christmas and Easter he
heard with satisfaction the singing at Metz and at Trèves,
but the next year when he visited the places where the twelve
had been placed, he noticed to his horror that the choirs were
singing off the key. When he had satisfied himself that this
was indeed the sad fact about all that had been taught by the
twelve, he complained to Pope Leo, who called the twelve
home and summarily punished them. Some were banished
and some were shut up in prison where they could harm no
one. But at the same time he wrote thus to Charles:

If I send you other teachers, they will behave as badly as these
because they will wish to gratify their spite upon you. But I will in
another way be at pains to fulfill your desires. Send me now from
your company two clergymen of great natural talent so that my
people shall not know they belong to you, and so, God willing, they
shall be fully instructed in the art that you so earnestly pursue.

Charles selected two priests accordingly and sent them to
Rome. In due time the Pope sent them back perfectly instructed. Charles kept one at his court to sing and to teach.
The other was begged of him by his natural son, Trogo, who
was Bishop of Metz, where he sang in the new church.[1]

As to poetry, his prose sometimes reveals a suggestive
power over figurative and imaginative language that must
have been valuable to him whenever he turned to verse-
making. In one of his letters [2] to Offa, King of Mercia, he
speaks of the divine spirit as 'a perfect and spotless dove with

[1] Monk of Saint Gall.   [2] No. 9 in von den Steinen.

248

wings of silver and body of glimmering gold,' which is a fair flight of fancy in a letter-writer that can also be so plain and direct. In a general circular [1] about vesper services, written in 783 or a little later, he says he has committed to Paulus Diaconus the work of revising and improving the service. 'He will diligently examine the words of the catholic fathers and at the same time will cull from their ample blossoms sundry flowers and from this available material wreathe a chaplet.'

Another letter to Offa [2] is half devoted to expressions of brotherly good will and exhortations to a pious life. Then he comes abruptly from religion to business and gives assurance that the merchants Offa has sent to Frankland will be protected and furthered in every way. And in case they should fall into any difficulties, let them turn at once to him or to one of his judges and they may be sure of righteous treatment, because he believes in commerce and desires to extend it. And in case any Frankish merchants encounter difficulties in England, he hopes Offa will look after them with the same diligence.

There is a priest that on his way back from Rome has fallen into some trouble and Charles bespeaks for him a fair trial and the operations of a court that shall not be too costly for him — it is odd to see the emphasis he places on this point. For, says he, 'What can be more satisfactory to us than when knowledge of Apostolic values enables us to decide a case in which the opinions of many had been irreconcilable?'

Then he reverts to business for a moment, but comes back to a moral reflection about the 'mortal treasures' that divine goodness has endowed him with, some of which he has distributed among the episcopal sees and some others he is now sending as gifts to his brother Offa 'with joy and thanksgiving to the Almighty' — an Avar sword and sword-belt, and two Syrian mantles — 'that everywhere among Christian people the divine favor may be recognized and the name

[1] No. 2.   [2] No. 10.

of Our Lord Jesus Christ be honored forever.' The connection between sword-belts and heavenly grace seems obscure to us, but must have loomed clear enough to his peculiar mentality.

A strong character — the lesions, as will be observed later, being as notable as the merits.

CHAPTER XVIII

THE HIGH–BORN FUGITIVE AND THE RIOT

A TALL man, towering not less than six feet, four inches; athletic in build, massive in the shoulder,[1] 'great-chested like a steed,' blue-eyed, tawny of hair, ruddy of countenance, with a broad, rather cheerful face; a manifestly over-vitalized man, abnormally active, incapable of fatigue, having that spirit of energy and mastership that even when it is in repose manages to overawe the timid and the quiescent — this is the portrait of Charles of the Franks, deduced from his contemporaries and from the two effigies believed to have been made of him in his lifetime. The worshipful long beard and the mattress of long red hair, once cherished as the emblems of royal state, had gone with the spineless Childeric III. This man wore in his earlier years the long mustaches of the Frank above a shaven chin. When he had passed fifty, he probably wore a full beard of moderate length.

The celebrated description of him by Einhard, so often quoted, so long taken for veritable, faded into the mythical when it was shown to be no more than a composite of five or six Roman emperors,[2] as drawn by the Einhards of their own times. But we are not obliged to follow the knee-crooking Secretary about these things. We have other authorities. The Chronicle of Saint-Denis [3] sets forth a description almost as minute and much more trustworthy. It appears from this that the continual references in legends, tales, and songs to the tall form and powerful arm of Charlemagne were justified;[4] that he had remarkable eyes, keen and eager, an affable and easy address. When Einhard says that his voice was higher

---

[1] Capefigue, p. 159.   [2] Halphen, pp. 93–94.   [3] Capefigue, p. 159.
[4] For example, Angilbert, quoted by Dr. Abel at page 31, 'Over all forth moved King Charles with his towering shoulders.'

251

and weaker than became one of so large a frame,[1] this may be accepted as probable, since the same phenomenon has been observed in others. His statement that Charlemagne was a fluent and impressive talker with a good command of language may be taken without too much reservation, for here are evidences of it throughout the Capitularies, those infallible indices of life and character.

In this powerful frame dwelt a powerful, restless, single-track mind, rather simple, yet having a peasant's shrewdness, not reflective, not given to speculation, habituated to plain dealing and plain speaking, not overdelicate in its sensibilities, and yet having a singular capacity for fine emotions. The lack of a power to weigh nicely, to consider both sides, to deliberate profoundly, must have been an advantage, in view of the work he had to do. No question as to the righteousness or the wisdom of a course could perplex such a mind. It is hard to conceive of him as beset with timidities or a time of hesitation. His government was a theocracy. He was its titular head, carrying out the divine will. How could he err? He had few objects; at them he drove with a confident tenacity that nothing could shake.[2]

That this mind so resolute was in some ways but ill tutored is laid bare in his continual efforts to make men good by legislation and imperial decrees. 'Let all men live together according to the command of God, justly and in accordance with righteous judgment,' he cries, and believes implicitly in a satisfactory result. 'Let the canons in canonical life scrupulously abstain from business and base gain. Let the nuns with diligence guard their life. Let the laity and those living in the world obey every law without fraud or deceit and in every particular live in perfect charity and peace.'

Thus he wrote many times, in season, out of season. He was of his age the champion letter-writer. Pen in hand he had no compeer. Lord Bacon might have cited him to verify the benefit of much writing. Exact he was; at least as to his

[1] *Life*, p. 32.   [2] Lucien Double, p. 3.

CHARLEMAGNE

By an unknown Dutch master of the Sixteenth Century. Now in the
Rathaus, Aachen. Photograph by Gerhard Mertens, Aachen.
Reproduction forbidden.

meaning. When aroused, he cast his thought into hard round shots.

About all things in Church and State he was a strict disciplinarian. More than once he incurred the soft reproofs of his gentle friend Alcuin because he was too rigid, and sometimes, in the good monk's view, excessively severe.[1] Again and again these letters disclose his masterful and overweening temperament. The compulsive religious fervor in him and his democratic conviction must have been for his generation an unspeakable boon. The two impulses are not really divisible. He was peasant in his democratic inclinings, but also something else. The splendid democracy of the New Testament had laid hold upon him, and bent him irresistibly into new ways. Otherwise he might have ranked among tyrants and been almost as granitic as they. Sometimes he was impatient of mere men, great or small, that lodged across his path, and, great or small, did not hesitate to rebuke them with almost ferocious energy — never forgetting that they were sinners in the sight of heaven and telling them so plainly. For example:

About the year 801, Theodulf, the learned Bishop of Orléans, who had been an honored member of the Aachen Academy, had grave cause to complain against one of his clergy.[2]

He had the priest arrested, tried, and sentenced to imprisonment.

The priest was of high birth and a powerful family. He objected to the punishment decreed upon him. Doubtless through the connivance of his keepers, he broke jail and fled to Tours, where he had many adherents of his family and where he took sanctuary in the Church of Saint Martin. There he is said to have confessed his faults, promised amendment, and asked for a safe-conduct to appear before Charlemagne and plead his case.

[1] He rebukes the King for harsh treatment of the Saxons. Mombert, p. 126.
[2] Von den Steinen, p. 97.

Meantime, Theodulf sent messengers demanding that the escaped prisoner be returned to him.

The monks of Saint Martin's were in a dilemma about this. Sanctuary for an ecclesiastical offender might still be deemed sanctuary as for anybody else. Yet there was the high authority of a bishop, presently reënforced. Their own Bishop, he of Tours, agreed with him of Orléans that the surrender must be made.

Of a sudden the whole case was raised to the dignity of a national issue by Charlemagne. He heard of the flight and sent an order that the fugitive should be given up.

Still the monks of Saint Martin's hesitated. It is conceivable that besides the law of sanctuary they were moved by the universal spirit of the guild; it was a man of their own order that had fled to them. To defy the King and Emperor was a strong step. The monks were hardly ready to take it. But they were willing to temporize.

Alcuin was there among them. He sided with his fellows and against his old friend and comrade the King. He writes that in the end it was decided to submit and to make the surrender.

But here another complication arose. The messengers from Orléans received the fugitive and were about to start homeward with him when a report flew about that on the road was a hostile force, probably of the accused man's relatives, that had formed an ambush and intended a rescue.

Thereupon, says Alcuin, 'they went away, leaving the man standing at the church door.' [1]

Alcuin ridicules the ambush story and says it was only pretended. The next day came events that make it seem of a different aspect.

Tours was invaded by a crowd of Orléanists that swarmed to the church to lay hands on the man they wanted. He flung himself upon the shrine of the blessed Saint Martin and lay there, quaking. The crowd attempted to take him thence.

[1] No. 15 in von den Steinen's collection.

The monks rallied and tried to expel the intruders. Something like a pitched battle, a thing most scandalous in the eyes of the severe Charles, took place in the very church.

At its height a vassal or retainer of the wealthy fugitive tried to defend his master. The Orléanists seized him and would have dealt hardly with him. His loud cries for help were heard on the outside. For some hours Tours had been disturbed with rumors that the men of Orléans were about to attack them. The report now ran that the Orléanists were in the church and sacking it or maybe destroying the tomb of the martyr. The whole city rushed together in a tumult.[1]

Within the church the monks succeeded in driving out the invaders. The trembling occasion of all this uproar could eat a safe supper in the refectory, but when the Orléanists reached the street, the battle was renewed with the citizens. There were hectic hours in quiet old Tours that night.

It is to a clergyman that Alcuin writes of these things. 'Of course,' he says, 'the Bishop's men have asserted many things that did not happen and exaggerated many that did. Judge, Your Reverence, if it is right for an accused person that has fled to the church to be torn thence with violence, or whether it is seemly that one that has appealed to the Emperor should not succeed in reaching him, or whether it is right that a quiet person that has confessed his sins should be robbed of all his goods, even to his shoe laces.

'To be sure, the man accused in this case has committed many sins and wicked crimes. Yet there are living priests to testify that he had made his confession before he was arrested and put into shackles and punished with the rack. Why then does the Lord Jesus say, "Condemn not that ye be not condemned"?'[2]

When all this came to the knowledge of Charles, he took his ready pen in hand and discharged a blast at the heads of the monks of Tours that must have startled them. It is to be

[1] Von den Steinen, p. 98.
[2] Alcuin's letter, printed at page 98 in von den Steinen.

noted that, utterly disagreeing with his old friend Alcuin, he still tries to protect him. The accused man in his appeal had likened himself to the Apostle Paul appealing to Cæsar from the judgment seat of Festus. It was all unlucky, that comparison. It touched Charles at two points upon which he was particularly susceptible. It involved the Bible, about which he believed he knew more than most men, and it involved a matter of church discipline, about which he believed himself the greatest living authority. The monks should have obeyed his order. The man should have been given up at once. As for the pretended analogy, he shatters that as if with one blow of his mighty fist. The cases were not in any way similar. Paul, as will be seen by reference to the holy text, had been accused by the Jews, but had not been tried nor convicted. He asked to have his case heard before Cæsar and won that right. But this priest had been tried, convicted, and was undergoing punishment, from which he had escaped, a condition totally different.[1]

Having disposed of this matter, he sternly rebukes the monks for failing to obey his instructions. They had written him a letter urging their side of the case. About the same time a letter reached him from Theodulf, giving the contrary view. He scarifies the monks again for the intemperate tone of their communication. It lacks the Christian restraint in which the Bishop wrote. Toward the end he proceeds with this specimen of unfettered speech:

You yourselves know perfectly well, you that are called members of the community of this monastery and — truthfully, let us hope — servants of God, how often your lives have been the subject of scandal, and not without reason. Often you have professed yourselves to be monks, often to be canons, often to be neither. To help you to better things and to cancel your bad reputation, we have sent you a distinguished scholar and leader whom we sought out and invited from a distant land, that with wise words and admonitions he might bring you into the right way of life, and because he was pious he might by example give you a basis for good conduct.

[1] Von den Steinen, pp. 100-01.

But deplorably, all this has gone for naught and the Devil has found in you his handy servants that he may sow discord where it is most unseemly, which is among the sages and teachers of the Church. Whereas you should have reprimanded and chastened these transgressors, you incite them to still farther offenses of malice and anger. Surely, with God's mercy, they will give no more heed to your wicked counsel.

You, however, who stand there as scorners of our commands, whether you call yourselves canons or monks, are to bring yourselves before our court according to the proclamation entrusted to these our messengers. And no matter whether your letter clears you from responsibility for the uproar and riot, you are to come nevertheless and cleanse yourselves through acceptable explanations from the disgrace of neglecting your duty.[1]

We owe so much to his letter-writing that it seems easy to overlook some slips, inconsistencies, and excesses. The habit was fixed in him; he began its practice when he and his reign were young. Doubt exists as to the date of his first Capitulary; some have believed it to be as early as 771, before he came into the undivided kingdom. It could not have been long thereafter. Like the rest, it bustles with reforms. In the interest of a better administration of justice, he wishes to have the procedure of the law courts remade. Then he passes to the state of the Church and admonishes the clergy concerning their duties and obligations, enjoining upon them due observation of the instructions of their bishops.[2] Perhaps nothing in these revelations is more significant than that he should have started so early upon such tasks. The sense of them must have been in him from the beginning.

Almost any occasion might be enough to produce a letter. About 781 a famine seems to have blighted northern Italy. Charles, arriving at that time, issued at Mantua a Capitulary to protect and rescue the poor freeholders that had been forced to sell their possessions at low prices. In the same document he strove, as so often on other occasions, to restrain the power of the nobles, to regulate and improve the

[1] All these letters are included under No. 15 in von den Steinen.
[2] Cited by Davis, p. 61.

257

administration of justice by the magistrates, to foster commerce. It throws another light upon the age to find that the same Capitulary prohibits the slave trade with the Saracens, which had grown to the proportions of a national scandal in Italy, and the trade in arms with the Greeks and the Avars,[1] which amounted to a kind of treason.

Naturally, he returns often to those prescriptive rights of the nobles that he so stubbornly combated. They give him many topics for his active pen. We could forgive much in a man that tries so persistently to side with the weak. One of these decrees or letters contains his famous eight-clause ban or prohibition, designed to this end. By its terms, these offenses are put upon equal footing:

To dishonor the Holy Church;
To act unjustly or oppressively toward widows;
To be cruel or unjust to orphans;
To deal unjustly with poor men, for these have no adequate power to defend themselves;
To carry off a free-born woman without her parents' consent;
To refuse, after having been summoned, to do military service against the enemy;
Arson;
Burglary.

For all these offenses, the penalty is the same.

We may never be done wondering that so many different impulses of reform should so persist in a man of war and booty, in no way to be advantaged by them. It is one of the strangest facts in history and ought to show man in new aspects of his complexities.

The most famous of the documents is known as the General Admonition. It was written in 798 [2] and proceeds thus:

In the reign of our Lord Jesus Christ, who ruleth forever, I, Charles, by the grace of God and favor of his mercy King and ruler of the Franks and the devoted defender and humble helper of the Holy Church, to all ranks of ecclesiastical piety and dignitaries of

---

[1] Cited by Davis, p. 62.   [2] No. 5 in von den Steinen's collection.

secular power the salutation of perpetual peace and blessedness in Christ our Lord, the God eternal.

Regarding with the peaceful consideration of a pious mind, together with our priests and counselors, the abundant clemency of Christ our King, toward us and our people, and how needful it is not only with the whole heart and mouth to show forth his praise, so that he who has conferred such great honor upon our realm may deign by his protection to preserve us and our kingdom forever; Wherefore it has pleased us to ask your ability, O pastors of the Church of Christ and leaders of his flock, most shining lights of the world, that by your watchful care and zealous admonition you strive earnestly to lead God's people to the pastures of eternal life, and to bring back the erring sheep to safety within the strong walls of the church, within the circle of your good examples and exhortations, lest the treacherous wolf, finding any outside, devour one that transgresses the canonical sanctions or goes beyond the paternal traditions of the universal councils. So by the great zeal of our devotion, admonishing and exhorting them, they must be compelled at once to remain within the paternal sanctions with a firm faith and perseverance; in which labor and zeal let your holiness most surely know that our diligence will coöperate with yours. Wherefore we have sent to you our *missi*, who by the authority of our name will with you correct all that needs correction. Moreover, we subjoin also some Capitula from the canonical institutions which seem to us most necessary.

Let no one, I ask, deem this pious admonition to be presumptuous whereby we desire to correct what is in error, to do away with what is superfluous and to strengthen that which is right, but let him receive it with a favorable and charitable disposition. For we read in the Books of the Kings how the holy Josiah, going about the kingdom given to him by God, correcting and admonishing, strove to recall the people to the worship of the true God. Not that I can make myself his equal in holiness, but that we must ever follow the example of the holy men everywhere, and, as far as we can, join in the endeavor after a good life to the praise and glory of our Lord Jesus Christ.

After this come eighty-one Capitula, being a series of particular admonitions.

First, 'that the Catholic faith may be diligently taught and preached to all the people by the bishops and presbyters, because this is the first commandment of the Lord God Almighty in the law, "Hear, O Israel, The Lord our God is one Lord; and thou shalt love the Lord thy God with all thine heart and with all thy soul, and with all thy mind, and with all thy strength."'

Next, 'that there may be peace and harmony and concord with all Christian people among bishops, abbots, counts, judges, and all people everywhere, the least as well as the greatest, because nothing is pleasing to God without peace, not even the gift of the holy oblation at the altar.'

Next, that the bishops shall diligently examine the clergy under their charge as to faith and practice and see that they well understand the mass; 'that the Psalms be properly sung according to the divisions of the verses,' that the clergy shall understand the Lord's Prayer 'and preach so as to be understood by all.' He gives particular directions as to the singing of the hymns, the priest and people to join. 'And by all means the presbyters and deacons must be told that they may not bear arms, but trust in the protection of God rather than in arms.'

He strictly enjoins upon the clergy the care of the church edifice 'that it be not accessible to dogs' nor subject to the least dishonor; 'that the vessels consecrated to God may be gathered up with great care and treated with respect by those who are worthy. Also that secular business and vain conversation be not carried on in the churches because the house of God should be a house of prayer and not a den of thieves; and that the people have minds intent upon God when they come to the solemn service of the mass, and let them not depart before the ending of the priest's benediction,' which may be deemed an illuminating commentary.

It concludes with this passage:

So, most beloved, let us with all our hearts prepare ourselves in the knowledge of the truth, that we may be able to resist those who deny the truth, and that the word of God, by the favor of Divine Grace, may increase and extend and be multiplied to the benefit of God's Holy Church, and to the salvation of our souls, and to the praise and glory of the name of our Lord Jesus Christ. Peace be to the preachers, grace to the obedient, and glory to our Lord Jesus Christ. Amen.[1]

After these appeals he could go forth and with fire and sword waste the lands of the Saxons or rejoice in the killing of many Avars. But we are to remember the spirit of the times. How often in the chronicles and annals at the end of an account of a campaign one encounters something like this!

When he had beaten the Gascons and captured the city of Thouars, King Pepin with the whole troops of Franks, under the leadership of Christ, returned home laden with plunder and spoils.[2]

And to his account of the terrible day at Verden, Einhard adds, all matter of fact:

After he had thus accomplished his revenge, the King took his way to Diedenhofen for the winter and celebrated there in his wonted manner Christmas and Easter.[3]

[1] Cited by Wells, pp. 227–31.
[2] Paulus Diaconus.   [3] *Annals*, p. 71.

CHAPTER XIX

THE IRON WILL

IN some of its phases, life at the imperial and royal court of Aachen could hardly be called austere, unless the stories afterward circulated about it did it injustice.[1] Yet there is no warrant for the assertion sometimes made [2] that it was notoriously profligate. In one sense all courts of that time were more or less profligate. When we compare that of Charlemagne with such stews of iniquity as existed at Constantinople in his own day, and had existed nearer home in still worse forms in the days of his predecessors, we are moved to humble thanks for the betterment.

One of the stories about the Charlemagne household that for centuries was diligently repeated and still occasionally returns to the printed page involved this same Einhard. According to the narrative, while he was secretary to Charlemagne he fell in love with one of the King's daughters, Emma by name, and used to visit her secretly at night. On one occasion, departing after midnight, he found that snow had fallen heavily and he was overwhelmed by the fact that his footsteps would be recorded in it as coming from the Princess's door. From this dilemma she rescued him by taking him in her arms and carrying him through the snow to a spot where his trail would arouse no suspicion and cause no scandal. But Charlemagne, who was often represented as waking when he should have slept, happened to be looking out of his window and saw these acrobatics. Whereupon the next day, instead of having Einhard beheaded, poignarded, poisoned, or banished, he married the young lovers.

Even if stressed, the fact that Charlemagne had no daugh-

[1] Dieffenbach and Vogt, p. 348.   [2] Davis, p. 238.

BRONZE STATUE OF CHARLEMAGNE MADE IN
THE CARLOVINGIAN PERIOD
Now in the Carnavalet Museum, Paris

ter Emma would probably not have discouraged the ingenious persons that invented and repeated this tale. Einhard's wife was indeed named Emma,[1] but she is well known to have been the sister of Bernhardt, Bishop of Worms.

But this story, though manifestly untrue, has in its details some significance because it again was of the order of the things that might have been. It is in keeping with what we know of the general trend of morals around the palace. The King himself set the example. Of all his defects in character his weakness for women was the most conspicuous. The sincere religious devotee in all other respects seems to have convinced himself that rules of conduct stopped short of the control of carnal impulses. Of the way in which he achieved this view he has unluckily left us no record; it would be more interesting than anything he put into his Capitularies. A fervent and manifestly honest religionist that without remorse, misgivings, or concealment lived in such a state as made a jest of a basic law of the creed he hotly embraced would be something of a psychological and moral curiosity. It is to be surmised that he found in David and Solomon a warrant for what would now be deemed his slips from a state of grace; perhaps it was not without significance that he chose David as his nickname at the Academy. But besides this, morals being so geographical, fugitive, and changing according to the age, it is easy to imagine that neither he nor his contemporaries saw any notable inconsistency in his conduct.

His adventure with Himiltrude at the beginning of his reign and the birth of her son Pepin we have recorded. After the abrupt dismissal of his first wife, Desiderata (if that was the lady's name), he married Hildegarde, the fair Alemannian, at that time little more than a girl. She bore him three sons, Charles, Pepin (first called Carloman), and Louis, and three daughters, Hrotrud, Bertha, and Gisla. When Hilde-

---

[1] After years of married life they retired from the world and entered upon lives of religious seclusion. Einhard became a priest and went to the Monastery of Seligenstadt, where he remained until his death in 840.

garde died, he was shaken with sorrow, for of all the women of his acquaintance it was she that he most loved. Yet a few months afterward he had sufficiently recovered from his bereavement to marry Fastrada, who by all accounts was neither fair nor wise, and in no respect resembled Hildegarde. She bore him two daughters, Theodorat and Hiltrude. About the same time by a mistress whose name has been lost he had a daughter named Hruohard. After the death of Fastrada, he married Liutgarde, another Alemannian princess. By her he had no children. Succeeding to her were four mistresses, who bore him, all told, three sons and two daughters. Altogether he left about eighteen children, of whom at least eight were legitimate. Vétault [1] makes a noble attempt to assert that the four alliances after the death of Liutgarde were morganatic marriages, but the thought is plainly born of the wish. Eighteen children — it will be seen that the impressive contingent since his time claiming descent from Charlemagne began to a good start. [2]

As to personal traits, we can make no question that he had in reserve a notable obstinacy. In him appeared nothing of the Napoleonic opportunism; he had no skill to watch the cracks and crannies of events, thrust in a hand and pluck forth the fruit of expectancy. His notion of policy was to forge ahead toward the single object. The war with the Saxons lasted thirty years. You do not discover in this man one sign of weariness, discouragement, or turning aside. He was like Washington, like William the Silent; his idea was to get on with the work in hand. Sometimes the Saxons wearied of the game; he did not. [3] Every year he took up the task again, often just where he had taken it up the year before. So long as the Saxons would continue to break their promises, he was there to hammer them back into a new submission. Yet

---

[1] Conf. Einhard, *Life*, pp. 27–28; Paulus Diaconus, p. 7.

[2] Nicoll, Maud Churchill, *The Descent of Phœnix Ingraham from Charlemagne, and Charlemagne's Descent from Arnoaldus, Major Domo to Clothaire II, King of the Salian Franks.*

[3] Hodgkin, pp. 110–11.

the man distinguished by this composure is the man that ordered the dreadful day of Verden when the barbarian instinct within him broke through all acquired restraint and he sated vengeance exactly after the manner of the heathen he condemned.

For all that, he must have had in his heart an instinctive leaning toward mercy and a kindness extraordinary for a ruler in his day. Einhard says so and we have much better witnesses in the records. By the law of the time, the prevailing custom, and the finding of the court, he would have been justified in putting to death Tassilo, Duke of Bavaria. Tassilo had repeatedly violated his oath of allegiance and his solemn promise, he had stirred enemies of the nation to attack it, he had himself headed a rebellion, he had made war upon his sovereign. Being tried for his offenses, he was condemned to death and Charles went out of his way to save him.

For none of his contemporaries had he profounder respect or more sincere affection than for Hadrian the Pope. When Arichis died, the unruly Lombardian Duke of Benevento, Charles was holding the Duke's son Grimoald as hostage. It would have been easy, in accordance with prevalent ethics, and deemed, indeed, commendable, to annex the Beneventan territories and allow Grimoald to whistle in his fist like Drayton's shepherd, or go shorn to a monastery. Charles had the most powerful incentives to such a course, including the prayers of his friend, the Pope. On no account, urged Hadrian, should he allow a member of the unspeakable Lombardian tribe to ascend that throne. But Charles released Grimoald and gave him his father's throne and possessions. There is no chance that policy dictated this course. Policy would have indicated annexation. It must have seemed to him the decent thing to do, and he did it, in the face of the protests of his dear friend Hadrian. Afterward he had reason to think his friend had been right.

The conquered Avars petitioned him that they might be

265

allowed to move upon some untilled land in Bavaria and make there a new start. They had deceived and betrayed him, and what they now asked would bring nearer to his capital a once dangerous and treacherous people, but he granted their request and encouraged them toward prosperity. Soon afterward they came again and asked to be allowed to have a change to the form of government to which they had been accustomed. In a conquered people what they asked was as much contrary to precedent as to Charles's own favorite notion of government by appointed representatives, but he let them have their wish.[1] They moved into the new territory and in a few generations were absorbed into the general population. If he had attempted to force upon them the Frankish system, they would in all probability have remained Avars and been driven to an enduring and perhaps perilous clannishness. It is incredible that the Jews would have retained their compact isolation of spirit if they had been decently treated.

When the Regensburg conspiracy against his life was disclosed, Charles had no punishment for his guilty son Pepin except to retire him to a monastery. If this clemency to his own kin seems nothing worth Einhard's praise, we may revert to history. Eight hundred years later there was another conspiracy against another king, and the picture of the Duke of Monmouth groveling at the feet of his uncle, the records of Sedgmoor, and the Bloody Assizes afford a startling contrast to Pepin peacefully pursuing horticulture in the monastery close. Yet the same mind that could be compassionate in one case could be fiercely cruel in another. The leaders of the Regensburg plot were punished with a merciless severity. According to accepted tradition, the fate of one of them was a notable example of vengeance. The region of which he was the titular lord was hilly. The highest of all the hills was chosen; on it was erected the highest gallows that had been seen in those parts, and the nobleman was hanged thereon.

[1] Hodgkin, p. 163.

It might be urged in palliation [1] that the King on a former and similar occasion had been much more lenient. In 785 a conspiracy had been organized by the Thuringian Count Hardrad, aiming to kill Charles and seize the throne. If we can place any dependence on Einhard, only three of the plotters lost their lives, and these only because when they were arrested they drew their swords and tried to kill the officers. [2] It is conceivable that Charles attributed the second conspiracy to his lenity about the first.

We may regret that we have not more information about this first episode. Einhard attributes the cause of the revolt to Queen Fastrada, whom he bitterly disliked, and to whom he charges most of the disastrous events of the time. There is a story to the effect that the real beginning of the difficulty was romantic. A Frankish knight had made suit to the daughter of a Thuringian count, had won her affections, and was betrothed to her. When the appointed day came, the young woman's father suddenly refused to allow the wedding. Thereupon trouble broke between the two factions. A much likelier surmise is that the revolt merely expressed the restless and untamable spirit of the age. [3]

The case of a religious zealot that is not also a religious fanatic would be enough to arrest our attention at any time. Charles was the grandson of The Hammer of Tours; he had fought often against Mohammedans; for years they harried his coasts and attacked his cities. Yet he maintained a warm and genuine friendship with Haroun-al-Rashid, the great Caliph of Bagdad, exchanged with him presents and affectionate greetings, manifestly viewed him with respect. [4] He must have had, too, a certain amplitude of soul in regard to matters more nearly personal. Paulus Diaconus, whom he induced to join his staff of teachers at Aachen, was a Lombard. His brother had been an active supporter of King

[1] Davis, p. 148.   [2] Conf. Davis, p. 135.
[3] Outlined by Hodgkin, p. 132.
[4] Einhard, *Life*, p. 24; Davis, pp. 198, 230–31.

Desiderius and was at one time a prisoner in the hands of Charles. Paulus was a worthy pedagogue, but a poor diplomat. He did not conceal at the court of the Franks that he was an ardent Lombard partisan. It is possible, also, that in the colder air of Aachen he mourned the loss of the balmy climate of Italy. In a short time his predilections became known, and Sir Superservice, then as always active about the powerful, goes headlong to Charles with the information that this imported tutor of his is a traitor. How a traitor? Why, he professes himself a loyal subject to Desiderius, arch-enemy of the Franks, and deserves the penalty for high treason, which in that gentle day might be blinding, followed by the cutting off of the hands, or the like simple remedies.

When the significance of this suggestion made its way into the royal mind, the King shook with indignation.

'What!' he cried aloud, 'shall I do thus to one that is an excellent poet and historian? God forbid!'

Peter of Pisa, the great teacher, and Paul Warnefrid, who was a poet, were likewise loyal Lombardians, but lived long at the Aachen court, undisturbed about their allegiance.[1] Both returned in peace to Lombardy when their ministrations at Aachen were done. Theodulf, the other favorite poet in the Academy, was a Goth from Spain. The Spanish Goths, as we have seen, had no love for the Frankish establishment, but Theodulf was welcomed none the less. In the end he was elevated to the Bishopric of Orléans, which seems to show that merit and accomplishments must have weighed much and nationality little.

At the Mayfield or national assembly, the Emperor-King was accustomed to go about dressed not otherwise than any other well-to-do Frank, and with no sign of his station except a staff tipped with gold. While he was absent at the Avar war, a certain bishop took refuge at Aachen, where he was courteously entertained by Queen Hildegarde. This made him so arrogant that he assumed the airs of royalty and,

[1] Vétault, p. 427.

268

taking the King's gold-tipped staff, appeared in public with it, using it as a bishop's crozier. When the King returned, horror-stricken lackeys told him of this performance. Instead of being affronted, he made light of it and sent the Bishop away with gifts.[1]

He took himself, his work, and what he believed to be his mission seriously, but he had a sense of humor, sometimes coarse, sometimes grim, but probably relishable by the not too dainty taste of the Franks.[2]

A revered old bishop having died, Charles appointed to the vacant see a rather youngish but promising clergyman. After the investiture, the new Bishop ordered his horse to be brought up. The groom for some reason was slow in obeying the order, and the new prelate lost his temper in rather unpriestly fashion. When at last the horse appeared, the fuming Bishop impatiently leaped upon it with such haste that he cleared the saddle and fell on the other side. Charles, who was observing all this, said:

'Good man, you are so quick and nimble, so active and swift-footed, that since, as you know, the kingdom is now beset with alarms of war on all sides and I need all men of such swift action, you will stay with me and go along with the troops, sharing our toils and actions so long as you are able to mount a horse as quickly as you can now.'[3]

On an occasion when he was journeying through the kingdom, he stopped of a Sunday at a church in one of the cities, and as usual took careful note of the quality of the singing. While the service was going on, an itinerant priest entered the church and joined the ecclesiastics in the chancel. He must have been from the country and innocent of the musical reforms that Charles had so diligently introduced, for he stood open-mouthed and took no part in the singing. The choir-master noticed him thus dumb in the tuneful throng, and smote him with his baton to move him to sing. The poor

[1] Monk of Saint Gall, p. 21.   [2] Davis, p. 244.
[3] Monk of Saint Gall, pp. 10–11.

priest was helplessly embarrassed, not knowing what to do, but to save himself from another visit of the baton, he stood opening and closing his mouth but making no sound.

No one else noticed this but Charlemagne. When the service was over, he had the priest brought before him.

'Let me thank you, good man, for your singing this morning,' said the ironical King; and then added, 'and also for your hard labor.' But the narrative adds that he salved the taunt with a piece of money.[1]

In humor his fancy must have been sardonic. After his dear friend Alcuin had retired to the monastery at Tours, they continued to correspond on terms of intimacy and affection. In one of his letters Alcuin attempts to show calculations by which the lunar and solar years could be brought into harmony. The King discovers a slip in the calculations. He turns them over to some of the boys that have been taught in the court school at Aachen, and they discover the same error. Then the King forwards their report to the learned professor with sarcastic comments about the pupils that have outrun their master, and Alcuin replies in the same spirit acknowledging his blunder. It is a mild order of repartee and wit, but we are to remind ourselves of the age. We are in luck to find anybody smiling at anything — or having anything to smile at! It appears also that the mind that ordered great armies and colossal operations over wide areas had queer little fancies for metrical trifles rather beneath the dignity of poor puns. There is extant verse in which riddles are exchanged between Charles and Paulus Diaconus, or between Charles and another, that would unspeakably bore a primary schoolboy of to-day.[2]

One of the favorite narratives drawn from the Monk of Saint Gall is The Bishop and the Mouse.

'I have told you how the glorious Charles elevated the humble,' says the Monk. 'I will now tell you how he humbled the proud.' There was a certain bishop in the kingdom that,

[1] Monk of Saint Gall, pp. 11–12.   [2] Hodgkin, pp. 218–19.

although immensely rich, would never give anything to the poor, but spent great sums upon luxury and his selfish pleasures. This disgusted the King, one of whose commonest preachments was charity. He sent for an itinerant merchant of his acquaintance and the Jewish persuasion, with whom he arranged a trick upon the Bishop.

Before long the merchant appeared at the episcopal palace with what he declared was the greatest curiosity of the age, a colored mouse that at great expense he had secured in Palestine.

The Bishop instantly demanded to see this wonder, and when it was produced, wished to possess it. He offered three silver pounds.

The merchant burst forth into wrathful exclamations.

'What! Only three pounds! I had rather throw my treasure into the sea.'

'Ten pounds,' said the Bishop.

The merchant waxed in indignation. 'O God of Abraham!' he cried, 'let me not lose my labor and the cost of the carriage of this wonder!'

The Bishop, now more than ever determined to have the wonderful thing, paid for it a bushel of silver. The merchant took the price to Charles, who called a conference of his bishops.

When all were assembled, he deposited the silver in the midst of them and said: 'Look you, what one of you has paid for a painted mouse!' and while the foolish Bishop sat scarlet-faced with confusion, he told the story and made it a text for a homily on apostolic poverty and the duty of the clergy to the poor.

Although he was at times as hard as granite, and could be as correspondingly cruel, he seems to have been ordinarily of a strong inclination against the blood-thirst that marked the men of the Clovian order. So, at least, the tales and legends represent him. It seems that he slept badly, which was natural enough in one of his peculiarly restless disposition, and his custom was to arise at night and go roaming about the camp. One night he found two young men, the sons of counts, that had been assigned to sentry duty, fast asleep on the ground, and, what was still worse to his mind, they were plainly drunk. He did not waken them, but the next day summoned his officers to a council.

'What shall that man deserve,' he asked, 'that betrays the Franks to their enemies?'

'Death!' shouted the assembly with one breath, which, of course, he had known would be the response. He then related what he had discovered the night before, and set the young men before them. Unanimously the council pronounced the mortal sentence upon sentries asleep at their posts, but we are told that Charles did not allow the young men to be put to death. He gave them instead 'harsh words,' and let them go.

The same mind that could thus bend to the side of mercy the ruthless discipline of war devised the savage Saxon Capitularies of 782. Relentless in 782, it was conspicuously mild and merciful in 797. These contrasts seem to shiver the image of a man all congruous and one-piece, but that perhaps is a loss we can bear with equanimity.

When into these indices, important or trivial, we fit the great pivotal fact that in an age half mad with lust for war he seems to have been something of a pacifist, we can see that the man is worth more than ordinary regard. Rather than have a war with the King of the Lombards, he offered an indemnity in a cause that was none of his. In the face of that singular gesture his incontinence, his obstinacy, and even his occasional cruelties are all outweighed. The founder of the public school system, the originator of the modern state, was also one of the earliest practical advocates of arbitration. His Frankish hose and tunic were of the ninth century, but the spirit within him was essentially of our own day.

His dogged tenacity of purpose went far beyond mere battle-winning, and included his resolution to rescue learn-

272

ing. It recurs continually in these letters. At some time after the year 780, but probably not long after, he sent out the first of his circular appeals to the clergy to use their utmost efforts to further education. He says:

> For we desire you to be, as it is fitting soldiers of the Church should be, decent in mind, learned in discourse, chaste in conduct, and eloquent in speech, so that whosoever shall seek to see you, out of reverence for God or your reputation for holy conduct, just as he is edified by your appearance may also be instructed by your wisdom, which he has learned from your reading or singing, and may go away joyfully, giving thanks to omnipotent God.[1]

He must have had great capacity for friendship and have been to his friends loyal and generous. Einhard says that he was deeply attached to Hadrian, and when the news came of the death of the great Pontiff, Charles wept as bitterly as if he had lost his dearest brother.[2] For Paulus Diaconus, Lombardian and all, he had an abiding affection,[3] while his twin-brother attachment for Alcuin is one of the idyls of the times. The few letters that remain of their correspondence show a deep-seated affection on both sides. 'My dearest David' and 'my dearest Albinus' are not with them perfunctory greetings. The King has laid aside all pomp and circumstance to be simple and natural with his good comrade.[4] Since David and Jonathan there has been no better story of the kind, and I do not now recall another instance of a man in Charlemagne's position, or anything like it, that could show so simple and sincere a spirit, as far from condescension as from vulgarity, always fine, always genuine.

That he was of a terrific and abnormal activity is obvious. The celerity of his excursions from one part of the empire to another, performed over atrocious roads and sometimes in

---

[1] From *Translations and Reprints from the Original Sources of European History*, published by the University of Pennsylvania, vol. 8, Series for 1899, pp. 12-13.

[2] Einhard, *Life*, p. 29.   [3] Hodgkin, p. 219.

[4] 'Always, however, the intercourse is friendly, sincere, elevating. The King does not patronize, and the deacon does not cringe. One cannot but feel in reading these letters that both men were made to be loved.' Hodgkin, p. 191.

bad weather, comes near the mysterious. Military experts have generally been unable to discern how he managed it with the facilities at his disposal. The alertness of his physical movements was only a reflex of his restless mind. In swift succession he could map a summer's campaign against the Saxons or the Avars, issue new regulations for the government of counts and bishops, write a letter rebuking a negligent officer, arrange for the founding of a new school, caution a sexton against allowing the least dirt or defilement to appear in a church,[1] count the eggs from his farm, catalogue with a housewife's care every plant in his garden, and compute the number of soldiers that ought to be furnished by a duchy, march, or county.

The Capitularies reveal him with the true reforming mind, dissatisfied with things as he found them, resolved to better them, and leaving most of them stamped with no more than his protest. Yet about many of his schemes of reform he was far from futile. He liked agriculture and operated a farm of his own. The art in general he found reduced to its most primitive terms, except where the beneficent monks had rescued it and labored it to grow. He undertook to spread through the kingdom the knowledge and skill theretofore confined to the monasteries. Not long afterward there came upon Europe a great revival of agriculture and a notable improvement in its methods. A learned German, Herr Imana-Sternegg, in an elaborate treatise [2] on this subject, is satisfied that all of this revival was due to the efforts of Charlemagne, whom he hails as the father of modern farming and the world's agricultural revolutionist. Another learned German, Herr Dopsch, in another elaborate treatise,[3] holds that Herr Imana-Sternegg is in error and the revival came from other sources and influences. As to this, no one will ever know definitely. But a ruler that in the eighth century wanted

[1] Einhard, *Life*, p. 35.
[2] *Deutsche Wirtschaffgeschichte*, published in Leipsic in 1879.
[3] *Die Wirtschafftsentwicklung der Karlingerperiode.*

his subjects to be good farmers and tried to make them so is enough of a wonder even if he failed. Charlemagne's interest is attested by his Capitularies devoted to the subject.

But Herr Dopsch, who thinks his influence upon agriculture was small, concedes that as to commerce he was the pioneer of the Middle Ages and the world is indebted to him for invaluable improvements in the manner and ways of exchange. In this he shows us again a psychological phenomenon; a simple, straight-working, fore-and-aft mind that could be so diverse in its viewpoints. He reformed the monetary system and introduced a universal coinage so that men from Metz could trade with men from Venice without going to the money-changer. Ten centuries ahead of the French National Assembly, he tried to reform the names of the months, which struck him as absurd. Why should Christian nations celebrate in their calendars heathen deities and Roman emperors? He devised new names for all the months, names based upon the characteristics of the season. This failed to last beyond his own day. He tried to better the nomenclature about the winds, giving them twelve names instead of four. This was a worse failure than the other.

When he became king he found each province in his dominion governed by its own set of laws, so to call them. Every wild tribe coming down from the woods brought its own customs, and these, when they had been softened in different degrees by contact with the irrepressible genius of Roman culture, took on the functions of law.[1] But such customs widely differed. Often the jungle inheritances were not easily sloughed off.[2] What was a crime in one province was nothing in another; recognized rights here were not known there. Charlemagne did not see so far as to a codification such as Napoleon and Justinian effected, but he purposed to reduce the laws to writing and reform the general features of the customs [3] throughout the kingdom so that a man need no

[1] Adams, *Civilization During the Middle Ages*, p. 14.
[2] Hallam, chap. IX, p. 487.   [3] Einhard, *Life*, p. 37.

longer be seized in one province for an offense that was no offense in another. But even in this he was chiefly defeated. The average administrative mind of his day could grasp neither the necessity for such a reform nor the way to bring it about.

But he did succeed in bettering the judicial proceeding, wresting it, doubtless, from the inertia that drags at the skirts of every reformer. The Franks, Lombards, and Saxons had a system by which every ten families had, or were supposed to have, a magistrate of their own to settle their differences and determine their causes. Above these were segregations of one hundred families each, with a still higher judicial officer. But the proceedings before these magistrates were irregular, unchecked, and leading to grave abuses. Charlemagne took from the hands of these irresponsible and arbitrary courts the determination of all causes in which life, liberty, lands, or servants were involved. In all such cases the count or governor of the district was made the judge, and even in cases still left in the jurisdiction of the lower courts an appeal was now possible.

To check the counts and prevent any abuse of their power, he introduced what were called *scabini*, who were jurors chosen by the people and sitting in the cases brought before the counts. Still more, the counts were under the close observation of those ever-moving inspectors, the *Missi Regii*, who had the power to dismiss any magistrate on proved charges of wrongdoing and must have exercised a great restraining hand upon nobles and placemen.[1] Finally, there was a universal right of appeal to the court of the King, and to the King himself.

The Capitularies tell the story. In 802 he sent out one of a general nature for the instruction, or maybe for the restraining, of the *Missi*, and says, speaking of himself in the third person:

[1] Hallam, chap. I, Part. I, p. 31.

276

Where anything that is not right and just has been enacted in the law, he has ordered them to inquire into this most diligently, and to inform him of it; he desires, God granting, to reform it. And let no man, through his cleverness or astuteness, dare to oppose or thwart the written law, as many are wont to do or the judicial sentence passed upon him, or do injury to the church of God or the poor, or the widows or the wards or any Christian. But all shall live entirely in accordance with God's precept, justly and under a just rule, and each shall be admonished to live in harmony with his fellows in his business or profession.[1]

After the passing of Charlemagne, the rising tide of feudalism and the increasing arrogance of the nobles erased all these great improvements and left the state of the poor apparently as hopeless as it had been before his day. But here as in so many other instances the reversion was only temporary (although it lasted longer than usual), and the curious can see in the system of checks, balances, and appeals instituted by Charlemagne the germs of the modern democratic systems by which justice is sought for all on even terms. It is plain enough that this was his conviction and desire, but here, as elsewhere, his skill to see was better than his way to perform.

Eleven centuries of commentators have held it a reproach to him that the physical empire he founded began to dissolve with his last breath and continued to break into fragments until little was left of it but a name and a memory. In this respect it differed in no way from all other physical empires that have ever existed or ever will exist. It is the fate of such concoctions; with toil and bloodshed, and usually with lies and hypocrisies, they are put together that they may fall apart in the eyes of all men. But the real empire of Charlemagne was not physical; it was spiritual, and still endures. His real service to civilization was not that he brought many separate tribes to acknowledge one domination; it went far beyond any such trivial and negligible triumphs.

Politically, he remade Europe by restoring to it, or devising

[1] Reprinted by Hodgkin at page 244.

for it, the ordered state, the conception of a responsible government, and the conception of government as existing for the benefit of the governed.[1] It is not too much to say that the state as we know it originated with him. Freytag and von den Steinen may be justified when they aver there is not a nation in Europe to-day that cannot trace back its roots to the policy and sagacity of Charlemagne.

Culturally, he conceived the public school, saw its immense importance to the state, introduced into a barbarian society its first notion of intellectual pursuits, started the new and composite European mind upon the road of intellectual development it has traveled ever since.

Sociologically, he, first among rulers and statesmen, suggested practically that the strength of a nation is the strength of its masses and the welfare of a nation is the welfare of its least fortunate.

[1] Hodgkin, pp. 243–50.

CHAPTER XX

THE LAST SCENES

For a brief but joyous period after that coronation at Rome, he and the conglomerate of wild men, wilder men, and half-wild men he governed had something that for them almost approximated peace. Except in name the new empire was not different from the old kingdom, nor the Emperor of the West from the King of the Franks. No territory went with the revived name, but an immense addition of prestige and power, with a new asset of security for the unfortunate generality. Charles might appropriately have taken up his residence in Rome and so refurbished with the galvanized title certain splendors long vanished but not forgotten. Instead, he went back to Aachen and the round of life he had led there, the Academy, the making of Capitularies, the dreams of reform, the simple dress, and the steady plodding after the old objects — with one that was new.

He had now to consider seriously whether what had been gained for his faith and his notions of progress could be held.

Among his distinctions from the general run of unflinching conquerors and empire-builders is this, that while, as we have noted, he took himself seriously as they always do, it was himself in relation to what he thought was his job and not himself in relation to the world and its spot-light. He seems to have had about as little of illusion as it is possible for a successful man to have and sunned not himself too much in the rays of his own glory. The one fact that from the beginning of his career he shunned ceremony, display, and parade is enough. We are not well accustomed in history to a shrinking Tamerlane.

His Waterloo came in segments and at different times, but

inevitably, as always. For one thing there was now falling upon him and all his works and all of civilization in Europe the shadow running before the next great disruptive influence that was to put to the test all that he had done. The Norsemen, the fierce, hardy, resolute people of Scandinavia, were threatening the Empire. About this time they were moving from their wooded islands to form the alliance we have mentioned with the tribes of the Northern Slavs, just south of them. Some of the aspects of this union must have been disquieting to anybody that knew the character of the allies. It appears that repeatedly they drove Charlemagne from his favorite pursuits, and when we record the failure of some of his pet reforms, we ought also to remember the gathering troubles that assailed him.

There is a foolish story told by the Monk of Saint Gall,[1] repeated by many commentators and perpetuated in a historical painting, that Charles being at one of his Mediterranean seaports saw the peculiar ships of the Norsemen passing on one of their raids. His companions took them to be merchantmen.

That Charles had the supernatural powers of a seer is one of the petted fantasies of the excellent Monk; so he makes his hero cry out:

'Alas! they are no merchantmen,' and he sheds tears.

His companions ask why he weeps, and he says:

'Alas! how much injury they will work to my successors and my successors' subjects!'

At that moment the Saracen corsairs were harassing the Mediterranean shores and the Norsemen were busy along the North Sea. If the honest Monk's story is true, therefore, Charles at Narbonne, south of France, saw the Norsemen ravaging Friesland — 'to the great scandal of the Emperor and the great astonishment of modern historians,' remarks Professor Halphen.[2]

More than a miraculous television was needed in this case.

[1] At page 71.   [2] *Études*, etc., p. 127.

After so many years and so much bloodshed, the Saxons had been beaten into quiescence and loyalty, but beyond the Saxons were the Danes, the first of these Norse tribes, habituated to a practice of annual invasion and pillage of the northern Saxon lands. By land or by sea, pillage was their vocation, highly developed by experience and careful attention. By sea they went in long, dragon-beaked pirate ships, the fashion and fame of which seem to have filled landsmen with a peculiar terror.[1] In repeated visits they harried the coast as far south as Brittany.

They had for ruler one Godofrid,[2] the perfect ideal of a viking, savage, resourceful, bold as a lion and nimble as a monkey. He had gifts for statecraft as well as for plunder. He knitted an alliance to the south of him with the Slavonic tribe known as the Wiltzes, whom we have previously encountered as trouble-makers and border raiders of the first class. Another Slavonic tribe in that region called the Abodrites had an alliance with the Franks. The Duke of the Abodrites was one Thrasko.

In 808 down came the Danes upon the Abodrites and captured an Abodrite chieftain named Godelaib,[3] whom they hanged on the spot before proceeding to overrun and oppress the adjacent territory.

Thrasko came to the scene with all his forces, and war ensued of the kind we sometimes read about in books on Zulus and Red Indians, the kind of war that is prosecuted with a consuming frenzy until one tribe or the other or both become extinct. Many battles were fought, with varying success, but one uniform result of great slaughter on both sides. At last out of the red mists the Danes emerged essentially victorious.

---

[1] Not always. It is related that in 812 a fleet of these marauders landed upon what is called in the chronicles 'the Scotch Island of Ireland,' with thought to do there the usual plundering and burning. But the natives, instead of fleeing before them, gave them battle, killed many, and drove the rest back to their ships, in which they made a swift return home. Einhard, *Annals*, p. 124.

[2] Monk of Saint Gall, p. 70; Vétault, p. 472.

[3] Einhard, *Annals*, pp. 115–17; Vétault, p. 472.

They drove Duke Thrasko and the remnant of his forces southward and then took their ease while they heaped up the plunder.

Thrasko appealed to Charles for help. The eldest son of the Emperor bore his name and was supposed to repeat his virtues. He was now dispatched at the head of a punitive expedition. The trained Frankish warriors had no great difficulty in cutting up the Danish line [1] wherever it could be found, but the case was much as it had been with the Saxons thirty years before. The Danes would be beaten in the field, vanish from sight into the woods and caves, and come out to kill, burn, and rob, whenever the occasion offered.

This, for an unexpected reason, did not endure long. King Godofrid of the Danes saw that at the moment he was hopelessly overmatched. Of a sudden he marched boldly southward, met a Frankish detachment, and professed a desire for peace and an interview with the Emperor. A curious and dramatic scene followed. [2] Charles on hearing the welcome news started from Aachen and made a swift journey to the frontier. At Baden Hiot, Holstein, he met Godofrid face to face and a conversation followed. Godofrid protested that he had not made the war nor desired it; what his heart was set upon was peace. All he wanted now was an amicable arrangement by which Danes, Abodrites, and aught else might live without blood-letting.

No doubt the Emperor heard with joy these protestations and responded to them. A treaty was arranged. Duke Thrasko of the Abodrites was induced to return to his country under a promise of security and the war seemed ended. Charles went back to his Academy and the bulk of the Frankish forces withdrew southward.

The rest of the story is like an old saga. Thrasko had given his son as a hostage into the keeping of Godofrid. Despite this fact and his promises, he suddenly invaded the land of the Wiltzes, allies of the Danes, 'wasted it with fire and

[1] Einhard, *Annals*, pp. 115, 118, 120.　　　　[2] Hodgkin, p. 209.

CHARLEMAGNE SURRENDERS THE CROWN TO HIS SON LOUIS THE PIOUS

Mural painting by Rethel in the Rathaus, Aachen

sword,' says the chronicle, 'and returned home laden with booty.'[1]

Then Godofrid sent an agent or hired assassin to Rerik, the Abodrites' capital. In the market-place he caught Duke Thrasko off his guard and stabbed him to death.[2]

This was the signal. At once the Danes, disregarding the treaty, returned upon the Abodrite country, seized and possessed it, and Godofrid launched for the southlands the greatest viking expedition that had so far left Scandinavia. Two hundred long ships comprised this armada. He captured Rerik and burned it. He sailed to Friesland, defeated its people, took possession of their country, looted it, laid tribute upon it, and threatened the regions to the south. According to the 'Annals'[3] of Metz, he boasted that this time he would drive the Franks beyond the Rhine, master all the country north of it, restore the old religion, and shut up Charles in Aachen itself.

At this news, which in view of his experiences could hardly have seemed novel to Charles, he roused himself once more from his peaceful pursuits in the Academy. All the old-time swiftness and sureness he manifested now. He gave orders for the building of a great fleet to annihilate the Danes upon the sea, a great fortress to overawe them on land, and in person he led the forces that were to combat them. Before he could carry out his plans, the situation underwent one of those kaleidoscopic changes that continually enliven the story of the Middle Ages. For the time being, the whole Danish menace collapsed. Godofrid paid in kind the penalty for his murder of Thrasko. On board his flagship he was assassinated by one of his own bandits.

The emotional and superstitious Danes instantly abandoned their expedition and returned home.[4] King Hemming, Godofrid's successor, was weak and short-lived. On his death there were two claimants for the throne, Sigifrid, who was

---

[1] Einhard, *Annals*, p. 117.   [2] *Ibid.*, p. 118.
[3] Cited by Vétault, p. 478.   [4] Einhard, *Annals*, p. 123.

Godofrid's nephew, and Anulo, nephew of a former king. Civil war followed. For some years the ferocious vikings were chiefly engaged in expending their ferocity upon one another. Sigifrid and Anulo arranged a combat. Each slew the other. The war went on. At last the party of Anulo had the best of it and placed his brothers Heriolo and Reginfrid on the throne.

But this did not end the strife. The defeated party continued to fight until, says the chronicle, 10,740 men had fallen in one battle.[1] Europe had a respite from the Norse peril, but it was to hear again from the dragon-beaked ships and the cow-horned marauders.

This was the last campaign of Charlemagne.

The blows now fell upon him in steady succession. The Moors continually attacked his southern coasts, his generals were not always successful in beating them off. Two of his sons, Charles, the first-born, Pepin the second, had proved on the field and otherwise their capacity and their gravity of character. Pepin, who had been operating with an army in an attempt to chasten Venice, contracted a fever there and died in July, 810. Hrotrud, the Emperor's oldest daughter, died in June of that year,[2] his eldest son Charles in December of the next year. In 806 he had outlined the division of his domain among his three sons, Charles, Pepin, and Louis. Only Louis was now left to inherit him, and the father, being so keen of eye and sure of judgment, could hardly have failed to discern the weakness of Louis's character.

For some time the health of Charlemagne had been failing, although he had seemed so strong. Because of his iron constitution and his temperate habits he had long passed the average span of life in his times, but he felt death drawing near. He settled the succession of the Empire upon his son, known in history as Louis the Pious, and he made his will,

[1] Einhard, *Annals*, p. 123.

[2] Hrotrud had been engaged to Constantine of the East. She never married but left a son that was afterward the Abbot of Saint Denis. Hodgkin, p. 227.

liberally providing for the poor, with minute instructions about the use to be made of his estates. In September, 813, feeling his infirmities growing upon him, he formally abdicated, and Louis took charge of the government.[1]

All his life his favorite pastime had been hunting. It was the end of him. In the midst of winter he went upon a hunting expedition in the forest of Ardennes and suffered an attack of gout. He returned to Aachen and added to the gout a severe cold. Physicians he scorned, partly because they prescribed a diet he liked not.[2] Fever set in, pleurisy developed. He had long believed that for all human ailments the sovereign medication was fasting. He applied it now and his physical strength could not withstand the ordeal. He felt himself failing and sent for his chaplain.

The end was worthy of the faith he had professed. In the evening he made his confession, partook of the sacrament, and listened to the exhortations of his spiritual adviser. The next morning, Saturday, January 28, 814, he was much weaker. About nine o'clock he roused himself, with his right hand made the sign of the cross, folded his hands upon his breast, and slipped gently out.[3] He had almost reached the age of seventy-two years.

He was buried [4] with great ceremony in the minster church. of Aachen, the building of which had been one of the achievements of his later years, the eight-sided Roman basilica that in 804 Pope Leo himself had come to consecrate.[5]

All the world rang with the news of the passing of this great figure. No other man for centuries before or after him filled so large a space in human affairs. Great as he really was, fiction, perfervid imagination, and the adulators speedily made him to appear much greater. To his renown a fortunate combina-

[1] Einhard, *Annals*, p. 125. The division of the Empire is to be found at pages 107–11.

[2] Einhard, *Life*, p. 39.

[3] Wells, p. 299; Einhard, *Annals*, p. 127.

[4] Einhard, *Life*, p. 32. *Vide* Appendix B for this strange story.

[5] Einhard, *Annals*, p. 106.

285

tion of physical, mental, and moral endowments contributed. The reports of his great strength, tall form, piercing eyes, inimitable courage, appealed powerfully to the common understanding; and the more thoughtful among men honored him because into the riotous tangle of affairs as he found them he had introduced moderation and a desire for justice. Such men spoke of his tolerant spirit, his innovations that at least looked toward progress, the novelty of his purpose to be of use, and his comparative indifference to his own glory.

Of one other quality he possessed enough to outshine both extravagant eulogy and subtle detraction. Even his enemies admitted that he had loved the truth. Some of them did more than admit the unclouded candor of his walk; they praised it. The Saracens mourned him. The Saxons, who for a generation had struggled against him, testified spontaneously to his honesty as to his prowess. 'The best man on earth and the bravest,' they said, 'was Charles. Truth and good faith he established and kept.' Most eloquent of all was the tribute that came from another paynim source. 'He has passed, the universal father,' they said, and lamented him as if he had been one of their own.[1]

Most of the reforms he tried to bring about failed with him. Those that remained have persisted, with always widening influence, to this day. Appraising his career at this distance and impartially, no wonder appears that he stumbled, took sometimes the wrong path, was inconsistent like any other mortal man, reverted at intervals to the standards of his ancestors, was dazzled with the false lights of empire, contended in vain against the rapacity, cruelty, and bestiality that surged around him. In all ways he was human. He worked by wit and not by witchcraft. But the real wonder, surpassing everything else in his story, moving the most indifferent to a kind of awe, and having no satisfactory explanation

[1] Monk Ademar of Chabannes, cited by Theodor Lindner, *Die Fabel von der Bestattung Karls des Grosses*, p. 8.

THE FIRST SARCOPHAGUS OF CHARLEMAGNE

An old marble brought by him from Italy. The relief represents
the rape of Proserpina

PERMANENT SARCOPHAGUS OF CHARLEMAGNE

short of the providential, is that out of the shambles and sanguinary muck heaps of the eighth century should have come a man so clear of spirit and so curiously well equipped to do for civilization the service it most needed.

THE END

APPENDICES

A. A CHARLEMAGNE CHRONOLOGY

A.D.

481   Clovis King of the Salian Franks.
496   Clovis baptized.
511   Death of Clovis.
511--690 Slow decline and ruin of the Merovingian line; rise of the mayors of the palace.
568   Lombards invade and conquer northern Italy.
614   Pepin of Landon Mayor of the Austrasian Palace.
690   Pepin of Heristal takes charge.
717   Charles Martel, illegitimate son of Pepin, becomes Mayor.
732   Battle of Tours; defeat of the Saracen invasion.
741   Pepin the Short becomes Mayor.
742   Birth of Charlemagne, April 2, although this date is not without question.
751   Deposition of Childeric III, crowning of Pepin the Short as King of the Franks. Birth of Carloman, Charlemagne's brother.
768   Death of Pepin the Short; accession of Charles and Carloman.
769   War with Aquitania.
770   Charles married to Desiderata, daughter of the King of Lombardy.
771   Death of Carloman; Desiderata sent home. Charles sole ruler of the Franks.
772   First Saxon war; destruction of the Irminsul. Hadrian becomes Pope.
773   War with Lombardy; end of the Lombard line. Charles's first visit to Rome.
774   New outbreak of the Saxons.
775--776 Saxon uprising.
777   Saxons apparently subdued; peace established.
778   Expedition to Spain; Roncesvalles. New Saxon uprising headed by Widukind.
779   Defeat of the Saxons.
780   Defeat of the Saxons; organization of the Saxon territory.
781   Second visit to Rome. Arrival of Alcuin.
782   Uprising of Saxons and Sorbs. Defeat at Süntel. The terrible day of Verden.
783   Uprising of the Saxons; battles of Detmold and the Hase. Death of Hildegarde; marriage with Fastrada.

289

784	Uprising of the Saxons and Frisians. Summer and winter campaigns.
785	Final defeat and surrender of Widukind. Thuringian conspiracy.
786	Peace. In the autumn to Italy.
787	Third visit to Rome. Expedition against Benevento. Suppression of Tassilo of Bavaria.
788	Annexation of Bavaria. Defeat of Irene's invasion. Trouble begins with the Avars.
789	War with the Wiltzes.
790	Peace.
791	Expedition against the Avars.
792	Conspiracy at Regensburg. New uprising of the Saxons.
793	Revolt of the Saxons. Attempt to build the Rhine–Danube canal.
794	Defeat of the Saxons. Death of Fastrada. Marriage with Liutgarde.
795	First Avar ring pierced. Death of Pope Hadrian. Leo III becomes Pope.
796	Expedition to Saxony. Final destruction of the Avar power.
797	New and milder Capitularies for Saxony. Expedition against the Northern Saxons.
798	Operations in North Saxony.
799	Accusations against Pope Leo III and his journey to Paderborn. Renewed operations in Saxony.
800	Death of Queen Liutgarde. Journey to Rome. Exoneration of the Pope. Crowning of Charles as Emperor of the West.
801	In Italy until summer.
802	Many reforms instituted in the state. Government made more democratic. Negotiations with Constantinople. Deposition of Irene.
803	Peace and reforms.
804	Death of Alcuin. Expedition to North Saxony. Deportation of the North Saxons.
805	Expedition against the Bohemians.
806	Plan prepared to divide the Empire. War with the Sorbs.
807	Peace.
808	Godofrid of Denmark makes war on the Abodrites.
809	Godofrid's pretended move for peace.
810	Death of Pepin. Death of Hrotrud. Charlemagne's last campaign. Murder of King Godofrid by one of his subjects.
811	Death of Prince Charles, Charlemagne's eldest son.
812	Peace.
813	Abdication of Charles. Accession of Louis, his third son.
814	Death of Charlemagne, January 28.

B. THE STRANGE STORY OF THE BURIAL OF CHARLEMAGNE

'Kaiser Karl was buried in Aachen in the basilica of the Church of Mary the Virgin, which he himself had built there. His body was aromatized [embalmed] and placed in a sitting position on a golden chair in the vault of the tomb, encircled with golden swords. He held in his hands and resting on his knees a golden copy of the Evangelists. One shoulder leaned against the throne. The head was raised into a lifelike posture because it was held by the diadem which in turn was fastened with a golden chain.

'In the diadem was laid a piece of the cross of Christ. The tomb was filled with perfumes, ointments, balsam, and musk, and with treasures of different sorts. The body was dressed in kingly robes and the face under the diadem was protected with a cloth. The golden scepter and golden shield that Pope Leo had consecrated for him were placed in front of him, and the tomb was sealed. No words can say how great was the sorrow in all lands because even by the heathen he was lamented. He died in peace, anointed with the holy oil, and comforted with the last rites of the Church.'

This is the authoritative account of the burial of Charlemagne as written by the monk Ademar of Angoulême, who died in 1035 — probably while on a pilgrimage to Jerusalem.

It was endorsed and supplemented in a report of the same occurrence found in the seventeenth century in the newly discovered 'Annals' of Novallo, which cover the period from 816 to 1048.

'The burial of the Emperor,' says this chronicle, 'was attended by his sons, among them the Abbot Hugo of Novallo.

'After many years the Emperor Otto III came to the city where the body of the Emperor Charles rested and took himself to the scene of the interment, accompanied by two bishops and the Count Otto von Lomello. The Count Lomello narrates what happened in the following words:

'"So we went to the burial-place of Emperor Charles. He did not lie at length, as is the custom with other corpses, but sat like a living person on a throne chair. He was crowned with a gold crown and held a scepter in his hands, which were covered with gloves. His nails projected beyond the ends of the glove fingers, having grown through. Over him was a canopy of marble and lime, excellently set together, through which we broke a hole in order to reach him. As we came in, we noticed a very strong odor. Nevertheless, we honored him on our knees. The Emperor Otto adorned the body with white wreaths. He cut off the projecting finger nails and rearranged everything faultlessly in place. No sign of decay appeared in the body, except that a bit of the tip of the nose was lacking, which the Emperor had replaced with gold. After he had drawn a tooth from the mouth of the corpse and again walled up the vault, we departed."'

291

APPENDICES

When this remarkable corroboration, so circumstantial and direct, being the testimony of an eye-witness, was made public, all doubt vanished, if any had existed, as to the account given by the monk of Angoulême, and history recorded the burial of Charlemagne in an upright position, seated upon his throne, the Evangelists in his hands. To account for the disappearance of the tomb and its contents was easy. The Norsemen had robbed the place and destroyed the tomb.

Thus the matter stood for centuries, and historical paintings of Otto III entering the tomb and of the body sitting on the throne sealed the general belief. No less a hand than von Kaulbach's added to this collection. See his work in the National Museum, Nürnberg.

There could hardly be a stronger illustration of the fabrication of history and the general acceptance of fictionalized records. Within the present generation the patient labors of Dr. Theodor Lindner, the antiquarian, have shown [1] that the whole story of the vault, the burial in the upright position, the breaking in by Otto III, and the rest is mere romancing. The Count von Lomello, indeed, was a historical character, but there is no reason to believe he ever sanctioned the fable that has been ascribed to him.

When the funeral rites were done, the body of Charlemagne was placed in a coffin in a reclining position, possibly in the stone sarcophagus that he had brought from Rome as a specimen of Grecian carving. This is not certain, but is now generally believed in Aachen.

So it rested until 1165, when at the command of Barbarossa it was placed in a wooden casket and buried in the center of the church. About fifty years later, the Emperor Frederick II had the remains placed in a magnificent shrine of silver gilt, a wonderful specimen of mediæval handicraft skill, and it is believed they still repose there. Not quite all, if report is true. A bone of the lower right leg, framed in gold, is preserved in the muniment room of the church and believed to be that of Charlemagne. Among the other unusual treasures of the same room is a silver gilt bust made in the sixteenth century and said to contain a piece of Charlemagne's skull.

Much of the church still stands as he built it. In the exterior wall may be traced the lines of his work, partly destroyed by the Norsemen, ably and thoroughly rebuilt. In the interior the central octagon is as he left it, except that the piers have been covered with marble and richly adorned.

The Rathaus of Aachen stands on the site of Charlemagne's palace, which originally was connected by a portico with the church. The Rathaus contains the famous mural paintings of Rethel depicting the life of Charlemagne, and many other mementoes of the great Emperor.

[1] *Die Fabel von der Bestattung Karls des Grosses*, by Theodor Lindner. Aachen, 1893.

C. THE SONG OF ROLAND

The probable date of the greatest and most famous of these Songs is about 1100. The best copy extant is in the Bodleian Library at Oxford, England. It is signed 'Turoldus,' but nothing is known of its author. In 1927, M. Joseph Bédier of the French Academy printed it in Paris with an inspiring introductory essay and a carefully edited text, accompanied with a literal version in modern French. It is, therefore, for the first time, accessible to all the world.

It is a poem of 4002 lines arranged in 291 stanzas of varying length and irregular rhyming. In general, the rhymes are based on the principle of assonance and many of them would not seem rhymes at all to the modern ear. Most of the poem deals with an imaginary account of what happened at Roncesvalles, where the Franks are betrayed by a false knight named Ganelon, and where Roland, nephew of King Charles, performs with his comrade Oliver deeds of surpassing valor. His horn, the 'oliphant,' and his good sword 'Durrendal,' are also highly extolled. At times the toiling two, Roland and Oliver, are joined and assisted against the masses of paynims by the doughty Turpin, Archbishop of Reims. To give a notion of the stanzaic arrangement and the themes if not the spirit of the composition, one stanza may be translated thus:

LXXXIII

Quoth Oliver: 'The heathen there are strong
And in my view we French but weak and few.
Sound, Comrade Roland, a note upon thy horn.
King Charles will bring the army at thy call.'
'A fool,' cried Roland, 'thou wouldst make of me!
Throughout dear France my name would earn but scorn.
Within the hour, I strike with Durrendal.
Red to its golden hilt its blade shall be.
These wicked heathen come but to their scathe.
I swear it, I, that all are marked for death.'

D. 'CHARLEMAGNE'S HYMN'

(From 'Saint Basil's Hymnal.' Compiled by the Basilian Fathers and published by the John P. Daleiden Company, Chicago. Copyright. Printed by permission.)

VENI, CREATOR SPIRITUS

1. Ve - ni, Cre - a - tor Spi - ri - tus,
2. Qui di - ce - ris Pa - ra - cli - tus,

Men-tes tu - o - rum vi - si - ta: Im - ple su - per - na gra - ti - a
Al - tis - si - mi do - num De - i, Fons vi - vus, ig - nis, ca - ri - tas,

Quae tu cre - a - sti pec - to - ra. A - men.
Et spi - ri - ta - lis unc - ti - o.

3	4	5
Tu septiformis munere,	Accende lumen sensibus,	Hostem repellas longius,
Digitus paternae dexterae,	Infunde amorem cordibus,	Pacemque dones protinus:
Tu rite promissum Patris,	Infirma nostri corporis	Ductore sic te praevio,
Sermone ditans guttura.	Virtute firmans perpeti.	Vitemus omne noxium.

6	7
Per te sciamus da Patrem	Deo Patri sit gloria,
Noscamus atque Filium,	Et Filio qui a mortuis
Teque utriusque Spiritum	Surrexit, ac Paraclito,
Credamus omni tempore.	In saeculorum saecula.

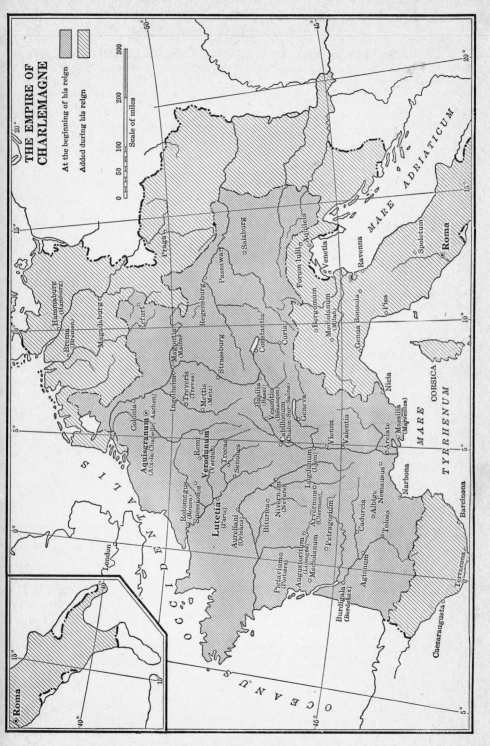

THE EMPIRE OF
CHARLEMAGNE

At the beginning of his reign

Added during his reign

Scale of miles

0   50   100   200   300

Hammaburg
(Hamburg)

Brema
(Bremen)

Magadaburg

Erfurt

Praga

Salzburg

Passawa

Regensburg

Colonia
(Cologne)

Ingelheim

Maguntia
(Mainz)

Treveris
(Treves)

Mettis
(Metz)

Strassburg

Confluentia

Curia

Aquisgranum
(Aix-la-Chapelle)
Aachen

Remi

Verodunum
(Verdun)

Treras

Senones

Basilia
(Basel)

Vesontio
(Besançon)

Cabillonum
(Chalon-sur-Saone)

Geneva

Vienna

Bergomum

Mediolanum
(Milan)

Genua Bononia

Pisa

Forum Iulii

Venetia

Aquileia

Ravenna

Spoletum

●Roma

MARE ADRIATICUM

MARE CORSICA TYRRHENUM

CORSICA

Nicia

Massilia
(Marseilles)

Arelato

Valentia

Narbona

Nemausus

Albiga

Cadurcia

Agrinum

Tolosa

Rotomagus
(Rouen)

Suessiones

Lutetia
(Paris)

Aurelani
(Orleans)

Bituriao

Niuernum
(Nevers)

Arvernum
(Clermont)

Petrogorium

Lugdunum
(Lyon)

Limoges

Pictavium
(Poitiers)

Augustorium

Mediolanum

Burdigala
(Bordeaux)

Terracona

Caesaraugusta

Barcinona

GALLIA OCCIDENTALIS

OCEANUS

London

●Roma

INDEX

INDEX

his sons Charles and Pepin and his daughter Hrotrud, 284; his last days and death, 285; estimates of his character and services, 286, 287.

Charles Martel (The Hammer, illegitimate son of Pepin of Heristal), 43; indicated for the Mayoralty, 44; imprisoned by Plectrudis, his father's widow, 44; escape from prison, 45; early defeats, 45; wins Battle of Ambléve, 45; victories over Raginfrid, 46; as mayor of Metz appealed to against the advancing Saracens, 51; victory at Tours over the Saracens, 52–53; other victories, 53; wars with the Saxons, 54; rules without a king, 54; difficulty of estimating his personal character, 55; indifference toward the Church, 55; conspiracy against in his last days, 56–57; death of (October 22, 751), 56–57

Charles, Prince, eldest son of Charlemagne, first appearance in war, 147; his death, 284.

Chieftains, barbarian, power of, 122.

Childeric, chief of the Salians, father of Clovis, alleged visions of on his wedding night, 15.

Childeric III, King of the Franks, deposed, 1, 3, 61; manner of his selection as king, 58; sequestered in a monastery, 61; general ignorance in his times, 81.

Chilperic, King of the Burgundians, murder of, 7.

Chilperic, King of Neustria, marriage with Galswinthe, 24; murdered, 25.

Chlothar, son of Fredegonde, King of Neustria, 28.

Christopher, defender of the Papacy against the Népi conspirators, 87; escapes from Rome, 87; appeals to King Desiderius, 87; leads army of liberation to Rome, 88; mobbed with his son, 90; fate, 90.

Civilization, under Roman Empire and barbarian invasion, 80; ignorance of the nobles, 81; indebtedness of, to the monks and monasteries, 81; eclipse of learning, 81; loss of ordinary arts, 82, 83; men and manners in the Dark Ages, 83–85.

Classical texts, copied and preserved by Charlemagne, 120.

Cloderic, son of King Sigebert, murderer of his father, 11; killed by order of Clovis, 12.

Clotilde the Fair, daughter of Chilperic, King of the Burgundians, wooed by Clovis, 7; escape from King Gondebaud, 8–9; converts King Clovis, 10.

Clovis (or Chlodovech), Chief of the Salians, King of the Franks, origin of, 5; his military genius, 6; invades Flanders, 6; wins Battle of Soissons, 6; rapid successes of, 6; woos and wins Clotilde, niece of King Gondebaud, 7–9; wins Battle of Dijon over Gondebaud, 9; annexes Burgundy, 9; conversion of, 10; annexes Visigoth kingdom, 11; his cruelty and duplicity, 10–14; annexes the Kingdom of the Ripuarian Franks, 12; his murder of Rignacaise and Rignier, 12–13; instigates the murder of King Sigebert, 11; orders the slaying of Cloderic, 12; murder of King Rignone, 13; story of the vase of Reims, 13; adventure with a follower, 13–14; his revenge, 14; his energy, 14; extent of his dominions, 14.

Columba, Saint, work of, 31.

Commerce, Charlemagne's great service to, 275.

Constantin, brother of the Duke of Népi, falsely declared Pope, 86; reigns as Pope, 87; his letters to King Pepin, 97; deposed and imprisoned, 88; blinded, 88.

Constantin V (Copronymus), Emperor of the East, career and traits, 179; his suspicious death, 180.

Constantin VI, Emperor of the East, subjugated by his mother, 180; infatuation with Hrotrud, 181–182; revolts against and imprisons his mother, 183–184; her counter-revolt, 184; captured and blinded by her order, 185.

D

Danes, irruption of, ninth century, 281.
Danube-Rhine Canal, failure of, 208–209

INDEX

Godofrid, King of the Danes, attacks the Abrodites, 281; launches his great Armada, 283; murdered by one of his own men, 283.

Gondebaud, King of the Burgundians, obtains the kingdom by murder and treachery, 7; outwitted by his niece Clotilde, 8–9; becomes vassal to Clovis, 9, 10.

Government, system of among the barbarians, 122.

Gregory of Tours, cited, 27; about the Saxons, 131.

Grifo, youngest son of Charles Martel, conspires against him, 56–57.

Grimoald, son of Arichis, Duke of Benevento, hostage to Charles, 161; placed upon his father's throne, 182–193.

Grimwald, son of Pepin of Heristal, assassinated, 43.

Grimwald, son of Pepin of Landon, Mayor of Austrasia (in 643), 37; deposes King Dagobert, 37; revolt against, 38; tortured to death, 38.

H

Hadrian I, Pope, his character, 95; attempts to save Afiarta, 96; his letter rebuking the Archbishop of Ravenna, 97; fortifies Rome against Desiderius and checks him with a threat of excommunication, 98; sends messenger to appeal to Charles, 98–99; encounter with Arichis, Duke of Benevento, 160; rebukes Tassilo of Bavaria, 162; death of (795), 220; his friendship with Charles, 275.

Halphen, Professor Louis, historical researches of, Pref. Note, v.

Hatto of Aquitania, imprisoned and blinded by his brother, 75.

Hegira, the, 46.

Helmichis, lover of Queen Rosamund, poisoned by her, 68.

Hildegarde, Queen, death and character of, 146; her beneficent influence upon Charles, 159.

Hrotrud, daughter of Charlemagne, sought in marriage by Constantin VI, 180–191.

Hunold, Duke of Aquitania, member of the conspiracy against Charles Martel, 56; alliance with King Aistulf against King Pepin, 74–75; quarrel with his brother Hatto, whom he imprisons and blinds, 75; his remorse, 75; succeeded by his son Waifar, 75; returns to the Aquitanian revolt after his son's death, 77.

I

Image worship, dissension in the Eastern Church over, 185–186.

Imperialism, effect of upon the inhabitants of Italy, 67.

Irene, Empress of the East, romantic story of, 179–180; married to Leo IV, 180; becomes sole ruler after the deaths of her father-in-law and husband, 180; intrigues of, 180; plans a marriage between her son and the daughter of Charlemagne, 180; organizes a combination against Charles, 182; defeated by Winighis, 182; horsewhips her son, the Emperor, 184; frightful cruelty to her brothers-in-law, 185; orders her son to be blinded, 185; her luxury and arrogance, 185; downfall and last days of, 187–188; influence of in bringing about the coronation of Charles, 217–219.

Irminsul, sacred image of the Saxons, destroyed by Charles, 13.

Iron Crown of the Lombards, the, fiction about, 111–112.

Istria, duchy of, seized by Charlemagne after the war with the East, 183; charges against the government of, 206–207; punishment of the Duke of, 208.

Italy, relations to Frankland, 63–69.

J

Jonas, Christian renegade, joins Islamites in siege of Damascus, 47; with Caled pursues the Christians, 48; suicide of his fiancée, 48.

L

Lambert, Saint, condemns the mistress of Pepin of Heristal, 43; assassinated therefor, 44.

INDEX

Lampegia, daughter of Eudo, Duke of Aquitaine, given in marriage to Munuza, the Saracen, 50.

Laon, Battle of, 40.

Laws, attempts to reform and unify, 275–276.

Lentulus, the King's steward, incident of, 197.

Leo III, Pope, successor to Hadrian, 220; plot against, 220–226; attacked in the streets and imprisoned, 220; romantic story of his rescue, 222; brought before Charles, 222–224; generosity toward his persecutors, 226.

Leo IV, Emperor of the East, son of Constantin V, infatuated with Irene, 180; succeeds his father, 180; suspicious death, 180.

Leodegarius (Saint Leger), Bishop of Autun, heads revolt against Mayor of Neustria, 39; defeated by the Bishop of Clermont and sent to a monastery, 39; blinded and slain by Ebroin, 40.

Libuin, Saint, daring protest against Saxon idolatry, 132; martyrdom of, 133.

Liutberga, Duchess of Bavaria, origin, 159; hatred of Charles, 159.

Lombards, origin of name, 63 and footnote; first mentioned in history, 63; appearance and terror they caused, 64; traits assigned to them by old writers, 64; mercenaries in the Roman army, 65; invade Italy, 66, 67; sudden panic of in battle, 68; extend their territories in Italy, 69; relations with the Papacy, 69; effects of the Italian climate upon their traits, 69, 114.

Lupus, leader of the Basques at Roncesvalles, 157.

M

Mahomet, birth of and pretensions to prophecy, 46; Hegira, the, 46; attack on Medina, 46.

Mainz, burning of the great bridge at, 209.

Manuza, Saracen chieftain, revolts against Abderrahman, 50–51.

Mayor of the Palace, the, beginning of his power, 16; prime minister and actual ruler, 17; the mayoralty scheme of government, 20–21.

Meginfrid, the King's chamberlain, 200–201.

Merovech, son of King Chilperic and Queen Audovera, captain of Rouen, falls in love with Queen Brunhilda, 25.

Merovingians, end of their dynasty, 2, 61; origin of the name, 5; decline of the descendants of Clovis, 15, 16; capitals of the Merovingian empire, 16.

Merwig, Chief of the Salians, instructor of Clovis, 5.

Minstral Guide, the, romantic tale of, 104.

Missi Regii, their function in the government of Charlemagne, 205, 206.

Monk of Saint Gall, The, untrustworthiness of, Pref. Note, v; apocryphal account of the siege of Pavia, 104–106; his foolish story about the Norsemen's ships, 280.

Monks of St. Martin, Tours, attempt of to protect a fugitive, 254.

Murder, rates of atonement for in the Dark Ages, 83.

Music, Charlemagne's interest in, 120, 243–248.

N

Népi, duke of, conspiracy of against the Papacy, 86–88; death of, 88.

Neustria, ancient name for much of what is now France, 19.

Neustrians, essentially Celt and Latin, 19–20.

Neustrians versus Austrasians, see French and Germans.

Nicephorus, conspirator against Irene, crowned Emperor, 187.

Norsemen, growing peril from, 280.

O

Odaocer the Hun, deposes Romulus Augustus, 3–5.

Offa, King of Mercia; Charles's letter to, 249, 250.

Otten, Mayor of Austrasia, assassinated, 37.

303

INDEX